RAINBOW
GOOD NEWS BIBLE

Canadian Bible Society

10 Carnforth Road
Toronto, Ontario
Canada M4A 2S4
www.biblesociety.ca

Through its ministry of translating, publishing and distributing the Scriptures, the Canadian Bible Society strives to fulfil its vision: to reach every person with the life-giving Word of God and to encourage its use.

Revenue from the sale of Scriptures by the Canadian Bible Society supports the distribution of the Word of God throughout the world.

For more information about the Canadian Bible Society or our Scripture products, please contact:
10 Carnforth Road, Toronto, ON M4A 2S4
Tel: (416) 757-4171   1-800-465-2425   info@biblesociety.ca
www.biblesociety.ca   www.biblescanada.com

101021077 Rainbow Bible HC
ISBN 978-0-88834-960-6   Printed in China   CBS-2014-2K

GOOD NEWS BIBLE

 Collins

 BIBLE SOCIETY

GOOD NEWS BIBLE

The Bible Societies/Collins, a division of HarperCollins*Publishers*

First edition published 1976
Second edition © 1994
Third edition © 2004
This edition © 2009

Text, illustrations and all helps are copyright
Anglicised text © the British and Foreign Bible Society 1976, 1994, 2004
Old Testament © American Bible Society 1976, 1992
New Testament © American Bible Society 1966, 1971, 1976, 1992
How to use the *Good News Bible*, Lists of passages and Reading plan © 2003 Collins
Maps © 2000 Collins
Timeline © The British and Foreign Bible Soceity from material from Craig Bartholomew

Title	Code	ISBN
Ghana orange	GNB 043P	978 9 96 400185 8
Uganda orange with pictures	GNB 043P	978 0 56 409533 9
Kenya	GNB 043P	978 9 96 648165 8
Kenya	GNB 042P	978 0 56 409994 8
Zambia	GNB 043P	978 0 56 409184 3

Typeset using Corel Ventura 10 by
Bookcraft Ltd. www.bookcraft.co.uk

Production management by
Bible Society Resources Ltd
www.bibleresources.org.uk

BSRL/200M/2013
Printed in China
APC-FT061809

The British and Foreign Bible Society is a member of the United Bible Societies which is a worldwide fellowship of National Bible Societies working in more than 180 countries. Their aim is to achieve the widest possible, effective and meaningful distribution of the Holy Scriptures, and to help people interact with the Word of God. More than 500 million Scriptures are distributed every year. You are invited to share in this work by your prayers and gifts. The Bible Society in your country will be very happy to provide details of its activity.

Contents

Books of the Bible in alphabetical order

v

How to use the *Good News Bible*

The *Good News Bible* is an easy-to-read translation of the Bible which aims to give today's readers maximum understanding of the content of the original texts. It does not follow the traditional vocabulary and style found in the historic English Bible versions. Instead it attempts to present the biblical content and message in standard, everyday, natural English. It is used by churches, individuals and schools throughout the world. In addition to being a truly easy-to-read translation, the *Good News Bible* also includes a range of added extras to help you get the most out of it. Here's a quick guide to how it all works.

The basics: The Bible is a collection of 66 separate books divided into two sections, the **Old Testament** (which tells the story of the people of Israel), and the **New Testament** (which tells the story of Jesus' birth, life, death and resurrection, and the early days of the church).

Bible references: Each Bible book is divided into chapters, and each chapter is divided into verses. To find a particular Bible passage, you need to look up the Bible book you want on the Contents page, then go to the relevant chapter, and then find the verse. As you navigate around the Bible you will find details of what part of the Bible you're in — page number, book name and chapter number — across the top of the page.

When you see a Bible reference written down it will look something like this:

John 3.16

The reference is always in the same order; the book, chapter and then verses. So to find this reference you would go to the book of John, Chapter 3 (marked with the large number at the beginning of a section) verse 16 (marked with a small number within the text).

Finding a particular passage: The Bible is full of famous stories, characters and sayings. Many of these are listed at the front of your Bible for you to find quickly, but there are many more that are not listed. As you become more familiar with the different books you will know where to go to find certain passages, characters or topics but there will be other occasions where you will need extra help. Some people use a concordance (a book or on the internet) which acts like a keyword search. You can then use the Bible reference to find the passage in your Bible (see above). You may also find the index at the back of this Bible helpful.

Starting to read the Bible: If you want to get an introduction to the Bible as a whole, you could just read a whole book from the beginning — either Genesis or one of the Gospels would probably be the best place to start. But there is also a three-week reading plan at the front of the Bible, which will help you get an overview.

Maps and word list: To help you further, there is a range of relevant maps and a word list at the back of the Bible.

The different parts of the Bible

Once you're ready to do some more exploring on your own, you might find the following summary of the different parts of the Bible helpful:

The Law: The first five books of the Bible set the scene, starting with creation and God's promises to Abraham, followed by the growth of Abraham's family into a nation, and their escape from captivity in Egypt to become God's chosen people.
Law books: *Genesis, Exodus, Leviticus, Numbers, Deuteronomy*

Historical books: Arrival in the Promised Land doesn't actually happen until the next book, Joshua. From Judges to Esther, these tell the story of the protectors of God's people — first judges, then kings, including David and Solomon — and how the people of Israel increasingly moved away from God and ended up in exile.
History books: *Joshua, Judges, Ruth, 1 Samuel, 2 Samuel, 1 Kings, 2 Kings, 1 Chronicles, 2 Chronicles, Ezra, Nehemiah, Esther*

Poetic books: These cover a wide range of themes, from Job's suffering and the existential despair of Ecclesiastes to the wisdom of Proverbs and the romance of Song of Songs. Then there are the Psalms, which contains all these themes and more in the one book!
Poetry: *Job, Psalms, Proverbs, Ecclesiastes, Song of Songs, Lamentations*

Prophecy: These books are divided into 'major' (to put it simply, the long ones) and 'minor' (the short ones), and between them cover the time from the later kings through to the exile, giving God's warnings to the people and promises for the future; there are also references which seem to be fulfilled by Jesus.
Prophecy: *Isaiah, Jeremiah, Ezekiel, Daniel, Hosea, Joel, Amos, Obadiah, Jonah, Micah, Nahum, Habakkuk, Zephaniah, Haggai, Zechariah, Malachi*

The Gospels and Acts: Four different writers give their own account of Jesus' life, death and resurrection, each emphasising a different aspect of his mission for their particular intended audience and enabling us to build up a more rounded view as a result. Then Luke goes on to tell the story of the early church in Acts.
Gospels and Acts: *Matthew, Mark, Luke, John, Acts*

Letters: These letters were written by leaders of the early church (Paul, mostly, but some by others) to the new churches they'd set up, which needed encouragement and guidance. They still have much to teach us today about how to live. Revelation ends the New Testament with a bang!
Letters: *Romans, 1 Corinthians, 2 Corinthians, Galatians, Ephesians, Philippians, Colossians, 1 Thessalonians, 2 Thessalonians , 1 Timothy , 2 Timothy, Titus, Philemon, Hebrews, James, 1 Peter, 2 Peter, 1 John, 2 John, 3 John, Jude, Revelation*

Introductory reading plan

Time needed Three weeks
Aim To grasp the basics of what comes where in the Bible

To help you begin reading the Bible, these three one-week reading courses cover the essentials of the story the Bible tells. The passages are chosen because they are often referred to, and, taken together, show the development of God's relationship with mankind, but also so as to be easy to read and understand.

1 The Old Testament (one week)
- ❏ Day 1 Genesis 1—2: Creation
- ❏ Day 2 Genesis 3: Human disobedience
- ❏ Day 3 Exodus 20: The Ten Commandments
- ❏ Day 4 1 Samuel 17: David and Goliath
- ❏ Day 5 Daniel 6: Daniel and the lions
- ❏ Day 6 Psalm 23: The Lord is my shepherd
- ❏ Day 7 Isaiah 53: The suffering servant

2 The Gospels (one week)
- ❏ Day 1 Luke 2: Jesus' birth
- ❏ Day 2 John 1: Jesus is baptized, and calls his first disciples
- ❏ Day 3 Matthew 5—6: Sermon on the Mount
- ❏ Day 4 Luke 15: Some of Jesus' parables
- ❏ Day 5 Mark 14: The last supper and the betrayal of Jesus
- ❏ Day 6 Mark 15: The crucifixion
- ❏ Day 7 Luke 24: Resurrection

3 The Early Church (one week)
- ❏ Day 1 Acts 2: The coming of the Holy Spirit
- ❏ Day 2 Acts 9: The conversion of Saul
- ❏ Day 3 Acts 10: Peter is shown that Christianity is for all nations
- ❏ Day 4 Romans 3: The essentials of Christian faith
- ❏ Day 5 Romans 8: Life in the spirit
- ❏ Day 6 1 Corinthians 13: Love
- ❏ Day 7 Galatians 5: The fruit of the spirit

A Time-Line of the Bible

Creation
earliest times | Humans created in God's image

Disobedience
earliest times | Humans fall into sin (Adam and Eve),
Cain and Abel, Noah and the flood, Tower of Babel

God's People — Israel

c. 2000 BC	Abraham is called and travels into Canaan
c. 1650 BC	The sons of Jacob move to Egypt
c. 1250 BC	Moses leads the Israelites out of Egypt, and God calls them to be the nation who will serve him
probably late 13th century BC	Conquering and settling in Canaan
12th and 11th centuries BC	Israel led by military liberators called "judges"
c. 1030–1010 BC	Israel ruled by King Saul
c. 1010–970 BC	Israel ruled by King David
c. 970–931 BC	Israel ruled by King Solomon
931 BC	Israel splits into two (Israel and Judah)
722/721 BC	The people of the north (Israel) go into exile in Assyria
587/586 BC	The people of the south (Judah) go into exile in Babylon
539 BC	The return from exile begins
	The time between the Old and the New Testaments
probably 6 BC	The coming of the king — Jesus' birth

about a thousand years

When the Christian calendar was worked out in the sixth century, a mistake in working back to the date of Jesus' birth meant that it was a few years out.

probably 30 AD	The death and resurrection of Jesus
c. 41–65 AD	The travels and ministry of Paul

Jesus recognized as king over everthing
the future | Jesus returns to set up the new heavens and earth

Important chapters from every book in the Bible

Old Testament

Genesis 1, 3, 12, 37
Exodus 3, 4, 12, 20
Leviticus 19
Numbers 11
Deuteronomy 4, 6, 8, 30
Joshua 1, 24
Judges 6, 7
Ruth 1
1 Samuel 3, 16, 24
2 Samuel 7, 11, 12
1 Kings 8, 12, 18
2 Kings 5, 6, 17, 25
1 Chronicles 29
2 Chronicles 20
Ezra 9
Job 1, 19, 42
Psalms 1, 23, 51, 139
Proverbs 3, 11, 28
Ecclesiastes 3, 12
Song of Songs 2
Isaiah 6, 43, 61
Lamentations 3
Jeremiah 1, 7, 17, 31
Ezekiel 2, 3, 34, 36, 37
Daniel 1, 6, 9
Hosea 6
Joel 3
Amos 5
Obadiah
Jonah 2
Micah 6
Nahum 1
Habakkuk 1, 2
Zephaniah 1, 2
Haggai 1
Zechariah 2
Malachi 3

New Testament

Matthew 6, 10, 16, 24, 28
Mark 1, 14
Luke 2, 12, 23
John 1, 3, 10, 14,
Acts 1, 2, 9, 17, 26
Romans 1, 3, 8, 12
1 Corinthians 1, 13, 15
2 Corinthians 1, 4, 5
Galatians 5
Ephesians 2
Philippians 3
Colossians 1
1 Thessalonians 5
2 Thessalonians 3
1 Timothy 1
2 Timothy 3
Titus 3
Philemon
Hebrews 11, 2
James 4
1 Peter 2
2 Peter 3
1 John 4
Jude
Revelation 1, 3, 5, 22

Passages for special occasions

The numbers in heavy type are page numbers.
OT Old Testament   NT New Testament

Baptism
Jesus' baptism
Matthew 3.13–17, **NT 5**
Mark 1.9–11, **NT 43**
Luke 3.21–22, **NT 75**
Nicodemus
John 3.1–10, **NT 115**
Ethiopian eunuch
Acts 8.26–39, **NT 153**
Philippian jailer
Acts 16.22–34, **NT 163**
Dead to sin but alive in union with Christ
Romans 6.1–4, **NT 185**

Bereavement
Comfort for mourners
Matthew 5.4, **NT 7**
Jesus the resurrection and the life
John 11.21–27, **NT 128**
The resurrection of Jesus
1 Corinthians 15.1–57, **NT 210**
The Lord's coming
1 Thessalonians 4.13–18, **NT 246**

Christmas
The sign of Immanuel
Isaiah 7.10–17, **OT 662**
The birth of Jesus is announced
Luke 1.26–38, **NT 71**
The shepherds are told of the birth of Jesus
Luke 2.8–20, **NT 73**
The birth of Jesus
Matthew 1.18–25, **NT 4**
Three wise men
Matthew 2.1–12, **NT 4**

Easter
Suffering servant
Isaiah 53, **OT 705**
Jesus' death and resurrection
Matthew 26—28, **NT 36**
Mark 14—16, **NT 64**
Luke 22—24, **NT 105**;
John 19—21, **NT 137**
United with him
Romans 6.1–14, **NT 185**
Obedient to death
Philippians 2.5–11, **NT 236**
Christ suffered for you
1 Peter 2.21–23, **NT 284**

Wedding Day
Adam and Eve
Genesis 2.18–25, **OT 5**
The capable wife
Proverbs 31.10–31, **OT 638**
Wedding in Cana
John 2.1–11, **NT 114**
Love
1 Corinthians 13, **NT 208**
Wives and husbands
Ephesians 5.22–33, **NT 233**
The old and the new life
Colossians 3.12–19, **NT 242**
How to please God
Hebrews 13.4, **NT 276**;
1 Peter 3.1–7, **NT 284**

Prayers from the Bible

Isaac's blessing
Genesis 27.28–29 **OT 28**

Moses thanks God after leaving Egypt
Exodus 15.1–18 **OT 69**

Moses asks to see God's glory
Exodus 33.12–23 **OT 88**

Aaron's Blessing
Numbers 6.24–27 **OT 131**

Deborah's song of thanksgiving and victory
Judges 5 **OT 229**

Elijah's prayer on Mount Carmel
1 Kings 18.36–39 **OT 343**

The prayer of Jabez
1 Chronicles 4.10 **OT 386**

Job seeks reasons for his suffering
Job 10 **OT 493**

David's prayer for forgiveness
Psalm 51 **OT 552**

Hezekiah's prayer in his illness
Isaiah 38.10–20 **OT 686**

Daniel's prayer about the king's dream
Daniel 2.20–23 **OT 836**

Jonah's prayer in the fish
Jonah 2 **OT 876**

Mary's Prayer of Thanksgiving (Magnificat)
Luke 1.46–55 **NT 71**

Simeon's prayer at the temple (Nunc Dimittis)
Luke 2.29–35 **NT 74**

The prayer of Zechariah (Bendictus)
Luke 1.68–79 **NT 72**

Jesus teaches the Lord's prayer
Matthew 6.9–13 **NT 9**,
Luke 11.2–4 **NT 89**

Jesus prays for all believers
John 17 **NT 135**

The prayer of Stephen as he is martyred
Acts 7.59–60 **NT 152**

Paul's praise of God
Romans 16.25–27 **NT 196**

Paul's prayer for the Christians in Ephesus
Ephesians 3.14–21 **NT 231**

A prayer for the Christians in Phillipi
Phillipians 1.1–11 **NT 235**

Events in the Bible

People in the Bible

Abraham
Genesis 11.26—25.10, **OT 13**

Adam
Genesis 2.7—5.5, **OT 5**

David
1 Samuel 16.1—31.13, **OT 271**
2 Samuel, **OT 288**
1 Kings 1.1—2.12, **OT 318**
1 Chronicles 11.1—29.30, **OT 394**

Elijah
1 Kings 17.1—2 Kings 2.15, **OT 341**
Matthew 17.3–13, **NT 24**
Romans 11.2–4, **NT 190**

Elisha
1 Kings 19.16–21, **OT 345**;
2 Kings 2.1—9.3, OT 351
2 Kings 13.14–21, OT 365

Eve
Genesis 2.22—4.1, **OT 5**
2 Corinthians 11.3, **NT 206**

Gideon
Judges 6.11—8.27, **OT 230**

Isaac
Genesis 21.1—28.5, **OT 20**

Jacob
Genesis 25.19—35.29, **OT 25**
Genesis 46—50.13, **OT 48**

Jesus
Matthew, **NT 3**
Mark, **NT 43**
Luke, **NT 70**
John, **NT 112**

John the Baptist
Matthew 3.1–15, **NT 5**
Matthew 11.2–15, **NT 15**
Matthew 14.2–12, **NT 20**
Matthew 21.25–32, **NT 29**
Mark 1.4–11, **NT 43**
Mark 6.14–29, **NT 51**
Mark 11.29–33, **NT 60**
Luke 1.5–80, **NT 70**
Luke 3.2–20, **NT 74**
Luke 7.18–33, **NT 81**
John 1.6–36, **NT 112**
John 3.23–30, **NT 115**

John the Apostle
Matthew 4.21, **NT 6**
Mark 1.29, **NT 44**
Mark 5.37, **NT 50**
Mark 9.2, 38, **NT 56**
Mark 10.35, 41, **NT 59**
Mark 13.3, **NT 62**
Luke 9.49, 54, **NT 87**
John, **NT 112**

Joshua
Acts 3.1–11, **NT 146**
Acts 4.13–21, **NT 147**
Acts 8.14–17, **NT 153**
Galatians 2.9, **NT 224**

Joshua
Exodus 17.8–13, **OT 72**
Numbers 13.1–16, **OT 137**
Numbers 27.18–23, **OT 153**
Deuteronomy 31.23, **OT 194**
Joshua, **OT 200**

Mary
Matthew 1.16, 18, 20, **NT 3**
Matthew 2.11, **NT 4**
Luke 1.27–56, **NT 71**
Luke 2.5, 16–19, 34, **NT 73**
John 19.25–27, **NT 138**

Moses
Exodus 2—21.22, **OT 55**
Exodus 24.1–18, **OT 78**
Exodus 32—40, **OT 85**
Numbers 1, **OT 125**;
Numbers 12—13.20, **OT 136**
Numbers 27.18–23, **OT 153**
Deuteronomy 1—4.40, **OT 163**
Deuteronomy 31—34, **OT 194**

Noah
Genesis 5.29—9.29, **OT 8**
Isaiah 54.9, **OT 706**
Hebrews 11.7, **NT 273**

Paul
Acts 8—9.30, **NT 152**
Acts 11.25—28.31, **NT 157**

Peter
Matthew 4.18, **NT 6**
Matthew 14.27—17.13, **NT 21**
Matthew 26.36—27.75, **NT 39**
Mark 8.27—9.13, **NT 55**
Luke 5.1–11, **NT 77**
Luke 9.18–36, **NT 85**
Luke 22.54–62, **NT 107**
John 1.41–42, **NT 114**
John 6.68–69, **NT 121**
John 21.2–24, **NT 140**
Acts 1.14—5.41, **NT 143**
Acts 9.32—12.9, **NT 155**
1 Peter **NT 282**
2 Peter **NT 287**

Samson
Judges 13.2–16, **OT 239**

Samuel
1 Samuel 1.19—4.1, **OT 254**
1 Samuel 7—12, **OT 261**
1 Samuel 15—16, **OT 269**
1 Samuel 25.1, **OT 281**

Solomon
1 Kings 1.11—11.43, **OT 319**

Miracles of Jesus

Man born blind
John 9, **NT 125**

Officer's servant
Matthew 8.5–13, **NT 11**

Raising of Jairus' daughter from the dead
Matthew 9.18–19, **NT 13**
Mark 5.22–24, **NT 50**
Luke 8.41–42, **NT 84**

Feeding of the five thousand
Matthew 14.15–21, **NT 21**
Mark 6.30–44, **NT 52**
Luke 9.12–17, **NT 85**
John 6.5–13, **NT 119**

Catch of fish
Luke 5.1–11, **NT 77**

Stilling of the storm
Matthew 8.23–27, **NT 12**
Mark 4.37–41, **NT 48**
Luke 8.22–25, **NT 120**

Walking on water
Matthew 14.25, **NT 21**
Mark 6.48–51, **NT 52**
John 6.19–21, **NT 120**

Turning water into wine
John 2.1–11, **NT 114**

Ten men with leprosy
Luke 17.11–19, **NT 98**

Jesus heals a possessed man
Mark 5.1–20, **NT 49**

The paralysed man
Luke 5.18–25, **NT 78**

Parables of Jesus

Gold coins
Luke 19.11–27, **NT 101**

Good Samaritan
Luke 10.29–37, **NT 88**

Great feast
Luke 14.15–24, **NT 95**

Hidden treasure
Matthew 13.44, **NT 20**

Lost coin, lost son, lost sheep
Matthew 18.10–14, **NT 25**
Luke 15, **NT 96**

Pearl, treasure in the field
Matthew 13.45–46, **NT 20**

Pharisee and the tax collector
Luke 18.9–14, **NT 99**

Sower
Matthew 13.3–9, 18–23, **NT 18**
Mark 4.3–8, 13–20, **NT 47**
Luke 8.5–8, 11–15, **NT 82**

Tenants in the vineyard
Matthew 20.1–16, **NT 27**
Matthew 21.33–46, **NT 30**

Two sons
Matthew 21.28–32, **NT 30**

House on rock and sand
Matthew 7.24–27, **NT 11**
Luke 6.47–49, **NT 80**

Where to find help in times of...

Failure
Psalm 51, **OT 552**
Matthew 18.21–35, **NT 26**
Luke 15.11–14, **NT 96**
Acts 13.26–39, **NT 159**
Romans 5.8, **NT 185**
Ephesians 4.31–32, **NT 233**

Temptation
Luke 4.1–13, **NT 76**
Ephesians 6.10–20, **NT 234**
Hebrews 4.15, **NT 267**
James 1.12–18, **NT 277**
1 Peter 5.8–9, **NT 286**

Doubt
Isaiah 40.27–28, **OT 689**
Matthew 11.1–6, **NT 15**
Mark 9.24, **NT 56**
John 20.19–29, **NT 140**
Acts 17.22–28, **NT 165**

Sadness
Matthew 6.25–34, **NT 9**
Matthew 11.28, **NT 16**
Philippians 4.4–7, **NT 238**
1 Peter 5.7, **NT 286**

Fear
Psalm 27, **OT 535**
Psalm 34.4, **OT 539**
Psalm 46, **OT 548**
Psalm 56, **OT 554**
Psalm 91, **OT 578**
Matthew 8.23–27, **NT 12**

Jealousy
Luke 15.25–32, **NT 97**
Galatians 5.19–26, **NT 228**
James 3.13–18, **NT 279**

Loneliness
Psalm 23, **OT 533**
Psalm 73.23–24, **OT 566**
Isaiah 41.10, **OT 690**
Isaiah 49.14–16, **OT 701**
John 14.15–21, **NT 132**

Illness
Psalm 103.1–4, **OT 584**
Romans 8.18–25, **NT 188**
2 Corinthians 4.16–18, **NT 216**
2 Corinthians 12.9, **NT 221**

Poverty
Matthew 6.24–33, **NT 9**
Mark 10.17–31, **NT 58**
1 Timothy 6.7–12, **NT 254**

Anger
Matthew 5.22–25, **NT 8**
James 1.19–21, **NT 278**

Betrayal
Psalm 41, **OT 545**

Bereavement
1 Thessalonians 4.13–18 **NT 286**
Revelation 21.3–5 **NT 314**

Decision-making
Matthew 6.25–34 **NT 9**
Romans 12.1–2 **NT 192**

Moving home
Psalm 121 **OT 602**
Mark 10.28–30 **NT 58**

Thankfulness
Psalm 100 **OT 583**
Ephesians 5.19–20 **NT 233**

Insomnia
Psalm 121.3–6 **OT 602**
Matthew 11.28 **NT 16**

A new start
Romans 12.3–11 **NT 192**
Colossians 3.23–24 **NT 243**
1 Thessalonians 5.12–18 **NT 287**

External Pressure
Psalm 37.1–7 **OT 541**
Exodus 18.17–23 **OT 73**

Where to find passages on...

Peace
Isaiah 26.3, **OT 676**
John 14.27 **NT 133**
Romans 5.1–5, **NT 184**
Philippians 4.4–7, **NT 238**

Love
1 Corinthians 13.1–3, **NT 208**
1 John 4.7–12, **NT 293**

Acceptance
Psalm 139, **OT 608**

Courage
Psalm 11, **OT 526**
Psalm 42, **OT 545**

Protection
Psalm 3, **OT 522**
Psalm 4, **OT 522**
Psalm 7, **OT 523**
Psalm 16, **OT 528**
Psalm 17, **OT 528**
Psalm 18, **OT 529**
Psalm 23, **OT 533**
Psalm 27, **OT 535**
Psalm 31, **OT 537**
Psalm 91, **OT 578**
Psalm 121, **OT 602**
Psalm 125, **OT 603**

Guidance
Psalm 1, **OT 521**
Psalm 5, **OT 522**
Psalm 15, **OT 528**
Psalm 19, **OT 531**
Psalm 25, **OT 534**
Psalm 32, **OT 538**
Psalm 86, **OT 574**

Patience
James 5.7–11, **NT 280**

Righteousness
Romans 3.10–26, **NT 183**
Romans 5.1–21, **NT 184**
Romans 6.11–23, **NT 186**
Romans 10.9–11, **NT 190**

Salvation
Romans 10.9–11, **NT 190**
Ephesians 2.4–9, **NT 230**
Titus 2.11–14, **NT 261**

Forgiveness
Matthew 18.21–35, **NT 26**
Acts 13.26–39, **NT 159**
Ephesians 4.31–32, **NT 233**

Faithfulness
Psalm 145.13–14 **OT 612**
Hebrews 6.10–12 **NT 268**

Justice
Micah 6.8 **OT 882**
Isaiah 61.8 **OT 712**

The Poor
Isaiah 58 6.9 **OT 709**
Proverbs 31.8–9 **OT 638**
Luke 4.16–21 **NT 76**

Hope
1 Timothy 4.9–10 **NT 253**
Romans 8.24–25 **NT 188**

Provision
Isaiah 58.11 **OT 709**
Matthew 6.25–34 **NT 9**

THE
OLD TESTAMENT

GENESIS

INTRODUCTION

The name *Genesis* means "origin". The book tells about the creation of the universe, the origin of the human race, the beginning of sin and suffering in the world, and about God's way of dealing with humanity. *Genesis* can be divided into two main parts: (1) The creation of the world and the early history of the human race. Here are the accounts of Adam and Eve, Cain and Abel, Noah and the flood, and the Tower of Babylon (chapters 1—11). (2) The history of the early ancestors of the Israelites. The first is Abraham, who was notable for his faith and his obedience to God. Then follow the stories of his son Isaac, and grandson Jacob (also called Israel), and of Jacob's twelve sons, who were the founders of the twelve tribes of Israel. Special attention is given to one of the sons, Joseph, and the events that brought Jacob and his other sons with their families to live in Egypt (chapters 12—50).

While this book tells stories about people, it is first and foremost an account of what God has done. It begins with the affirmation that God created the universe, and it ends with a promise that God will continue to show his concern for his people. Throughout the book the main character is God, who judges and punishes those who do wrong, leads and helps his people, and shapes their history. This ancient book was written to record the story of a people's faith and to help keep that faith alive.

Outline of Contents

The Story of Creation

1 In the beginning, when God created the universe,* ² the earth was formless and desolate. The raging ocean that covered everything was engulfed in total darkness, and the Spirit of God* was moving over the water. ³ Then God commanded, "Let there be light" — and light appeared. ⁴ God was pleased with what he saw. Then he separated the light from the darkness, ⁵ and he named the light "Day" and the darkness "Night". Evening passed and morning came — that was the first day.

⁶⁻⁷ Then God commanded, "Let there be a dome to divide the water and to keep it in two separate places" — and it was done. So God made a dome, and it separated the water under it from the water above it. ⁸ He named the dome "Sky". Evening passed and morning came — that was the second day.

⁹ Then God commanded, "Let the water below the sky come together in one place,

---

1.1 In the beginning... the universe; *or* In the beginning God created the universe; *or* When God began to create the universe.
1.2 the Spirit of God; *or* the power of God; *or* a wind from God; *or* an awesome wind.

See also: 1.3: 2 Cor 4.6

See also: 1.6–8: 2 Pet 3.5

Let the earth produce all kinds of plants ... creatures that live in the water (1.11,21)

so that the land will appear" — and it was done. 10 He named the land "Earth", and the water which had come together he named "Sea". And God was pleased with what he saw. 11 Then he commanded, "Let the earth produce all kinds of plants, those that bear grain and those that bear fruit" — and it was done. 12 So the earth produced all kinds of plants, and God was pleased with what he saw. 13 Evening passed and morning came — that was the third day.

14 Then God commanded, "Let lights appear in the sky to separate day from night and to show the time when days, years, and religious festivals* begin; 15 they will shine in the sky to give light to the earth" — and it was done. 16 So God made the two larger lights, the sun to rule over the day and the moon to rule over the night; he also made the stars. 17 He placed the lights in the sky to shine on the earth, 18 to rule over the day and the night, and to separate light from darkness. And God was pleased with what he saw. 19 Evening passed and morning came — that was the fourth day.

20 Then God commanded, "Let the water be filled with many kinds of living beings, and let the air be filled with birds." 21 So God created the great sea monsters, all kinds of creatures that live in the water,

and all kinds of birds. And God was pleased with what he saw. 22 He blessed them all and told the creatures that live in the water to reproduce, and to fill the sea, and he told the birds to increase in number. 23 Evening passed and morning came — that was the fifth day.

24 Then God commanded, "Let the earth produce all kinds of animal life: domestic and wild, large and small" — and it was done. 25 So God made them all, and he was pleased with what he saw.

26 Then God said, "And now we will make human beings; they will be like us and resemble us. They will have power over the fish, the birds, and all animals, domestic and wild,* large and small." 27 So God created human beings, making them to be like himself. He created them male and female, 28 blessed them, and said, "Have many children, so that your descendants will live all over the earth and bring it under their control. I am putting you in charge of the fish, the birds, and all the wild animals. 29 I have provided all kinds of grain and all kinds of fruit for you to eat; 30 but for all the wild animals and for all the birds I have provided grass and leafy plants for food" — and it was done. 31 God looked at everything he had made, and he was very pleased. Evening passed and morning came — that was the sixth day.

2 And so the whole universe was completed. 2 By the seventh day God finished what he had been doing and stopped working. 3 He blessed the seventh day and set it apart as a special day, because by that day he had completed his creation* and stopped working. 4 And that is how the universe was created.

The Garden of Eden

When the LORD* God made the universe, 5 there were no plants on the earth and no seeds had sprouted, because he had not sent any rain, and there was no one to

---

1.14 religious festivals; *or* seasons.

1.26 *One ancient translation* animals, domestic and wild; *Hebrew* domestic animals and all the earth.
2.3 by that day he had completed his creation; *or* on that day he completed his creation.
2.4 THE LORD: *See* LORD *in Word List*

See also: **1.26:** 1 Cor 11.7   **1.27:** Mt 19.4; Mk 10.6
1.27–28: Gen 5.1–2   **2.2:** Heb 4.4, 10
2.2–3: Ex 20.11

cultivate the land; 6 but water would come up from beneath the surface and water the ground.

7 Then the LORD God took some soil from the ground* and formed a man* out of it; he breathed life-giving breath into his nostrils and the man began to live.

8 Then the LORD God planted a garden in Eden, in the East, and there he put the man he had formed. 9 He made all kinds of beautiful trees grow there and produce good fruit. In the middle of the garden stood the tree that gives life and the tree that gives knowledge of what is good and what is bad.*

10 A stream flowed in Eden and watered the garden; beyond Eden it divided into four rivers. 11 The first river is the Pishon; it flows round the country of Havilah. 12 (Pure gold is found there and also rare perfume and precious stones.) 13 The second river is the Gihon; it flows round the country of Cush.* 14 The third river is the Tigris, which flows east of Assyria, and the fourth river is the Euphrates.

15 Then the LORD God placed the man in the Garden of Eden to cultivate it and guard it. 16 He said to him, "You may eat the fruit of any tree in the garden, 17 except the tree that gives knowledge of what is good and what is bad.* You must not eat the fruit of that tree; if you do, you will die the same day."

18 Then the LORD God said, "It is not good for the man to live alone. I will make a suitable companion to help him." 19 So he took some soil from the ground and formed all the animals and all the birds. Then he brought them to the man to see what he would name them; and that is how they all got their names. 20 So the man named all the birds and all the animals; but not one of them was a suitable companion to help him.

21 Then the LORD God made the man fall into a deep sleep, and while he was sleeping, he took out one of the man's ribs and closed up the flesh. 22 He formed a woman

out of the rib and brought her to him. 23 Then the man said,

"At last, here is one of my own kind —
Bone taken from my bone, and flesh
    from my flesh.
'Woman' is her name because she
    was taken out of man."*

24 That is why a man leaves his father and mother and is united with his wife, and they become one.

25 The man and the woman were both naked, but they were not embarrassed.

Human Disobedience

3 Now the snake was the most cunning animal that the LORD God had made. The snake asked the woman, "Did God really tell you not to eat fruit from any tree in the garden?"

2 "We may eat the fruit of any tree in the garden," the woman answered, 3 "except the tree in the middle of it. God told us not to eat the fruit of that tree or even touch it; if we do, we will die."

4 The snake replied, "That's not true; you will not die. 5 God said that, because he knows that when you eat it you will be like God* and know what is good and what is bad."*

How wonderful it would be to become wise (3.6)

6 The woman saw how beautiful the tree was and how good its fruit would be to eat, and she thought how wonderful it would be to become wise. So she took some of the fruit and ate it. Then she gave some to her husband, and he also ate it. 7 As soon as they had eaten it, they were

---

2.7 GROUND... MAN: *The Hebrew words for "man" and "ground" have similar sounds.*

2.9, 2.17 knowledge of what is good and what is bad; *or* knowledge of everything.

2.13 Cush (of Mesopotamia); *or* Ethiopia.

See also: 2.7: 1 Cor 15.45   **2.9:** Rev 2.7, 22.2, 14

2.23 WOMAN... MAN: *The Hebrew words for "woman" and "man" have similar sounds.*

3.5 God; *or* the gods.

3.5 know what is good and what is bad; *or* know everything.

See also: 2.24: Mt 19.5; Mk 10.7–8; 1 Cor 6.16; Eph 5.31   **3.1:** Rev 12.9, 20.2

given understanding and realized that
they were naked; so they sewed fig leaves
together and covered themselves.

8 That evening they heard the Lᴏʀᴅ God
walking in the garden, and they hid from
him among the trees. 9 But the Lᴏʀᴅ God
called out to the man, "Where are you?"

10 He answered, "I heard you in the garden; I was afraid and hid from you, because
I was naked."

11 "Who told you that you were naked?"
God asked. "Did you eat the fruit that I told
you not to eat?"

12 The man answered, "The woman
you put here with me gave me the fruit,
and I ate it."

13 The Lᴏʀᴅ God asked the woman,
"Why did you do this?"

She replied, "The snake tricked me into
eating it."

God Pronounces Judgement

14 Then the Lᴏʀᴅ God said to the snake,
"You will be punished for this; you alone of
all the animals must bear this curse: from
now on you will crawl on your belly, and
you will have to eat dust as long as you
live. 15 I will make you and the woman
hate each other; her offspring and yours
will always be enemies. Her offspring will
crush your head, and you will bite her offspring's* heel."

16 And he said to the woman, "I will
increase your trouble in pregnancy and
your pain in giving birth. In spite of this,
you will still have desire for your husband,
yet you will be subject to him."

17 And he said to the man, "You listened to your wife and ate the fruit
which I told you not to eat. Because of
what you have done, the ground will be
under a curse. You will have to work hard
all your life to make it produce enough
food for you. 18 It will produce weeds
and thorns, and you will have to eat wild
plants. 19 You will have to work hard and
sweat to make the soil produce anything, until you go back to the soil from
which you were formed. You were made
from soil, and you will become soil
again."

20 Adam* named his wife Eve,* because
she was the mother of all human beings.
21 And the Lᴏʀᴅ God made clothes out of
animal skins for Adam and his wife, and he
clothed them.

Adam and Eve are Sent Out of the Garden

22 Then the Lᴏʀᴅ God said, "Now the
man has become like one of us and has
knowledge of what is good and what is
bad.* He must not be allowed to take fruit
from the tree that gives life, eat it, and live
for ever." 23 So the Lᴏʀᴅ God sent him out
of the Garden of Eden and made him cultivate the soil from which he had been
formed. 24 Then at the east side of the garden he put living creatures* and a flaming
sword which turned in all directions. This
was to keep anyone from coming near the
tree that gives life.

Cain and Abel

4 Then Adam had intercourse with his
wife, and she became pregnant. She
bore a son and said, "By the Lᴏʀᴅ's help I
have acquired a son." So she named him
Cain.* 2 Later she gave birth to another son,
Abel. Abel became a shepherd, but Cain
was a farmer. 3 After some time, Cain
brought some of his harvest and gave it as
an offering to the Lᴏʀᴅ. 4 Then Abel brought
the first lamb born to one of his sheep,
killed it, and gave the best parts of it as an
offering. The Lᴏʀᴅ was pleased with Abel
and his offering, 5 but he rejected Cain and
his offering. Cain became furious, and he
scowled in anger. 6 Then the Lᴏʀᴅ said to
Cain, "Why are you angry? Why that scowl
on your face? 7 If you had done the right
thing, you would be smiling; * but because
you have done evil, sin is crouching at your
door. It wants to rule you, but you must
overcome it."

3.15 her offspring's; or their.
See also: 3.13: 2 Cor 11.3; 1 Tim 2.14
3.15: Rev 12.17 3.17–18: Heb 6.8

3.20 ADAM: This name in Hebrew means "humanity".
3.20 EVE: This name sounds similar to the Hebrew
word for "living", which is rendered in this context
as "human beings".
3.22 knowledge of what is good and what is bad; or
knowledge of everything.
3.24 LIVING CREATURES: See Word List.
4.1 CAIN: This name sounds like the Hebrew for
"acquired".
4.7 you would be smiling; or I would have accepted
your offering.
See also: 3.22: Rev 22.14 4.4: Heb 11.4

Why that scowl on your face? (4.6)

8 Then Cain said to his brother Abel, "Let's go out in the fields."* When they were out in the fields, Cain turned on his brother and killed him.

9 The LORD asked Cain, "Where is your brother Abel?"

He answered, "I don't know. Am I supposed to take care of my brother?"

10 Then the LORD said, "Why have you done this terrible thing? Your brother's blood is crying out to me from the ground, like a voice calling for revenge. 11 You are placed under a curse and can no longer farm the soil. It has soaked up your brother's blood as if it had opened its mouth to receive it when you killed him. 12 If you try to grow crops, the soil will not produce anything; you will be a homeless wanderer on the earth."

13 And Cain said to the LORD, "This punishment is too hard for me to bear. 14 You are driving me off the land and away from your presence. I will be a homeless wanderer on the earth, and anyone who finds me will kill me."

15 But the LORD answered, "No. If anyone kills you, seven lives will be taken in revenge." So the LORD put a mark on Cain to warn anyone who met him not to kill him.

16 And Cain went away from the LORD's presence and lived in a land called "Wandering", which is east of Eden.

The Descendants of Cain

17 Cain and his wife had a son and named him Enoch. Then Cain built a city and named it after his son. 18 Enoch had a son named Irad, who was the father of Mehujael, and Mehujael had a son named Methushael, who was the father of Lamech. 19 Lamech had two wives, Adah and Zillah. 20 Adah gave birth to Jabal, who was the ancestor of those who raise livestock and live in tents. 21 His brother was Jubal, the ancestor of all musicians who play the harp and the flute. 22 Zillah gave birth to Tubal Cain, who made all kinds of tools* out of bronze and iron. The sister of Tubal Cain was Naamah.

23 Lamech said to his wives,

"Adah and Zillah, listen to me: I have killed a young man because he struck me.
24 If seven lives are taken to pay for killing Cain,
Seventy-seven will be taken if anyone kills me."

Seth and Enosh

25 Adam and his wife had another son. She said, "God has given me a son to replace Abel, whom Cain killed." So she named him Seth.* 26 Seth had a son whom he named Enosh. It was then that people began using the LORD's holy name in worship.

The Descendants of Adam
(1 Chr 1.1–4)

5 This is the list of the descendants of Adam. (When God created human beings, he made them like himself. 2 He created them male and female, blessed them, and named them "Humanity".) 3 When Adam was 130 years old, he had a son who was like him, and he named him Seth. 4 After that, Adam lived another 800 years. He had other children 5 and died at the age of 930.

4.8 *Some ancient translations* Let's go out in the fields; *Hebrew does not have these words.*
See also: 4.8: Mt 23.35; Lk 11.51; 1 Jn 3.12
4.10: Heb 12.24

4.22 who made all kinds of tools; *one ancient translation* ancestor of all metalworkers.
4.25 SETH: *This name sounds like the Hebrew for "has given".*
See also: 4.24: Mt 18.22   **5.1–2:** Gen 1.27–28
5.2: Mt 19.4; Mk 10.6

6 When Seth was 105, he had a son, Enosh, 7 and then lived another 807 years. He had other children 8 and died at the age of 912.

9 When Enosh was 90, he had a son, Kenan, 10 and then lived another 815 years. He had other children 11 and died at the age of 905.

12 When Kenan was 70, he had a son, Mahalalel, 13 and then lived another 840 years. He had other children 14 and died at the age of 910.

15 When Mahalalel was 65, he had a son, Jared, 16 and then lived another 830 years. He had other children 17 and died at the age of 895.

18 When Jared was 162, he had a son, Enoch, 19 and then lived another 800 years. He had other children 20 and died at the age of 962.

21 When Enoch was 65, he had a son, Methuselah. 22 After that, Enoch lived in fellowship with God for 300 years and had other children. 23 He lived to be 365 years old. 24 He spent his life in fellowship with God, and then he disappeared, because God took him away.

25 When Methuselah was 187, he had a son, Lamech, 26 and then lived another 782 years. He had other children 27 and died at the age of 969.

28 When Lamech was 182, he had a son, 29 and said, "From the very ground on which the LORD put a curse, this child will bring us relief from all our hard work"; so he named him Noah.* 30 Lamech lived another 595 years. He had other children 31 and died at the age of 777.

32 After Noah was 500 years old, he had three sons, Shem, Ham, and Japheth.

Human Wickedness

6 When the human race had spread all over the world, and daughters were being born, 2 some of the heavenly beings* saw that these young women were beautiful, so they took the ones they liked. 3 Then the LORD said, "I will not allow people to live for ever; they are mortal.

From now on they will live no longer than a hundred and twenty years." 4 In those days, and even later, there were giants on the earth who were descendants of human women and the heavenly beings.* They were the great heroes and famous men of long ago.

5 When the LORD saw how wicked everyone on earth was and how evil their thoughts were all the time, 6 he was sorry that he had ever made them and put them on the earth. He was so filled with regret 7 that he said, "I will wipe out these people I have created, and also the animals and the birds, because I am sorry that I made any of them." 8 But the LORD was pleased with Noah.

Noah

9–10 This is the story of Noah. He had three sons, Shem, Ham, and Japheth. Noah had no faults and was the only good man of his time. He lived in fellowship with God, 11 but everyone else was evil in God's sight, and violence had spread everywhere. 12 God looked at the world and saw that it was evil, for the people were all living evil lives.

13 God said to Noah, "I have decided to put an end to the whole human race. I will destroy them completely, because the world is full of their violent deeds. 14 Build a boat for yourself out of good timber; make rooms in it and cover it with tar inside and out. 15 Make it 133 metres long, 22 metres wide, and 13 metres high. 16 Make a roof* for the boat and leave a space of 44 centimetres between the roof* and the sides. Build it with three decks and put a door in the side. 17 I am going to send a flood on the earth to destroy every living being. Everything on the earth will die, 18 but I will make a covenant with you. Go into the boat with your wife, your sons, and their wives. 19–20 Take into the boat with you a male and a female of every kind of animal and of every kind of bird, in order to keep them alive. 21 Take along all kinds of food for you and for them." 22 Noah did everything that God commanded.

5.29 NOAH: *This name sounds like the Hebrew for "relief"*.

6.2, 6.4 heavenly beings; *or* sons of the gods; *or* sons of God.

See also: **5.24:** Heb 11.5; Jude 14   **6.1–4:** Job 1.6, 2.1

6.4, 6.2 heavenly beings; *or* sons of the gods; *or* sons of God.

6.16 roof; *or* window.

See also: **6.4:** Num 13.33   **6.5–8:** Mt 24.37; Lk 17.26; 1 Pet 3.20   **6.9:** 2 Pet 2.5   **6.22:** Heb 11.7

Every kind of animal and bird ... went into the boat (7.8,9)

The Flood

7 The LORD said to Noah, "Go into the boat with your whole family; I have found that you are the only one in all the world who does what is right. 2 Take with you seven pairs of each kind of ritually clean animal, but only one pair of each kind of unclean animal. 3 Take also seven pairs of each kind of bird. Do this so that every kind of animal and bird will be kept alive to reproduce again on the earth. 4 Seven days from now I am going to send rain that will fall for forty days and nights, in order to destroy all the living beings that I have made." 5 And Noah did everything that the LORD commanded.

6 Noah was 600 years old when the flood came on the earth. 7 He and his wife, and his sons and their wives, went into the boat to escape the flood. 8 A male and a female of every kind of animal and bird, whether ritually clean or unclean, 9 went into the boat with Noah, as God had commanded. 10 Seven days later the flood came.

11 When Noah was 600 years old, on the seventeenth day of the second month all the outlets of the vast body of water beneath the earth burst open, all the floodgates of the sky were opened, 12 and rain fell on the earth for 40 days and nights. 13 On that same day Noah and his wife went into the boat with their three sons, Shem, Ham, and Japheth, and their wives. 14 With them went every kind of animal, domestic and wild, large and small, and every kind of bird. 15 A male and a female of each kind of living being went into the boat with Noah, 16 as God had commanded. Then the LORD shut the door behind Noah.

17 The flood continued for 40 days, and the water became deep enough for the boat to float. 18 The water became deeper, and the boat drifted on the surface. 19 It became so deep that it covered the highest mountains; 20 it went on rising until it was about seven metres above the tops of the mountains. 21 Every living being on the earth died — every bird, every animal, and every person. 22 Everything on earth that breathed died. 23 The LORD destroyed all living beings on the earth — human beings, animals, and birds. The only ones left were

See also: 7.7: Mt 24.38–39; Lk 17.27
7.11: 2 Pet 3.6

Everything on earth that breathed died (7.22)

Noah and those who were with him in the boat. 24 The water did not start going down for 150 days.

The End of the Flood

8 God had not forgotten Noah and all the animals with him in the boat; he caused a wind to blow, and the water started going down. 2 The outlets of the water beneath the earth and the floodgates of the sky were closed. The rain stopped, 3 and the water gradually went down for 150 days. 4 On the seventeenth day of the seventh month the boat came to rest on a mountain in the Ararat range. 5 The water kept going down, and on the first day of the tenth month the tops of the mountains appeared.

6 After 40 days Noah opened a window 7 and sent out a raven. It did not come back, but kept flying around until the water was completely gone. 8 Meanwhile, Noah sent out a dove to see if the water had gone down, 9 but since the water still covered all the land, the dove did not find a place to alight. It flew back to the boat, and Noah reached out and took it in. 10 He waited another seven days and sent out the dove again. 11 It returned to him in the evening with a fresh olive leaf in its beak. So Noah knew that the water had gone down. 12 Then he waited another seven days and sent out the dove once more; this time it did not come back.

13 When Noah was 601 years old, on the first day of the first month, the water was gone. Noah removed the covering of the boat, looked round, and saw that the ground was getting dry. 14 By the 27th day of the second month the earth was completely dry.

So Noah knew that the water had gone down (8.11)

15 God said to Noah, 16 "Go out of the boat with your wife, your sons, and their wives. 17 Take all the birds and animals out with you, so that they may reproduce and spread over all the earth." 18 So Noah went out of the boat with his wife, his sons, and their wives. 19 All the animals and birds went out of the boat in groups of their own kind.

Noah Offers a Sacrifice

20 Noah built an altar to the Lord; he took one of each kind of ritually clean animal and bird, and burnt them whole as a sacrifice on the altar. 21 The odour of the sacrifice pleased the Lord, and he said to himself, "Never again will I put the earth under a curse because of what people do; I know that from the time they are young their thoughts are evil. Never again will I destroy all living beings, as I have done this time. 22 As long as the world exists, there will be a time for planting and a time for harvest. There will always be cold and heat, summer and winter, day and night."

God's Covenant with Noah

9 God blessed Noah and his sons and said, "Have many children, so that your descendants will live all over the earth. 2 All the animals, birds, and fish will live in fear of you. They are all placed under your power. 3 Now you can eat them, as well as green plants; I give them all to you for food. 4 The one thing you must not eat is meat with blood still in it; I forbid this because the life is in the blood. 5 If anyone takes human life, he will be punished. I will punish with death any animal that takes a human life. 6 Human beings were made like God, so whoever murders one of them will be killed by someone else.

7 "You must have many children, so that your descendants will live all over the earth."

8 God said to Noah and his sons, 9 "I am now making my covenant with you and with your descendants, 10 and with all living beings — all birds and all animals — everything that came out of the boat with you. 11 With these words I make my covenant with you: I promise that never again will all

See also: **9.1:** Gen 1.28   **9.4:** Gen 7.26–27, 17.10–14; Lev 19.26; Deut 12.16, 23, 15.23   **9.6:** Gen 1.26; Ex 20.13   **9.7:** Gen 1.28

living beings be destroyed by a flood; never again will a flood destroy the earth. 12 As a sign of this everlasting covenant which I am making with you and with all living beings, 13 I am putting my bow in the clouds. It will be the sign of my covenant with the world. 14 Whenever I cover the sky with clouds and the rainbow appears, 15 I will remember my promise to you and to all the animals that a flood will never again destroy all living beings. 16 When the rainbow appears in the clouds, I will see it and remember the everlasting covenant between me and all living beings on earth. 17 That is the sign of the promise which I am making to all living beings."

The sign of my covenant with the world   (9.13)

Noah and his Sons

18 The sons of Noah who went out of the boat were Shem, Ham, and Japheth. (Ham was the father of Canaan.) 19 These three sons of Noah were the ancestors of all the people on earth.

20 Noah, who was a farmer, was the first man to plant a vineyard. 21 After he drank some of the wine, he became drunk, took off his clothes, and lay naked in his tent. 22 When Ham, the father of Canaan, saw that his father was naked, he went out and told his two brothers. 23 Then Shem and Japheth took a robe and held it behind them on their shoulders. They walked backwards into the tent and covered their father, keeping their faces turned away so as not to see him naked. 24 When Noah was sober again and learnt what his youngest son had done to him, 25 he said,

"A curse on Canaan!
He will be a slave to his brothers.
26 Give praise to the Lord, the God of Shem!
Canaan will be the slave of Shem.

27 May God cause Japheth* to increase!
May his descendants live with the people of Shem!
Canaan will be the slave of Japheth."

28 After the flood Noah lived for 350 years 29 and died at the age of 950.

The Descendants of Noah's Sons
(1 Chr 1.5–23)

10 These are the descendants of Noah's sons, Shem, Ham, and Japheth. These three had sons after the flood.

2 The sons of Japheth — Gomer, Magog, Madai, Javan, Tubal, Meshech, and Tiras — were the ancestors of the peoples who bear their names. 3 The descendants of Gomer were the people of Ashkenaz, Riphath, and Togarmah. 4 The descendants of Javan were the people of Elishah, Spain, Cyprus, and Rhodes; 5 they were the ancestors of the people who live along the coast and on the islands. These are the descendants of Japheth, living in their different tribes and countries, each group speaking its own language.

6 The sons of Ham — Cush, Egypt, Libya and Canaan — were the ancestors of the peoples who bear their names. 7 The descendants of Cush were the people of Seba, Havilah, Sabtah, Raamah, and Sabteca. The descendants of Raamah were the people of Sheba and Dedan. 8 Cush had a son named Nimrod, who became the world's first great conqueror. 9 By the Lord's help he was a great hunter, and that is why people say, "May the Lord make you as great a hunter as Nimrod!" 10 At first his kingdom included Babylon, Erech, and Accad, all three of them in Babylonia. 11 From that land he went to Assyria and built the cities of Nineveh, Rehoboth Ir, Calah, 12 and Resen, which is between Nineveh and the great city of Calah.

13 The descendants of Egypt were the people of Lydia, Anam, Lehab, Naphtuh, 14 Pathrus, Casluh, and of Crete, from whom the Philistines are descended.*

9.27 JAPHETH: *This name sounds like the Hebrew for "increase".*

10.14 *Probable text* and of Crete… descended; *Hebrew* from whom the Philistines are descended, and Crete.

15 Canaan's sons — Sidon, the eldest, and Heth — were the ancestors of the peoples who bear their names. 16 Canaan was also the ancestor of the Jebusites, the Amorites, the Girgashites, 17 the Hivites, the Arkites, the Sinites, 18 the Arvadites, the Zemarites, and the Hamathites. The different tribes of the Canaanites spread out, 19 until the Canaanite borders reached from Sidon southwards to Gerar near Gaza, and eastwards to Sodom, Gomorrah, Admah, and Zeboiim near Lasha. 20 These are the descendants of Ham, living in their different tribes and countries, each group speaking its own language.

21 Shem, the elder brother of Japheth, was the ancestor of all the Hebrews. 22 Shem's sons — Elam, Asshur, Arpachshad, Lud, and Aram — were the ancestors of the peoples who bear their names. 23 The descendants of Aram were the people of Uz, Hul, Gether, and Meshek. 24 Arpachshad was the father of Shelah, who was the father of Eber. 25 Eber had two sons: one was named Peleg,* because during his time the people of the world were divided; and the other was named Joktan. 26 The descendants of Joktan were the people of Almodad, Sheleph, Hazarmaveth, Jerah, 27 Hadoram, Uzal, Diklah, 28 Obal, Abimael, Sheba, 29 Ophir, Havilah, and Jobab. All of them were descended from Joktan. 30 The land in which they lived extended from Mesha to Sephar in the eastern hill country. 31 These are the descendants of Shem, living in their different tribes and countries, each group speaking its own language.

32 All these peoples are the descendants of Noah, nation by nation, according to their different lines of descent. After the flood all the nations of the earth were descended from the sons of Noah.

The Tower of Babylon

11 At first, the people of the whole world had only one language and used the same words. 2 As they wandered about in the East, they came to a plain in Babylonia and settled there. 3 They said to one another, "Come on! Let's make bricks and bake them hard." So they had bricks to build with and tar to hold them together. 4 They said, "Now let's build a city with a tower that reaches the sky, so that we can make a name for ourselves and not be scattered all over the earth."

5 Then the LORD came down to see the city and the tower which those men had built, 6 and he said, "Now then, these are all one people and they speak one language; this is just the beginning of what they are going to do. Soon they will be able to do anything they want! 7 Let us go down and mix up their language so that they will not understand one another." 8 So the LORD scattered them all over the earth, and they stopped building the city. 9 The city was called Babylon,* because there the LORD mixed up the language of all the people, and from there he scattered them all over the earth.

The Descendants of Shem
(1 Chr 1.24–27)

10 These are the descendants of Shem. Two years after the flood, when Shem was 100 years old, he had a son, Arpachshad. 11 After that, he lived another 500 years and had other children.

12 When Arpachshad was 35 years old, he had a son, Shelah; 13 after that, he lived another 403 years and had other children.

14 When Shelah was 30 years old, he had a son, Eber; 15 after that, he lived another 403 years and had other children.

16 When Eber was 34 years old, he had a son, Peleg; 17 after that, he lived another 430 years and had other children.

18 When Peleg was 30 years old, he had a son, Reu; 19 after that, he lived another 209 years and had other children.

20 When Reu was 32 years old, he had a son, Serug; 21 after that, he lived another 207 years and had other children.

22 When Serug was 30 years old, he had a son, Nahor; 23 after that, he lived another 200 years and had other children.

24 When Nahor was 29 years old, he had a son, Terah; 25 after that, he lived another 119 years and had other children.

26 After Terah was 70 years old, he became the father of Abram, Nahor, and Haran.

10.25 PELEG: *This name sounds like the Hebrew for "divide".*

11.9 BABYLON: *This name sounds like the Hebrew for "mixed up".*

The Descendants of Terah

27 These are the descendants of Terah, who was the father of Abram, Nahor, and Haran. Haran was the father of Lot, 28 and Haran died in his native city, Ur in Babylonia, while his father was still living. 29 Abram married Sarai, and Nahor married Milcah, the daughter of Haran, who was also the father of Iscah. 30 Sarai was not able to have children.

31 Terah took his son Abram, his grandson Lot, who was the son of Haran, and his daughter-in-law Sarai, Abram's wife, and with them he left the city of Ur in Babylonia to go to the land of Canaan. They went as far as Haran and settled there. 32 Terah died there at the age of 205.

God's Call to Abram

12 The Lord said to Abram, "Leave your country, your relatives, and your father's home, and go to a land that I am going to show you. 2 I will give you many descendants, and they will become a great nation. I will bless you and make your name famous, so that you will be a blessing.

3 I will bless those who bless you,
    But I will curse those who curse you.
    And through you I will bless all the
        nations."*

4 When Abram was 75 years old, he started out from Haran, as the Lord had told him to do; and Lot went with him. 5 Abram took his wife Sarai, his nephew Lot, and all the wealth and all the slaves they had acquired in Haran, and they started out for the land of Canaan.

When they arrived in Canaan, 6 Abram travelled through the land until he came to the sacred tree of Moreh, the holy place at Shechem. (At that time the Canaanites were still living in the land.) 7 The Lord appeared to Abram and said to him, "This is the country that I am going to give to your descendants." Then Abram built an altar there to the Lord, who had appeared to him. 8 After that, he moved on south to the hill country east of the city of Bethel and set up his camp between Bethel on the west and Ai on the east. There also he built an altar and worshipped the Lord. 9 Then he moved on from place to place, going towards the southern part of Canaan.

Abram in Egypt

10 But there was a famine in Canaan, and it was so bad that Abram went farther south to Egypt, to live there for a while. 11 When he was about to cross the border into Egypt, he said to his wife Sarai, "You are a beautiful woman. 12 When the Egyptians see you, they will assume that you are my wife, and so they will kill me and let you live. 13 Tell them that you are my sister; then because of you they will let me live and treat me well." 14 When he crossed the border into Egypt, the Egyptians did see that his wife was beautiful. 15 Some of the court officials saw her and told the king how beautiful she was; so she was taken to his palace. 16 Because of her the king treated Abram well and gave him flocks of sheep and goats, cattle, donkeys, slaves, and camels.

17 But because the king had taken Sarai, the Lord sent terrible diseases on him and on the people of his palace. 18 Then the king sent for Abram and asked him, "What have you done to me? Why didn't you tell me that she was your wife? 19 Why did you say that she was your sister, and let me take her as my wife? Here is your wife; take her and get out!" 20 The king gave orders to his men, so they took Abram and put him out of the country, together with his wife and everything he owned.

Abram and Lot Separate

13 Abram went north out of Egypt to the southern part of Canaan with his wife and everything he owned, and Lot went with him. 2 Abram was a very rich man, with sheep, goats, and cattle, as well as silver and gold. 3 Then he left there and moved from place to place, going towards Bethel. He reached the place between Bethel and Ai where he had camped before 4 and had built an altar. There he worshipped the Lord.

5 Lot also had sheep, goats, and cattle, as well as his own family and servants. 6 And so there was not enough pasture

---

12.3 And through... nations; or All the nations will ask me to bless them as I have blessed you.
See also: 12.1: Acts 7.2–3; Heb 11.8   **12.3:** Gal 3.8
12.7: Acts 7.5; Gal 3.16

See also: 12.13: Gen 20.2, 26.7

land for the two of them to stay together, because they had too many animals. 7 So quarrels broke out between the men who took care of Abram's animals and those who took care of Lot's animals. (At that time the Canaanites and the Perizzites were still living in the land.)

8 Then Abram said to Lot, "We are relatives, and your men and my men shouldn't be quarrelling. 9 So let's separate. Choose any part of the land you want. You go one way, and I'll go the other."

10 Lot looked round and saw that the whole Jordan Valley, all the way to Zoar, had plenty of water, like the Garden of the LORD* or like the land of Egypt. (This was before the LORD had destroyed the cities of Sodom and Gomorrah.) 11 So Lot chose the whole Jordan Valley for himself and moved away towards the east. That is how the two men parted. 12 Abram stayed in the land of Canaan, and Lot settled among the cities in the valley and camped near Sodom, 13 whose people were wicked and sinned against the LORD.

Abram Moves to Hebron

14 After Lot had left, the LORD said to Abram, "From where you are, look carefully in all directions. 15 I am going to give you and your descendants all the land that you see, and it will be yours for ever. 16 I am going to give you so many descendants that no one will be able to count them all; it would be as easy to count all the specks of dust on earth! 17 Now, go and look over the whole land, because I am going to give it all to you." 18 So Abram moved his camp and settled near the sacred trees of Mamre at Hebron, and there he built an altar to the LORD.

Abram Rescues Lot

14 Four kings, Amraphel of Babylonia, Arioch of Ellasar, Chedorlaomer of Elam, and Tidal of Goiim, 2 went to war against five other kings: Bera of Sodom, Birsha of Gomorrah, Shinab of Admah, Shemeber of Zeboiim, and the king of Bela (or Zoar). 3 These five kings had formed an alliance and joined forces in the Valley of Siddim, which is now the Dead Sea. 4 They had been under the control of Chedorlaomer for twelve years, but in the thirteenth year they rebelled against him. 5 In the fourteenth year Chedorlaomer and his allies came with their armies and defeated the Rephaim in Ashteroth Karnaim, the Zuzim in Ham, the Emim in the plain of Kiriathaim, 6 and the Horites in the mountains of Edom, pursuing them as far as Elparan on the edge of the desert. 7 Then they turned round and came back to Kadesh (then known as Enmishpat). They conquered all the land of the Amalekites and defeated the Amorites who lived in Hazazon Tamar.

8 Then the kings of Sodom, Gomorrah, Admah, Zeboiim, and Bela drew up their armies for battle in the Valley of Siddim and fought 9 against the kings of Elam, Goiim, Babylonia, and Ellasar, five kings against four. 10 The valley was full of tar pits, and when the kings of Sodom and Gomorrah tried to run away from the battle, they fell into the pits; but the other three kings escaped to the mountains. 11 The four kings took everything in Sodom and Gomorrah, including the food, and went away. 12 Lot, Abram's nephew, was living in Sodom, so they took him and all his possessions.

13 But a man escaped and reported all this to Abram, the Hebrew, who was living near the sacred trees belonging to Mamre the Amorite. Mamre and his brothers Eshcol and Aner were Abram's allies. 14 When Abram heard that his nephew had been captured, he called together all the fighting men in his camp, 318 in all, and pursued the four kings all the way to Dan. 15 There he divided his men into groups, attacked the enemy by night, and defeated them. He chased them as far as Hobah, north of Damascus, 16 and recovered the loot that had been taken. He also brought back his nephew Lot and his possessions, together with the women and the other prisoners.

Melchizedek Blesses Abram

17 When Abram came back from his victory over Chedorlaomer and the other kings, the king of Sodom went out to meet him in the Valley of Shaveh (also called the King's Valley). 18 And Melchizedek, who

---

13.10 GARDEN OF THE LORD: *a reference to the Garden of Eden.*

See also: **13.10**: Gen 2.10　**13.15**: Acts 7.5

See also: **14.18–20**: Heb 7.1–10

was king of Salem and also a priest of the
Most High God, brought bread and wine
to Abram, 19 blessed him, and said, "May
the Most High God, who made heaven
and earth, bless Abram! 20 May the Most
High God, who gave you victory over your
enemies, be praised!" And Abram gave
Melchizedek a tenth of all the loot he had
recovered.

21 The king of Sodom said to Abram,
"Keep the loot, but give me back all my
people."

22 Abram answered, "I solemnly swear
before the LORD, the Most High God,
Maker of heaven and earth, 23 that I will
not keep anything of yours, not even a
thread or a sandal strap. Then you can
never say, 'I am the one who made Abram
rich.' 24 I will take nothing for myself. I will
accept only what my men have used. But
let my allies, Aner, Eshcol, and Mamre,
take their share."

God's Covenant with Abram

15 After this, Abram had a vision and
heard the LORD say to him, "Do not
be afraid, Abram. I will shield you from
danger and give you a great reward."

2 But Abram answered, "Sovereign LORD,
what good will your reward do me, since I
have no children? My only heir is Eliezer of
Damascus.* 3 You have given me no children, and one of my slaves will inherit my
property."

4 Then he heard the LORD speaking to
him again: "This slave Eliezer will not
inherit your property; your own son will be
your heir." 5 The LORD took him outside
and said, "Look at the sky and try to count
the stars; you will have as many descendants as that."

6 Abram put his trust in the LORD, and
because of this the LORD was pleased with
him and accepted him.

7 Then the LORD said to him, "I am the
LORD, who led you out of Ur in Babylonia,
to give you this land as your own."

8 But Abram asked, "Sovereign LORD,
how can I know that it will be mine?"

9 He answered, "Bring me a cow, a goat,
and a ram, each of them three years old,

and a dove and a pigeon." 10 Abram
brought the animals to God, cut them in
half, and placed the halves opposite each
other in two rows; but he did not cut up
the birds. 11 Vultures came down on the
bodies, but Abram drove them off.

12 When the sun was going down,
Abram fell into a deep sleep, and fear
and terror came over him. 13 The LORD
said to him, "Your descendants will be
strangers in a foreign land; they will be
slaves there and will be treated cruelly
for four hundred years. 14 But I will punish the nation that enslaves them, and
when they leave that foreign land, they
will take great wealth with them. 15 You
yourself will live to a ripe old age, die in
peace, and be buried. 16 It will be four
generations before your descendants
come back here, because I will not drive
out the Amorites until they become so
wicked that they must be punished."

17 When the sun had set and it was
dark, a smoking fire-pot and a flaming
torch suddenly appeared and passed
between the pieces of the animals.
18 Then and there the LORD made a covenant with Abram. He said, "I promise to
give your descendants all this land from
the border of Egypt to the River Euphrates, 19 including the lands of the Ken-
ites, the Kenizzites, the Kadmonites,
20 the Hittites, the Perizzites, the Rephaim, 21 the Amorites, the Canaanites, the
Girgashites, and the Jebusites."

Hagar and Ishmael

16 Abram's wife Sarai had not borne
him any children. But she had an
Egyptian slave woman named Hagar,
2 and so she said to Abram, "The LORD has
kept me from having children. Why don't
you sleep with my slave? Perhaps she can
have a child for me." Abram agreed with
what Sarai said. 3 So she gave Hagar to
him to be his concubine. (This happened
after Abram had lived in Canaan for ten
years.) 4 Abram had intercourse with
Hagar, and she became pregnant. When
she found out that she was pregnant, she
became proud and despised Sarai.

15.2 My... Damascus; *Hebrew unclear.*
See also: 15.5: Rom 4.18; Heb 11.12
15.6: Rom 4.3; Gal 3.6; Jas 2.23

See also: 15.12: Job 4.13, 14   **15.13:** Ex 1.1–14;
Acts 7.6   **15.14:** Ex 12.40–41; Acts 7.7
15.18: Acts 7.5

5 Then Sarai said to Abram, "It's your fault that Hagar despises me.* I myself gave her to you, and ever since she found out that she was pregnant, she has despised me. May the LORD judge which of us is right, you or me!"

6 Abram answered, "Very well, she is your slave and under your control; do whatever you want with her." Then Sarai treated Hagar so cruelly that she ran away.

7 The angel of the LORD met Hagar at a spring in the desert on the road to Shur 8 and said, "Hagar, slave of Sarai, where have you come from and where are you going?"

She answered, "I am running away from my mistress."

9 He said, "Go back to her and be her slave." 10 Then he said, "I will give you so many descendants that no one will be able to count them. 11 You are going to have a son, and you will name him Ishmael,* because the LORD has heard your cry of distress. 12 But your son will live like a wild donkey; he will be against everyone, and everyone will be against him. He will live apart from all his relatives."

13 Hagar asked herself, "Have I really seen God and lived to tell about it?"* So she called the LORD who had spoken to her "A God who Sees". 14 That is why people call the well between Kadesh and Bered "The Well of the Living One who Sees Me".

15 Hagar bore Abram a son, and he named him Ishmael. 16 Abram was 86 years old at the time.

Circumcision, the Sign of the Covenant

17 When Abram was 99 years old, the LORD appeared to him and said, "I am the Almighty God. Obey me and always do what is right. 2 I will make my covenant with you and give you many descendants." 3 Abram bowed down with his face touching the ground, and God said, 4 "I make this covenant with you: I promise that you will be the ancestor of

many nations. 5 Your name will no longer be Abram, but Abraham,* because I am making you the ancestor of many nations. 6 I will give you many descendants, and some of them will be kings. You will have so many descendants that they will become nations.

7 "I will keep my promise to you and to your descendants in future generations as an everlasting covenant. I will be your God and the God of your descendants. 8 I will give to you and to your descendants this land in which you are now a foreigner. The whole land of Canaan will belong to your descendants for ever, and I will be their God."

9 God said to Abraham, "You also must agree to keep the covenant with me, both you and your descendants in future generations. 10 You and your descendants must all agree to circumcise every male among you. 11–12 From now on you must circumcise every baby boy when he is eight days old, including slaves born in your homes and slaves bought from foreigners. This will show that there is a covenant between you and me. 13 Each one must be circumcised, and this will be a physical sign to show that my covenant with you is everlasting. 14 Any male who has not been circumcised will no longer be considered one of my people, because he has not kept the covenant with me."

15 God said to Abraham, "You must no longer call your wife Sarai; from now on her name is Sarah.* 16 I will bless her, and I will give you a son by her. I will bless her, and she will become the mother of nations, and there will be kings among her descendants."

17 Abraham bowed down with his face touching the ground, but he began to laugh when he thought, "Can a man have a child when he is a hundred years old? Can Sarah have a child at ninety?" 18 He asked God, "Why not let Ishmael be my heir?"

19 But God said, "No. Your wife Sarah will bear you a son and you will name

---

16.5 It's your fault… me; or May you suffer for this wrong done against me.
16.11 ISHMAEL: *This name in Hebrew means "God hears".*
16.13 *Probable text* lived to tell about it?; *Hebrew unclear.*

See also: 16.15: Gal 4.22

17.5 ABRAHAM: *This name sounds like the Hebrew for "ancestor of many nations".*
17.15 SARAH: *This name in Hebrew means "princess".*

See also: 17.5: Rom 4.17   **17.7:** Lk 1.55
17.8: Acts 7.5   **17.10:** Acts 7.8; Rom 4.11

him Isaac.* I will keep my covenant with him and with his descendants for ever. It is an everlasting covenant. 20 I have heard your request about Ishmael, so I will bless him and give him many children and many descendants. He will be the father of twelve princes, and I will make a great nation of his descendants. 21 But I will keep my covenant with your son Isaac, who will be born to Sarah about this time next year." 22 When God finished speaking to Abraham, he left him.

23 On that same day Abraham obeyed God and circumcised his son Ishmael and all the other males in his household, including the slaves born in his home and those he had bought. 24 Abraham was 99 years old when he was circumcised, 25 and his son Ishmael was thirteen. 26 They were both circumcised on the same day, 27 together with all Abraham's slaves.

A Son is Promised to Abraham

18 The LORD appeared to Abraham at the sacred trees of Mamre. As Abraham was sitting at the entrance of his tent during the hottest part of the day, 2 he looked up and saw three men standing there. As soon as he saw them, he ran out to meet them. Bowing down with his face touching the ground, 3 he said, "Sirs, please do not pass by my home without stopping; I am here to serve you. 4 Let me bring some water for you to wash your feet; you can rest here beneath this tree. 5 I will also bring a bit of food; it will give you strength to continue your journey. You have honoured me by coming to my home, so let me serve you."

They replied, "Thank you; we accept."

6 Abraham hurried into the tent and said to Sarah, "Quick, take a sack of your best flour, and bake some bread." 7 Then he ran to the herd and picked out a calf that was tender and fat, and gave it to a servant, who hurried to get it ready. 8 He took some cream, some milk, and the meat, and set the food before the men. There under the tree he served them himself, and they ate.

9 Then they asked him, "Where is your wife Sarah?"

"She is there in the tent," he answered.

10 One of them said, "Nine months from now* I will come back, and your wife Sarah will have a son."

Sarah was behind him, at the door of the tent, listening. 11 Abraham and Sarah were very old, and Sarah had stopped having her monthly periods. 12 So Sarah laughed to herself and said, "Now that I am old and worn out, can I still enjoy sex? And besides, my husband is old too."

13 Then the LORD asked Abraham, "Why did Sarah laugh and say, 'Can I really have a child when I am so old?' 14 Is anything too hard for the LORD? As I said, nine months from now I will return, and Sarah will have a son."

15 Because Sarah was afraid, she denied it. "I didn't laugh," she said.

"Yes, you did," he replied. "You laughed."

Abraham Pleads for Sodom

16 Then the men left and went to a place where they could look down at Sodom, and Abraham went with them to send them on their way. 17 And the LORD said to himself, "I will not hide from Abraham what I am going to do. 18 His descendants will become a great and mighty nation, and through him I will bless all the nations.* 19 I have chosen him in order that he may command his sons and his descendants to obey me and to do what is right and just. If they do, I will do everything for him that I have promised."

20 Then the LORD said to Abraham, "There are terrible accusations against Sodom and Gomorrah, and their sin is very great. 21 I must go down to find out whether or not the accusations which I have heard are true."

22 Then the two men left and went on towards Sodom, but the LORD remained with Abraham. 23 Abraham approached the LORD and asked, "Are you really going to destroy the innocent with the guilty? 24 If there are fifty innocent people in the city, will you destroy the whole city? Won't you spare it in order to save the fifty? 25 Surely you won't kill the innocent with

---

18.10 Nine months from now; *or* This time next year.
18.18 through… nations; *or* all the nations will ask me to bless them as I have blessed him.

See also: **18.10:** Rom 9.9 **18.12:** 1 Pet 3.6
18.14: Lk 1.37

17.19 ISAAC: *This name in Hebrew means "he laughs".*
See also: **18.2a:** Heb 13.2

the guilty. That's impossible! You can't do that. If you did, the innocent would be punished along with the guilty. That is impossible. The judge of all the earth has to act justly."

26 The LORD answered, "If I find fifty innocent people in Sodom, I will spare the whole city for their sake."

27 Abraham spoke again: "Please forgive my boldness in continuing to speak to you, Lord. I am only a man and have no right to say anything. 28 But perhaps there will be only forty-five innocent people instead of fifty. Will you destroy the whole city because there are five too few?"

The LORD answered, "I will not destroy the city if I find forty-five innocent people."

29 Abraham spoke again: "Perhaps there will be only forty."

He replied, "I will not destroy it if there are forty."

30 Abraham said, "Please don't be angry, Lord, but I must speak again. What if there are only thirty?"

He said, "I will not do it if I find thirty."

31 Abraham said, "Please forgive my boldness in continuing to speak to you, Lord. Suppose that only twenty are found?"

He said, "I will not destroy the city if I find twenty."

32 Abraham said, "Please don't be angry, Lord, and I will speak just once more. What if only ten are found?"

He said, "I will not destroy it if there are ten." 33 After he had finished speaking with Abraham, the LORD went away, and Abraham returned home.

The Sinfulness of Sodom

19 When the two angels came to Sodom that evening, Lot was sitting at the city gate. As soon as he saw them, he got up and went to meet them. He bowed down before them 2 and said, "Sirs, I am here to serve you. Please come to my house. You can wash your feet and stay the night. In the morning you can get up early and go on your way."

But they answered, "No, we will spend the night here in the city square."

3 He kept on urging them, and finally they went with him to his house. Lot ordered his servants to bake some bread and prepare a fine meal for the guests. When it was ready, they ate it.

4 Before the guests went to bed, the men of Sodom surrounded the house. All the men of the city, both young and old, were there. 5 They called out to Lot and asked, "Where are the men who came to stay with you tonight? Bring them out to us!" The men of Sodom wanted to have sex with them.

6 Lot went outside and closed the door behind him. 7 He said to them, "Friends, I beg you, don't do such a wicked thing! 8 Look, I have two daughters who are still virgins. Let me bring them out to you, and you can do whatever you want with them. But don't do anything to these men; they are guests in my house, and I must protect them."

9 But they said, "Get out of our way, you foreigner! Who are you to tell us what to do? Out of our way, or we will treat you worse than them." They pushed Lot back and moved up to break down the door. 10 But the two men inside reached out, pulled Lot back into the house, and shut the door. 11 Then they struck all the men outside with blindness, so that they couldn't find the door.

Lot Leaves Sodom

12 The two men said to Lot, "If you have anyone else here — sons, daughters, sons-in-law, or any other relatives living in the city — get them out of here, 13 because we are going to destroy this place. The LORD has heard the terrible accusations against these people and has sent us to destroy Sodom."

14 Then Lot went to the men that his daughters were going to marry, and said, "Hurry up and get out of here; the LORD is going to destroy this place." But they thought he was joking.

15 At dawn the angels tried to make Lot hurry. "Quick!" they said. "Take your wife and your two daughters and get out, so that you will not lose your lives when the city is destroyed." 16 Lot hesitated. The LORD, however, had pity on him; so the men took him, his wife, and his two daughters by the hand and led them out of the city. 17 Then one of the angels said, "Run for your lives! Don't look back and

See also: **19.5–8:** Judg 19.22–24
19.11: 2 Kgs 6.18 **19.16:** 2 Pet 2.7

don't stop in the valley. Run to the hills, so that you won't be killed."

18 But Lot answered, "No, please don't make us do that, sir. 19 You have done me a great favour and saved my life. But the hills are too far away; the disaster will overtake me, and I will die before I get there. 20 Do you see that little town? It is near enough. Let me go over there — you can see it is just a small place — and I will be safe."

21 He answered, "All right, I agree. I won't destroy that town. 22 Hurry! Run! I can't do anything until you get there."

Because Lot called it small, the town was named Zoar.*

The Destruction of Sodom and Gomorrah

23 The sun was rising when Lot reached Zoar. 24 Suddenly the Lord rained burning sulphur on the cities of Sodom and Gomorrah 25 and destroyed them and the whole valley, along with all the people there and everything that grew on the land. 26 But Lot's wife looked back and was turned into a pillar of salt.

27 Early the next morning Abraham hurried to the place where he had stood in the presence of the Lord. 28 He looked down at Sodom and Gomorrah and the whole valley and saw smoke rising from the land, like smoke from a huge furnace. 29 But when God destroyed the cities of the valley where Lot was living, he kept Abraham in mind and allowed Lot to escape to safety.

The Origin of the Moabites and Ammonites

30 Because Lot was afraid to stay in Zoar, he and his two daughters moved up into the hills and lived in a cave. 31 The elder daughter said to her sister, "Our father is getting old, and there are no men in the whole world* to marry us so that we can have children. 32 Come on, let's make our father drunk, so that we can sleep with him and have children by him." 33 That night they gave him wine to drink, and the elder daughter had intercourse with him. But he was so drunk that he didn't know it.

34 The next day the elder daughter said to her sister, "I slept with him last night; now let's make him drunk again tonight, and you sleep with him. Then each of us will have a child by our father." 35 So that night they made him drunk, and the younger daughter had intercourse with him. Again he was so drunk that he didn't know it. 36 In this way both of Lot's daughters became pregnant by their own father. 37 The elder daughter had a son, whom she named Moab.* He was the ancestor of the present-day Moabites. 38 The younger daughter also had a son, whom she named Benammi.* He was the ancestor of the present-day Ammonites.

Abraham and Abimelech

20 Abraham moved from Mamre to the southern part of Canaan and lived between Kadesh and Shur. Later, while he was living in Gerar, 2 he said that his wife Sarah was his sister. So King Abimelech of Gerar had Sarah brought to him. 3 One night God appeared to him in a dream and said: "You are going to die, because you have taken this woman; she is already married."

4 But Abimelech had not come near her, and he said, "Lord, I am innocent! Would you destroy me and my people? 5 Abraham himself said that she was his sister, and she said the same thing. I did this with a clear conscience, and I have done no wrong."

6 God replied in the dream, "Yes, I know that you did it with a clear conscience; so I kept you from sinning against me and did not let you touch her. 7 But now, give the woman back to her husband. He is a prophet, and he will pray for you, so that you will not die. But if you do not give her back, I warn you that you are going to die, you and all your people."

8 Early the next morning Abimelech called all his officials and told them what had happened, and they were terrified.

19.22 Zoar: *This name sounds like the Hebrew for "small".*

19.31 the whole world; *or* this land.

See also: 19.24–25: Mt 10.15, 11.23–24; Lk 10.12, 17.29; 2 Pet 2.6; Jude 7   **19.26:** Lk 17.32

19.37 Moab: *This name sounds like the Hebrew for "from my father".*

19.38 Benammi: *This name in Hebrew means "son of my relative" and sounds like the Hebrew for "Ammonite".*

See also: 20.2: Gen 12.13, 26.7

9 Then Abimelech called Abraham and asked, "What have you done to us? What wrong have I done to you to make you bring this disaster on me and my kingdom? No one should ever do what you have done to me. 10 Why did you do it?"

11 Abraham answered, "I thought that there would be no one here who has reverence for God and that they would kill me to get my wife. 12 She really is my sister. She is the daughter of my father, but not of my mother, and I married her. 13 So when God sent me from my father's house into foreign lands, I said to her, 'You can show how loyal you are to me by telling everyone that I am your brother.' "

14 Then Abimelech gave Sarah back to Abraham, and at the same time he gave him sheep, cattle, and slaves. 15 He said to Abraham, "Here is my whole land; live anywhere you like." 16 He said to Sarah, "I am giving your brother a thousand pieces of silver as proof to all who are with you that you are innocent; everyone will know that you have done no wrong."

17-18 Because of what had happened to Sarah, Abraham's wife, the LORD had made it impossible for any woman in Abimelech's palace to have children. So Abraham prayed for Abimelech, and God healed him. He also healed his wife and his slave women, so that they could have children.

The Birth of Isaac

21 The LORD blessed Sarah, as he had promised, 2 and she became pregnant and bore a son to Abraham when he was old. The boy was born at the time God had said he would be born. 3 Abraham named him Isaac, 4 and when Isaac was eight days old, Abraham circumcised him, as God had commanded. 5 Abraham was a hundred years old when Isaac was born. 6 Sarah said, "God has brought me joy and laughter.* Everyone who hears about it will laugh with me." 7 Then she added, "Who would have said to Abraham that Sarah would nurse children? Yet I have borne him a son in his old age."

8 The child grew, and on the day that he was weaned, Abraham gave a great feast.

Hagar and Ishmael are Sent Away

9 One day Ishmael, whom Hagar the Egyptian had borne to Abraham, was playing with* Sarah's son Isaac.* 10 Sarah saw them and said to Abraham, "Send this slave and her son away. The son of this woman must not get any part of your wealth, which my son Isaac should inherit." 11 This troubled Abraham very much, because Ishmael was also his son. 12 But God said to Abraham, "Don't be worried about the boy and your slave Hagar. Do whatever Sarah tells you, because it is through Isaac that you will have the descendants I have promised. 13 I will also give many children to the son of the slave woman, so that they will become a nation. He too is your son."

14 Early the next morning Abraham gave Hagar some food and a leather bag full of water. He put the child on her back and sent her away. She left and wandered about in the wilderness of Beersheba. 15 When the water was all gone, she left the child under a bush 16 and sat down about a hundred metres away. She said to herself, "I can't bear to see my child die." While she was sitting there, she* began to cry.

17 God heard the boy crying, and from heaven the angel of God spoke to Hagar, "What are you troubled about, Hagar? Don't be afraid. God has heard the boy crying. 18 Get up, go and pick him up, and comfort him. I will make a great nation out of his descendants." 19 Then God opened her eyes, and she saw a well. She went and filled the leather bag with water and gave some to the boy. 20 God was with the boy as he grew up; he lived in the wilderness of Paran and became a skilful hunter. 21 His mother found an Egyptian wife for him.

21.6 LAUGHTER: *The name Isaac in Hebrew means "he laughs" (see also 17.17–19).*

See also: 21.2: Heb 11.11   **21.4:** Gen 17.12; Acts 7.8

21.9 playing with; *or* making fun of.
21.9 *Some ancient translations* with Sarah's son Isaac; *Hebrew does not have these words.*
21.16 she; *one ancient translation* the child.
See also: 21.10: Gal 4.29–30   **21.12:** Rom 9.7; Heb 11.18

The Agreement between Abraham and Abimelech

22 At that time Abimelech went with Phicol, the commander of his army, and said to Abraham, "God is with you in everything you do. 23 So make a vow here in the presence of God that you will not deceive me, my children, or my descendants. I have been loyal to you, so promise that you will also be loyal to me and to this country in which you are living."

24 Abraham said, "I promise."

25 Abraham complained to Abimelech about a well which the servants of Abimelech had seized. 26 Abimelech said, "I don't know who did this. You didn't tell me about it, and this is the first I have heard of it." 27 Then Abraham gave some sheep and cattle to Abimelech, and the two of them made an agreement. 28 Abraham separated seven lambs from his flock, 29 and Abimelech asked him, "Why did you do that?"

30 Abraham answered, "Accept these seven lambs. By doing this, you admit that I am the one who dug this well." 31 And so the place was called Beersheba,* because it was there that the two of them made a vow.

32 After they had made this agreement at Beersheba, Abimelech and Phicol went back to Philistia. 33 Then Abraham planted a tamarisk tree in Beersheba and worshipped the LORD, the Everlasting God. 34 Abraham lived in Philistia for a long time.

God Commands Abraham to Offer Isaac

22 Some time later God tested Abraham; he called to him, "Abraham!" And Abraham answered, "Yes, here I am!"

2 "Take your son," God said, "your only son, Isaac, whom you love so much, and go to the land of Moriah. There on a mountain that I will show you, offer him as a sacrifice to me."

3 Early the next morning Abraham cut some wood for the sacrifice, loaded his donkey, and took Isaac and two servants with him. They started out for the place that God had told him about. 4 On the third day Abraham saw the place in the distance. 5 Then he said to the servants, "Stay here with the donkey. The boy and I will go over there and worship, and then we will come back to you."

6 Abraham made Isaac carry the wood for the sacrifice, and he himself carried a knife and live coals for starting the fire. As they walked along together, 7 Isaac said, "Father!"

He answered, "Yes, my son?"

Isaac asked, "I see that you have the coals and the wood, but where is the lamb for the sacrifice?"

8 Abraham answered, "God himself will provide one." And the two of them walked on together.

9 When they came to the place which God had told him about, Abraham built an altar and arranged the wood on it. He tied up his son and placed him on the altar, on top of the wood. 10 Then he picked up the knife to kill him. 11 But the angel of the LORD called to him from heaven, "Abraham, Abraham!"

He answered, "Yes, here I am."

Now I know that you honour and obey God (22.12)

12 "Don't hurt the boy or do anything to him," he said. "Now I know that you honour and obey God, because you have not kept back your only son from him."

21.31 BEERSHEBA: *This name in Hebrew means "Well of the Vow" or "Well of Seven" (see also 26.33).*
See also: **21.22**: Gen 26.26
22.1–13: Heb 11.17–19   **22.2**: 2 Chr 3.1

See also: **22.9**: Jas 2.21

13 Abraham looked round and saw a ram caught in a bush by its horns. He went and got it and offered it as a burnt offering instead of his son. 14 Abraham named that place "The LORD Provides".* And even today people say, "On the LORD's mountain he provides."*

15 The angel of the LORD called to Abraham from heaven a second time, 16 "I make a vow by my own name — the LORD is speaking — that I will richly bless you. Because you did this and did not keep back your only son from me, 17 I promise that I will give you as many descendants as there are stars in the sky or grains of sand along the seashore. Your descendants will conquer their enemies. 18 All the nations will ask me to bless them as I have blessed your descendants — all because you obeyed my command." 19 Abraham went back to his servants, and they went together to Beersheba, where Abraham settled.

The Descendants of Nahor

20 Some time later Abraham learnt that Milcah had borne eight children to his brother Nahor: 21 Uz the firstborn, Buz his brother, Kemuel the father of Aram, 22 Chesed, Hazo, Pildash, Jidlaph, and Bethuel, 23 Rebecca's father. Milcah bore these eight sons to Nahor, Abraham's brother. 24 Reumah, Nahor's concubine, bore Tebah, Gaham, Tahash, and Maacah.

Sarah Dies and Abraham Buys a Burial Ground

23 Sarah lived to be 127 years old. 2 She died in Hebron in the land of Canaan, and Abraham mourned her death.

3 He left the place where his wife's body was lying, went to the Hittites, and said, 4 "I am a foreigner living here among you; sell me some land, so that I can bury my wife."

5 They answered, 6 "Listen to us, sir. We look upon you as a mighty leader; bury your wife in the best grave that we have. Any of us would be glad to give you a grave, so that you can bury her."

7 Then Abraham bowed before them 8 and said, "If you are willing to let me bury my wife here, please ask Ephron son of Zohar 9 to sell me Machpelah Cave, which is near the edge of his field. Ask him to sell it to me for its full price, here in your presence, so that I can own it as a burial ground."

10 Ephron himself was sitting with the other Hittites at the meeting place at the city gate; he answered in the hearing of everyone there, 11 "Listen, sir; I will give you the whole field and the cave that is in it. Here in the presence of my own people, I will give it to you, so that you can bury your wife."

12 But Abraham bowed before the Hittites 13 and said to Ephron, so that everyone could hear, "May I ask you, please, to listen. I will buy the whole field. Accept my payment, and I will bury my wife there."

14 Ephron answered, 15 "Sir, land worth only four hundred pieces of silver — what is that between us? Bury your wife in it." 16 Abraham agreed and weighed out the amount that Ephron had mentioned in the hearing of the people — 400 pieces of silver, according to the standard weights used by the merchants.

17 That is how the property which had belonged to Ephron at Machpelah, east of Mamre, became Abraham's. It included the field, the cave which was in it, and all the trees in the field up to the edge of the property. 18 It was recognized as Abraham's property by all the Hittites who were there at the meeting.

19 Then Abraham buried his wife Sarah in that cave in the land of Canaan. 20 So the field which had belonged to the Hittites, and the cave in it, became the property of Abraham for a burial ground.

A Wife for Isaac

24 Abraham was now very old, and the LORD had blessed him in everything he did. 2 He said to his oldest servant, who was in charge of all that he had, "Place your hand between my thighs* and make a vow. 3 I want you to make a vow in the name of the LORD, the God of heaven and earth, that you will not choose a wife for my son from the people here in Canaan. 4 You must go back to the country

---

22.14 Provides; or Sees.
22.14 provides; or is seen.
See also: 22.16–17: Heb 6.13–14
22.17: Heb 11.12   22.18: Acts 3.25
23.4: Heb 11.9, 13; Acts 7.16

24.2 PLACE... THIGHS: This was the way in which a vow was made absolutely unchangeable.

where I was born and get a wife for my son Isaac from among my relatives."

5 But the servant asked, "What if the young woman will not leave home to come with me to this land? Shall I send your son back to the land you came from?"

6 Abraham answered, "Make sure that you don't send my son back there! 7 The LORD, the God of heaven, brought me from the home of my father and from the land of my relatives, and he solemnly promised me that he would give this land to my descendants. He will send his angel before you, so that you can get a wife there for my son. 8 If the young woman is not willing to come with you, you will be free from this promise. But you must not under any circumstances take my son back there." 9 So the servant put his hand between the thighs of Abraham, his master, and made a vow to do what Abraham had asked.

10 The servant, who was in charge of Abraham's property, took ten of his master's camels and went to the city where Nahor had lived in northern Mesopotamia. 11 When he arrived, he made the camels kneel down at the well outside the city. It was late afternoon, the time when women came out to get water. 12 He prayed, "LORD, God of my master Abraham, give me success today and keep your promise to my master. 13 Here I am at the well where the young women of the city will be coming to get water. 14 I will say to one of them, 'Please, lower your jar and let me have a drink.' If she says, 'Drink, and I will also bring water for your camels,' may she be the one that you have chosen for your servant Isaac. If this happens, I will know that you have kept your promise to my master."

15 Before he had finished praying, Rebecca arrived with a water jar on her shoulder. She was the daughter of Bethuel, who was the son of Abraham's brother Nahor and his wife Milcah. 16 She was a very beautiful young woman and still a virgin. She went down to the well, filled her jar, and came back. 17 The servant ran to meet her and said, "Please give me a drink of water from your jar."

18 She said, "Drink, sir," and quickly lowered her jar from her shoulder and held it while he drank. 19 When he had finished, she said, "I will also bring water for your camels and let them have all they want."

20 She quickly emptied her jar into the animals' drinking-trough and ran to the well to get more water, until she had watered all his camels. 21 The man kept watching her in silence, to see if the LORD had given him success.

22 When she had finished, the man took an expensive gold ring and put it in her nose and put two large gold bracelets on her arms. 23 He said, "Please tell me who your father is. Is there room in his house for my men and me to spend the night?"

24 "My father is Bethuel son of Nahor and Milcah," she answered. 25 "There is plenty of straw and fodder at our house, and there is a place for you to stay."

26 Then the man knelt down and worshipped the LORD. 27 He said, "Praise the LORD, the God of my master Abraham, who has faithfully kept his promise to my master. The LORD has led me straight to my master's relatives."

28 The young woman ran to her mother's house and told the whole story. 29 Now Rebecca had a brother named Laban, and he ran outside to go to the well where Abraham's servant was. 30 Laban had seen the nose-ring and the bracelets on his sister's arms and had heard her say what the man had told her. He went to Abraham's servant, who was standing by his camels at the well, 31 and said, "Come home with me. You are a man whom the LORD has blessed. Why are you standing out here? I have a room ready for you in my house, and there is a place for your camels."

32 So the man went into the house, and Laban unloaded the camels and gave them straw and fodder. Then he brought water for Abraham's servant and his men to wash their feet. 33 When food was brought, the man said, "I will not eat until I have said what I have to say."

Laban said, "Go on and speak."

34 "I am the servant of Abraham," he began. 35 "The LORD has greatly blessed my master and made him a rich man. He has given him flocks of sheep and goats, cattle, silver, gold, male and female slaves, camels, and donkeys. 36 Sarah, my master's wife, bore him a son when she was old, and my master has given everything he owns to him. 37 My master made me promise with a vow to obey his command. He said, 'Do not choose a wife for my son from the young

women in the land of Canaan. 38 Instead, go to my father's people, to my relatives, and choose a wife for him.' 39 And I asked my master, 'What if she will not come with me?' 40 He answered, 'The LORD, whom I have always obeyed, will send his angel with you and give you success. You will get for my son a wife from my own people, from my father's family. 41 There is only one way for you to be free from your vow: if you go to my relatives and they refuse you, then you will be free.'

42 "When I came to the well today, I prayed, 'LORD, God of my master Abraham, please give me success in what I am doing. 43 Here I am at the well. When a young woman comes out to get water, I will ask her to give me a drink of water from her jar. 44 If she agrees and also offers to bring water for my camels, may she be the one that you have chosen as the wife for my master's son.' 45 Before I had finished my silent prayer, Rebecca came with a water jar on her shoulder and went down to the well to get water. I said to her, 'Please give me a drink.' 46 She quickly lowered her jar from her shoulder and said, 'Drink, and I will also water your camels.' So I drank, and she watered the camels. 47 I asked her, 'Who is your father?' And she answered, 'My father is Bethuel son of Nahor and Milcah.' Then I put the ring in her nose and the bracelets on her arms. 48 I knelt down and worshipped the LORD. I praised the LORD, the God of my master Abraham, who had led me straight to my master's relative, where I found his daughter for my master's son. 49 Now, if you intend to fulfil your responsibility towards my master and treat him fairly, please tell me; if not, say so, and I will decide what to do."

50 Laban and Bethuel answered, "Since this matter comes from the LORD, it is not for us to make a decision. 51 Here is Rebecca; take her and go. Let her become the wife of your master's son, as the LORD himself has said." 52 When the servant of Abraham heard this, he bowed down and worshipped the LORD. 53 Then he brought out clothing and silver and gold jewellery, and gave them to Rebecca. He also gave expensive gifts to her brother and to her mother.

54 Then Abraham's servant and the men with him ate and drank, and spent the night there. When they got up in the morning, he said, "Let me go back to my master."

55 But Rebecca's brother and her mother said, "Let her stay with us a week or ten days, and then she may go." 56 But he said, "Don't make us stay. The LORD has made my journey a success; let me go back to my master." 57 They answered, "Let's call her and find out what she has to say." 58 So they called Rebecca and asked, "Do you want to go with this man?"

"Yes," she answered.

59 So they let Rebecca and her old family servant go with Abraham's servant and his men. 60 And they gave Rebecca their blessing in these words:

"May you, sister, become the mother of millions!
May your descendants conquer the cities of their enemies!"

61 Then Rebecca and her young women got ready and mounted the camels to go with Abraham's servant, and they all started out.

62 Isaac had come into the wilderness of* "The Well of the Living One who Sees Me" and was staying in the southern part of Canaan. 63 He went out in the early evening to take a walk in the fields and saw camels coming. 64 When Rebecca saw Isaac, she got down from her camel 65 and asked Abraham's servant, "Who is that man walking towards us in the field?"

"He is my master," the servant answered. So she took her scarf and covered her face.

66 The servant told Isaac everything he had done. 67 Then Isaac brought Rebecca into the tent that his mother Sarah had lived in, and she became his wife. Isaac loved Rebecca, and so he was comforted for the loss of his mother.

Other Descendants of Abraham
(1 Chr 1.32–33)

25 Abraham married another wife, whose name was Keturah. 2 She bore him Zimran, Jokshan, Medan, Midian, Ishbak, and Shuah. 3 Jokshan was the father of Sheba and Dedan, and the descendants of Dedan were the Asshurim, the Letushim, and the Leummim. 4 The sons of Midian were Ephah, Epher, Hanoch, Abida, and Eldaah. All these were Keturah's descendants.

24.62 *Some ancient translations* into the wilderness of; *Hebrew* from coming.

5 Abraham left everything he owned to Isaac; 6 but while he was still alive, he gave presents to the sons his other wives had borne him. Then he sent these sons to the land of the East, away from his son Isaac.

The Death and Burial of Abraham

7-8 Abraham died at the ripe old age of 175. 9 His sons Isaac and Ishmael buried him in Machpelah Cave, in the field east of Mamre that had belonged to Ephron son of Zohar the Hittite. 10 It was the field that Abraham had bought from the Hittites; both Abraham and his wife Sarah were buried there. 11 After the death of Abraham, God blessed his son Isaac, who lived near "The Well of the Living One who Sees Me".

The Descendants of Ishmael
(1 Chr 1.28–31)

12 Ishmael, whom Hagar, the Egyptian slave of Sarah, bore to Abraham, 13 had the following sons, listed in the order of their birth: Nebaioth, Kedar, Adbeel, Mibsam, 14 Mishma, Dumah, Massa, 15 Hadad, Tema, Jetur, Naphish, and Kedemah. 16 They were the ancestors of twelve tribes, and their names were given to their villages and camping places. 17 Ishmael was 137 years old when he died. 18 The descendants of Ishmael lived in the territory between Havilah and Shur, to the east of Egypt on the way to Assyria. They lived apart from the other descendants of Abraham.

The Birth of Esau and Jacob

19 This is the story of Abraham's son Isaac. 20 Isaac was 40 years old when he married Rebecca, the daughter of Bethuel (an Aramean from Mesopotamia) and sister of Laban. 21 Because Rebecca had no children, Isaac prayed to the LORD for her. The LORD answered his prayer, and Rebecca became pregnant. 22 She was going to have twins, and before they were born, they struggled against each other in her womb. She said, "Why should something like this happen to me?" So she went to ask the LORD for an answer.

23 The LORD said to her,

"Two nations are within you;
You will give birth to two rival
     peoples.

See also: 25.10: Gen 23.3–16   25.23: Rom 9.12

One will be stronger than the other;
The older will serve the younger."

24 The time came for her to give birth, and she had twin sons. 25 The first one was reddish, and his skin was like a hairy robe, so he was named Esau.* 26 The second one was born holding on tightly to the heel of Esau, so he was named Jacob.* Isaac was 60 years old when they were born.

Esau Sells his Rights as the Firstborn Son

27 The boys grew up, and Esau became a skilled hunter, a man who loved the outdoor life, but Jacob was a quiet man who stayed at home. 28 Isaac preferred Esau, because he enjoyed eating the animals Esau killed, but Rebecca preferred Jacob.

Then Jacob gave him ... some of the soup   (25.34)

29 One day while Jacob was cooking some bean soup, Esau came in from hunting. He was hungry 30 and said to Jacob, "I'm starving; give me some of that red stuff." (That is why he was called Edom.*)

31 Jacob answered, "I will give it to you if you give me your rights as the firstborn son."

25.25 ESAU: *This name is taken to refer to Seir, the territory later inhabited by Esau's descendants; Seir sounds like the Hebrew for "hairy".*

25.26 JACOB: *This name sounds like the Hebrew for "heel".*

25.30 EDOM: *This name sounds like the Hebrew for "red".*

32 Esau said, "All right! I am about to die; what good will my rights do me then?"

33 Jacob answered, "First make a vow that you will give me your rights."

Esau made the vow and gave his rights to Jacob. 34 Then Jacob gave him some bread and some of the soup. He ate and drank and then got up and left. That was all Esau cared about his rights as the firstborn son.

Isaac Lives at Gerar

26 There was another famine in the land besides the earlier one during the time of Abraham. Isaac went to Abimelech, king of the Philistines, at Gerar. 2 The LORD had appeared to Isaac and had said, "Do not go to Egypt; stay in this land, where I tell you to stay. 3 Live here, and I will be with you and bless you. I am going to give all this territory to you and to your descendants. I will keep the promise I made to your father Abraham. 4 I will give you as many descendants as there are stars in the sky, and I will give them all this territory. All the nations will ask me to bless them as I have blessed your descendants. 5 I will bless you, because Abraham obeyed me and kept all my laws and commands."

6 So Isaac lived at Gerar. 7 When the men there asked about his wife, he said that she was his sister. He would not admit that she was his wife, because he was afraid that the men there would kill him to get Rebecca, who was very beautiful. 8 When Isaac had been there for some time, King Abimelech looked down from his window and saw Isaac and Rebecca making love. 9 Abimelech sent for Isaac and said, "So she is your wife! Why did you say she was your sister?"

He answered, "I thought I would be killed if I said she was my wife."

10 "What have you done to us?" Abimelech said. "One of my men might easily have slept with your wife, and you would have been responsible for our guilt." 11 Abimelech warned all the people: "Anyone who ill-treats this man or his wife will be put to death."

12 Isaac sowed seed in that land, and that year he harvested a hundred times as much as he had sown, because the LORD

blessed him. 13 He continued to prosper and became a very rich man. 14 Because he had many herds of sheep and cattle and many servants, the Philistines were jealous of him. 15 So they filled in all the wells which the servants of his father Abraham had dug while Abraham was alive.

16 Then Abimelech said to Isaac, "Leave our country. You have become more powerful than we are." 17 So Isaac left and set up his camp in the Valley of Gerar, where he stayed for some time. 18 He dug once again the wells which had been dug during the time of Abraham and which the Philistines had stopped up after Abraham's death. Isaac gave the wells the same names that his father had given them.

19 Isaac's servants dug a well in the valley and found water. 20 The shepherds of Gerar quarrelled with Isaac's shepherds and said, "This water belongs to us." So Isaac named the well "Quarrel".

21 Isaac's servants dug another well, and there was a quarrel about that one also, so he named it "Enmity". 22 He moved away from there and dug another well. There was no dispute about this one, so he named it "Freedom". He said, "Now the LORD has given us freedom to live in the land, and we will be prosperous here."

23 Isaac left and went to Beersheba. 24 That night the LORD appeared to him and said, "I am the God of your father Abraham. Do not be afraid; I am with you. I will bless you and give you many descendants because of my promise to my servant Abraham." 25 Isaac built an altar there and worshipped the LORD. Then he set up his camp there, and his servants dug another well.

The Agreement between Isaac and Abimelech

26 Abimelech came from Gerar with Ahuzzath his adviser and Phicol the commander of his army to see Isaac. 27 So Isaac asked, "Why have you now come to see me, when you were so unfriendly to me before and made me leave your country?"

28 They answered, "Now we know that the LORD is with you, and we think that there should be a solemn agreement between us. We want you to promise 29 that you will not harm us, just as we did not harm you.

See also: 25.33: Heb 12.16   **26.3–4:** Gen 22.16–18   **26.7:** Gen 12.13, 20.2

See also: 26.26: Gen 21.22

We were kind to you and let you leave peacefully. Now it is clear that the LORD has blessed you." 30 Isaac prepared a feast for them, and they ate and drank. 31 Early next morning each man made his promise and sealed it with a vow. Isaac said goodbye to them, and they parted as friends.

32 On that day Isaac's servants came and told him about the well which they had dug. They said, "We have found water." 33 He named the well "Vow". That is how the city of Beersheba* got its name.

Esau's Foreign Wives

34 When Esau was 40 years old, he married two Hittite women, Judith the daughter of Beeri, and Basemath the daughter of Elon. 35 They made life miserable for Isaac and Rebecca.

Isaac Blesses Jacob

27 Isaac was now old and had become blind. He sent for his elder son Esau and said to him, "My son!"

"Yes," he answered.

2 Isaac said, "You see that I am old and may die soon. 3 Take your bow and arrows, go out into the country, and kill an animal for me. 4 Cook me some of that tasty food that I like, and bring it to me. After I have eaten it, I will give you my final blessing before I die."

5 While Isaac was talking to Esau, Rebecca was listening. So when Esau went out to hunt, 6 she said to Jacob, "I have just heard your father say to Esau, 7 'Bring me an animal and cook it for me. After I have eaten it, I will give you my blessing in the presence of the LORD before I die.' 8 Now, my son," Rebecca continued, "listen to me and do what I say. 9 Go to the flock and pick out two fat young goats, so that I can cook them and make some of that food your father likes so much. 10 You can take it to him to eat, and he will give you his blessing before he dies."

11 But Jacob said to his mother, "You know that Esau is a hairy man, but I have smooth skin. 12 Perhaps my father will touch me and find out that I am deceiving him; in this way I will bring a curse on myself instead of a blessing."

13 His mother answered, "Let any curse against you fall on me, my son; just do as I say, and go and get the goats for me." 14 So he went to get them and brought them to her, and she cooked the kind of food that his father liked. 15 Then she took Esau's best clothes, which she kept in the house, and put them on Jacob. 16 She put the skins of the goats on his arms and on the hairless part of his neck. 17 She handed him the tasty food, together with the bread she had baked.

18 Then Jacob went to his father and said, "Father!"

"Yes," he answered. "Which of my sons are you?"

19 Jacob answered, "I am your elder son Esau; I have done as you told me. Please sit up and eat some of the meat that I have brought you, so that you can give me your blessing."

20 Isaac said, "How did you find it so quickly, my son?"

Jacob answered, "The LORD your God helped me to find it."

21 Isaac said to Jacob, "Please come closer so that I can touch you. Are you really Esau?" 22 Jacob moved closer to his father, who felt him and said, "Your voice sounds like Jacob's voice, but your arms feel like Esau's arms." 23 He did not recognize Jacob, because his arms were hairy like Esau's. He was about to give him his blessing, 24 but asked again, "Are you really Esau?"

"I am," he answered.

25 Isaac said, "Bring me some of the meat. After I have eaten it, I will give you my blessing." Jacob brought it to him, and he also brought him some wine to drink. 26 Then his father said to him,

He gave him his blessing (27.27)

"Come closer and kiss me, my son."
27 As he came up to kiss him, Isaac smelt his clothes — so he gave him his blessing. He said, "The pleasant smell of my son is like the smell of a field which the LORD has blessed. 28 May God give you dew from heaven and make your fields fertile! May he give you plenty of corn and wine! 29 May nations be your servants, and may peoples bow down before you. May you rule over all your relatives, and may your mother's descendants bow down before you. May those who curse you be cursed, and may those who bless you be blessed."

Esau Begs for Isaac's Blessing

30 Isaac finished giving his blessing, and as soon as Jacob left, his brother Esau came in from hunting. 31 He also cooked some tasty food and took it to his father. He said, "Please, father, sit up and eat some of the meat that I have brought you, so that you can give me your blessing."

32 "Who are you?" Isaac asked.

"Your elder son Esau," he answered.

33 Isaac began to tremble and shake all over, and he asked, "Who was it, then, who killed an animal and brought it to me? I ate it just before you came. I gave him my final blessing, and so it is his for ever."

34 When Esau heard this, he cried out loudly and bitterly and said, "Give me your blessing also, father!"

35 Isaac answered, "Your brother came and deceived me. He has taken away your blessing."

36 Esau said, "This is the second time that he has cheated me. No wonder his name is Jacob.* He took my rights as the firstborn son, and now he has taken away my blessing. Haven't you saved a blessing for me?"

37 Isaac answered, "I have already made him master over you, and I have made all his relatives his slaves. I have given him corn and wine. Now there is nothing that I can do for you, my son!"

38 Esau continued to plead with his father: "Have you only one blessing, father? Bless me too, father!" He began to cry.

39 Then Isaac said to him,
"No dew from heaven for you,
No fertile fields for you.
40 You will live by your sword,
But be your brother's slave.
Yet when you rebel,*
You will break away from his control."

41 Esau hated Jacob, because his father had given Jacob the blessing. He thought, "The time to mourn my father's death is near; then I will kill Jacob."

42 But when Rebecca heard about Esau's plan, she sent for Jacob and said, "Listen, your brother Esau is planning to get even with you and kill you. 43 Now, my son, do what I say. Go at once to my brother Laban in Haran, 44 and stay with him for a while, until your brother's anger cools down 45 and he forgets what you have done to him. Then I will send someone to bring you back. Why should I lose both my sons on the same day?"

Isaac Sends Jacob to Laban

46 Rebecca said to Isaac, "I am sick and tired of Esau's foreign wives. If Jacob also marries one of these Hittite women, I might as well die."

28 Isaac called Jacob, greeted him, and said to him, "Don't marry a Canaanite woman. 2 Go instead to Mesopotamia, to the home of your grandfather Bethuel, and marry one of the young women there, one of your uncle Laban's daughters. 3 May Almighty God bless your marriage and give you many children, so that you will become the father of many nations! 4 May he bless you and your descendants as he blessed Abraham, and may you take possession of this land, in which you have lived and which God gave to Abraham!" 5 Isaac sent Jacob away to Mesopotamia, to Laban, who was the son of Bethuel the Aramean and the brother of Rebecca, the mother of Jacob and Esau.

Esau Takes Another Wife

6 Esau learnt that Isaac had blessed Jacob and sent him away to Mesopotamia to find a wife. He also learnt that when

---

27.36 JACOB: *This name sounds like the Hebrew for "cheat".*

See also: **27.27–29:** Heb 11.20 **27.29:** Gen 12.3 **27.36:** Gen 25.29–34 **27.38:** Heb 12.17

27.40 rebel; *or* grow restless.

See also: **27.39–40:** Heb 11.20 **27.40:** Gen 36.8; 2 Kgs 8.20 **28.4:** Gen 17.4–8

Isaac blessed him, he commanded him not to marry a Canaanite woman. 7 He found out that Jacob had obeyed his father and mother and had gone to Mesopotamia. 8 Esau then understood that his father Isaac did not approve of Canaanite women. 9 So he went to Ishmael son of Abraham and married his daughter Mahalath, who was the sister of Nebaioth.

Jacob's Dream at Bethel

10 Jacob left Beersheba and started towards Haran. 11 At sunset he came to a holy place* and camped there. He lay down to sleep, resting his head on a stone. 12 He dreamt that he saw a stairway reaching from earth to heaven, with angels going up and coming down on it. 13 And there was the Lord standing beside him.* "I am the Lord, the God of Abraham and Isaac," he said. "I will give to you and to your descendants this land on which you are lying. 14 They will be as numerous as the specks of dust on the earth. They will extend their territory in all directions, and through you and your descendants I will bless all the nations.* 15 Remember, I will be with you and protect you wherever you go, and I will bring you back to this land. I will not leave you until I have done all that I have promised you."

16 Jacob woke up and said, "The Lord is here! He is in this place, and I didn't know it!" 17 He was afraid and said, "What a terrifying place this is! It must be the house of God; it must be the gate that opens into heaven."

18 Jacob got up early next morning, took the stone that was under his head, and set it up as a memorial. Then he poured olive oil on it to dedicate it to God. 19 He named the place Bethel.* (The town there was once known as Luz.) 20 Then Jacob made a vow to the Lord: "If you will be with me and protect me on the journey I am making and give me food and clothing, 21 and

A stairway ... from earth to heaven (28.12)

if I return safely to my father's home, then you will be my God. 22 This memorial stone which I have set up will be the place where you are worshipped, and I will give you a tenth of everything you give me."

Jacob Arrives at Laban's Home

29 Jacob continued on his way and went towards the land of the East. 2 Suddenly he came upon a well out in the fields with three flocks of sheep lying round it. The flocks were watered from this well, which had a large stone over the opening. 3 Whenever all the flocks came together there, the shepherds would roll

---

28.11 a holy place; *or* a place.
28.13 beside him; *or* on it.
28.14 through you... nations; *or* all the nations will ask me to bless them as I have blessed you and your descendants.
28.19 BETHEL: *This name in Hebrew means "house of God".*

See also: 28.12: Jn 1.51   **28.13:** Gen 13.14–15
28.14: Gen 12.3, 22.18

the stone back and water them. Then they would put the stone back in place.

4 Jacob asked the shepherds, "My friends, where are you from?"

"From Haran," they answered.

5 He asked, "Do you know Laban, grandson of Nahor?"

"Yes, we do," they answered.

6 "Is he well?" he asked.

"He is well," they answered. "Look, here comes his daughter Rachel with his flock."

7 Jacob said, "Since it is still broad daylight and not yet time to bring the flocks in, why don't you water them and take them back to pasture?"

8 They answered, "We can't do that until all the flocks are here and the stone has been rolled back; then we will water the flocks."

9 While Jacob was still talking to them, Rachel arrived with the flock. 10 When Jacob saw Rachel with his uncle Laban's flock, he went to the well, rolled the stone back, and watered the sheep. 11 Then he kissed her and began to cry for joy. 12 He told her, "I am your father's relative, the son of Rebecca."

She ran to tell her father; 13 and when he heard the news about his nephew Jacob, he ran to meet him, hugged him and kissed him, and brought him into the house. When Jacob told Laban everything that had happened, 14 Laban said, "Yes, indeed, you are my own flesh and blood." Jacob stayed there a whole month.

Jacob Serves Laban for Rachel and Leah

15 Laban said to Jacob, "You shouldn't work for me for nothing just because you are my relative. How much pay do you want?" 16 Laban had two daughters; the elder was named Leah, and the younger Rachel. 17 Leah had lovely* eyes, but Rachel was shapely and beautiful.

18 Jacob was in love with Rachel, so he said, "I will work seven years for you, if you will let me marry Rachel."

19 Laban answered, "I would rather give her to you than to anyone else; stay here with me." 20 Jacob worked seven years so

that he could have Rachel, and the time seemed like only a few days to him, because he loved her.

21 Then Jacob said to Laban, "The time is up; let me marry your daughter." 22 So Laban gave a wedding feast and invited everyone. 23 But that night, instead of Rachel, he took Leah to Jacob, and Jacob had intercourse with her. 24 (Laban gave his slave woman Zilpah to his daughter Leah as her maid.) 25 Not until the next morning did Jacob discover that it was Leah. He went to Laban and said, "Why did you do this to me? I worked to get Rachel. Why have you tricked me?"

26 Laban answered, "It is not the custom here to give the younger daughter in marriage before the elder. 27 Wait until the week's marriage celebrations are over, and I will give you Rachel, if you will work for me another seven years."

28 Jacob agreed, and when the week of marriage celebrations was over, Laban gave him his daughter Rachel as his wife. 29 (Laban gave his slave woman Bilhah to his daughter Rachel as her maid.) 30 Jacob had intercourse with Rachel also, and he loved her more than Leah. Then he worked for Laban another seven years.

The Children Born to Jacob

31 When the LORD saw that Leah was loved less than Rachel, he made it possible for her to have children, but Rachel remained childless. 32 Leah became pregnant and gave birth to a son. She said, "The LORD has seen my trouble, and now my husband will love me"; so she named him Reuben.* 33 She became pregnant again and gave birth to another son. She said, "The LORD has given me this son also, because he heard that I was not loved"; so she named him Simeon.* 34 Once again she became pregnant and gave birth to another son. She said, "Now my husband will be bound more tightly to me, because I have borne him three sons"; so she named him Levi.* 35 Then she became pregnant again and gave

---

29.17 lovely; or weak.

29.32 REUBEN: *This name sounds like the Hebrew for "see, a son" and "has seen my trouble".*
29.33 SIMEON: *This name sounds like the Hebrew for "hear".*
29.34 LEVI: *This name sounds like the Hebrew for "bound".*

birth to another son. She said, "This time I will praise the LORD"; so she named him Judah.* Then she stopped having children.

30 But Rachel had not borne Jacob any children, and so she became jealous of her sister and said to Jacob, "Give me children, or I will die."

2 Jacob became angry with Rachel and said, "I can't take the place of God. He is the one who keeps you from having children."

3 She said, "Here is my slave Bilhah; sleep with her, so that she can have a child for me. In this way I can become a mother through her." 4 So she gave Bilhah to her husband, and he had intercourse with her. 5 Bilhah became pregnant and bore Jacob a son. 6 Rachel said, "God has judged in my favour. He has heard my prayer and has given me a son"; so she named him Dan.* 7 Bilhah became pregnant again and bore Jacob a second son. 8 Rachel said, "I have fought a hard fight with my sister, but I have won"; so she named him Naphtali.*

9 When Leah realized that she had stopped having children, she gave her slave Zilpah to Jacob as his wife. 10 Then Zilpah bore Jacob a son. 11 Leah said, "I have been lucky"; so she named him Gad.* 12 Zilpah bore Jacob another son, 13 and Leah said, "How happy I am! Now women will call me happy"; so she named him Asher.*

14 During the wheat harvest Reuben went into the fields and found mandrakes,* which he brought to his mother Leah. Rachel said to Leah, "Please give me some of your son's mandrakes."

15 Leah answered, "Isn't it enough that you have taken away my husband? Now you are even trying to take away my son's mandrakes."

Rachel said, "If you will give me your son's mandrakes, you can sleep with Jacob tonight."

16 When Jacob came in from the fields in the evening, Leah went out to meet him and said, "You are going to sleep with me tonight, because I have paid for you with my son's mandrakes." So he had intercourse with her that night.

17 God answered Leah's prayer, and she became pregnant and bore Jacob a fifth son. 18 Leah said, "God has given me my reward, because I gave my slave to my husband"; so she named her son Issachar.* 19 Leah became pregnant again and bore Jacob a sixth son. 20 She said, "God has given me a fine gift. Now my husband will accept me, because I have borne him six sons"; so she named him Zebulun.* 21 Later she bore a daughter, whom she named Dinah.

22 Then God remembered Rachel; he answered her prayer and made it possible for her to have children. 23 She became pregnant and gave birth to a son. She said, "God has taken away my disgrace by giving me a son. 24 May the LORD give me another son"; so she named him Joseph.*

Jacob's Bargain with Laban

25 After the birth of Joseph, Jacob said to Laban, "Let me go, so that I can return home. 26 Give me my wives and children that I have earned by working for you, and I will leave. You know how well I have served you."

27 Laban said to him, "Let me say this: I have learnt by divination that the LORD has blessed me because of you. 28 Name your wages, and I will pay them."

29 Jacob answered, "You know how I have worked for you and how your flocks have prospered under my care. 30 The little you had before I came has grown enormously, and the LORD has blessed you wherever I went.* Now it is time for me to look out for my own interests."

31 "What shall I pay you?" Laban asked.

Jacob answered, "I don't want any wages. I will continue to take care of your flocks if you agree to this suggestion: 32 Let me go through all your flocks today and take every black lamb* and every spotted or

29.35 JUDAH: *This name sounds like the Hebrew for "praise".*

30.6 DAN: *This name sounds like the Hebrew for "judge in favour".*

30.8 NAPHTALI: *This name sounds like the Hebrew for "fight".*

30.11 GAD: *This name in Hebrew means "luck".*

30.13 ASHER: *This name in Hebrew means "happy".*

30.14 MANDRAKES: *Plants which were believed to produce fertility and were used as love-charms.*

30.18 ISSACHAR: *This name sounds like the Hebrew for "a man is hired" and "there is reward".*

30.20 ZEBULUN: *This name sounds like the Hebrew for "accept" and "gift".*

30.24 JOSEPH: *This name sounds like the Hebrew for "may he give another" and "he has taken away".*

30.30 wherever I went; *or* because of me.

30.32 *One ancient translation* every black lamb; *Hebrew* every spotted and speckled lamb, and every black lamb.

speckled young goat. That is all the wages I want. 33 In the future you can easily find out if I have been honest. When you come to check up on my wages, if I have any goat that isn't speckled or spotted or any sheep that isn't black, you will know that it has been stolen."

34 Laban answered, "Agreed. We will do as you suggest." 35 But that day Laban removed the male goats that had stripes or spots and all the females that were speckled and spotted or which had white on them; he also removed all the black sheep. He put his sons in charge of them, 36 and then went away from Jacob with this flock as far as he could travel in three days. Jacob took care of the rest of Laban's flocks.

37 Jacob got green branches of poplar, almond, and plane trees and stripped off some of the bark so that the branches had white stripes on them. 38 He placed these branches in front of the flocks at their drinking troughs. He put them there, because the animals mated when they came to drink. 39 So when the goats bred in front of the branches, they produced young that were streaked, speckled, and spotted.

40 Jacob kept the sheep separate from the goats and made them face in the direction of the streaked and black animals of Laban's flock. In this way he built up his own flock and kept it apart from Laban's.

41 When the healthy animals were mating, Jacob put the branches in front of them at the drinking troughs, so that they would breed among the branches. 42 But he did not put the branches in front of the weak animals. Soon Laban had all the weak animals, and Jacob all the healthy ones. 43 In this way Jacob became very wealthy. He had many flocks, slaves, camels, and donkeys.

Jacob Flees from Laban

31 Jacob heard that Laban's sons were saying, "Jacob has taken everything that belonged to our father. All his wealth has come from what our father owned." 2 He also saw that Laban was no longer as friendly as he had been earlier. 3 Then the LORD said to him, "Go back to the land of your fathers and to your relatives. I will be with you."

4 So Jacob sent word to Rachel and Leah to meet him in the field where his flocks

were. 5 He said to them, "I have noticed that your father is not as friendly towards me as he used to be; but my father's God has been with me. 6 You both know that I have worked for your father with all my strength. 7 Yet he has cheated me and changed my wages ten times. But God did not let him harm me. 8 Whenever Laban said, 'The speckled goats shall be your wages,' all the flocks produced speckled young. When he said, 'The striped goats shall be your wages,' all the flocks produced striped young. 9 God has taken flocks away from your father and given them to me.

10 "During the breeding season I had a dream, and I saw that the male goats that were mating were striped, spotted, and speckled. 11 The angel of God spoke to me in the dream and said, 'Jacob!' 'Yes,' I answered. 12 'Look,' he continued, 'all the male goats that are mating are striped, spotted, and speckled. I am making this happen because I have seen all that Laban is doing to you. 13 I am the God who appeared to you at Bethel, where you dedicated a stone as a memorial by pouring olive oil on it and where you made a vow to me. Now get ready to go back to the land where you were born.' "

14 Rachel and Leah answered Jacob, "There is nothing left for us to inherit from our father. 15 He treats us like foreigners. He sold us, and now he has spent all the money he was paid for us. 16 All this wealth which God has taken from our father belongs to us and to our children. Do whatever God has told you."

17–18 So Jacob got ready to go back to his father in the land of Canaan. He put his children and his wives on the camels, and drove all his flocks ahead of him, with everything that he had acquired in Mesopotamia. 19 Laban had gone to shear his sheep, and during his absence Rachel stole the household gods that belonged to her father. 20 Jacob deceived Laban by not letting him know that he was leaving. 21 He took everything he owned and left in a hurry. He crossed the River Euphrates and started for the hill country of Gilead.

See also: 31.13: Gen 28.18–22

Jacob … drove all his flocks ahead of him   (31.18)

Laban Pursues Jacob

22 Three days later Laban was told that Jacob had fled. 23 He took his men with him and pursued Jacob for seven days until he caught up with him in the hill country of Gilead. 24 In a dream that night God came to Laban and said to him, "Be careful not to threaten Jacob in any way." 25 Jacob had set up his camp on a mountain, and Laban set up his camp with his relatives in the hill country of Gilead.

26 Laban said to Jacob, "Why did you deceive me and carry off my daughters like women captured in war? 27 Why did you deceive me and slip away without telling me? If you had told me, I would have sent you on your way with rejoicing and singing to the music of tambourines and harps. 28 You did not even let me kiss my grandchildren and my daughters goodbye. That was a foolish thing to do! 29 I have the power to do you harm, but last night the God of your father warned me not to threaten you in any way. 30 I know that you left because you were so anxious to get back home, but why did you steal my household gods?"

31 Jacob answered, "I was afraid, because I thought that you might take your daughters away from me. 32 But if you find that anyone here has your gods, he will be put to death. Here, with our men as witnesses, look for anything that belongs to you and take what is yours." Jacob did not know that Rachel had stolen Laban's gods.

33 Laban went and searched Jacob's tent; then he went into Leah's tent, and the tent of the two slave women, but he did not find his gods. Then he went into Rachel's tent. 34 Rachel had taken the household gods and put them in a camel's saddlebag and was sitting on them. Laban searched through the whole tent, but did not find them. 35 Rachel said to her father, "Do not be angry with me, sir, but I am not able to stand up in your presence; I am having my monthly period." Laban searched but did not find his household gods.

36 Then Jacob lost his temper. "What crime have I committed?" he asked angrily. "What law have I broken that gives you the right to hunt me down? 37 Now that you have searched through all my belongings, what household article have you found that belongs to you? Put it out here where your men and mine can see it, and let them decide which one of us is right. 38 I have been with you now for twenty years; your sheep and your goats have not failed to reproduce, and I have not eaten any rams from your flocks. 39 Whenever a sheep was killed by wild animals, I always bore the loss myself. I didn't take it to you to show that it was not my fault. You demanded that I make good anything that was stolen during the day or during the night. 40 Many times I suffered from the heat during the day and from the cold at night. I was not able to sleep. 41 It was like that for the whole twenty years I was with you. For fourteen

years I worked to win your two daughters — and six years for your flocks. And even then, you changed my wages ten times. 42 If the God of my fathers, the God of Abraham and Isaac, had not been with me, you would have already sent me away empty-handed. But God has seen my trouble and the work I have done, and last night he gave his judgement."

The Agreement between Jacob and Laban

43 Laban answered Jacob, "These young women are my daughters; their children belong to me, and these flocks are mine. In fact, everything you see here belongs to me. But since I can do nothing to keep my daughters and their children, 44 I am ready to make an agreement with you. Let us make a pile of stones to remind us of our agreement."

45 So Jacob took a stone and set it up as a memorial. 46 He told his men to gather some rocks and pile them up. Then they ate a meal beside the pile of rocks. 47 Laban named it Jegar Sahadutha,* while Jacob named it Galeed.* 48 Laban said to Jacob, "This pile of rocks will be a reminder for both of us." That is why that place was named Galeed. 49 Laban also said, "May the LORD keep an eye on us while we are separated from each other." So the place was also named Mizpah.* 50 Laban went on, "If you ill-treat my daughters or if you marry other women, even though I don't know about it, remember that God is watching us. 51 Here are the rocks that I have piled up between us, and here is the memorial stone. 52 Both this pile and this memorial stone are reminders. I will never go beyond this pile to attack you, and you must never go beyond it or beyond this memorial stone to attack me. 53 The God of Abraham and the God of Nahor* will judge between us." Then, in the name of the God whom his father Isaac worshipped, Jacob solemnly vowed to keep this promise.

31.47 JEGAR SAHADUTHA: *This name in Aramaic means "a pile to remind us".*
31.47 GALEED: *This name in Hebrew means "a pile to remind us".*
31.49 MIZPAH: *This name sounds like the Hebrew for "place from which to watch".*
31.53 ABRAHAM... NAHOR: *Abraham was Jacob's grandfather and Nahor was Laban's grandfather.*

54 He killed an animal, which he offered as a sacrifice on the mountain, and he invited his men to the meal. After they had eaten, they spent the night on the mountain. 55 Early the next morning Laban kissed his grandchildren and his daughters goodbye, and left to go back home.

Jacob Prepares to Meet Esau

32 As Jacob went on his way, some angels met him. 2 When he saw them, he said, "This is God's camp"; so he called the place Mahanaim.*

3 Jacob sent messengers ahead of him to his brother Esau in the country of Edom. 4 He instructed them to say: "I, Jacob, your obedient servant, report to my master Esau that I have been staying with Laban and that I have delayed my return until now. 5 I own cattle, donkeys, sheep, goats, and slaves. I am sending you word, sir, in the hope of gaining your favour."

6 When the messengers came back to Jacob, they said, "We went to your brother Esau, and he is already on his way to meet you. He has four hundred men with him." 7 Jacob was frightened and worried. He divided into two groups the people who were with him, and also his sheep, goats, cattle, and camels. 8 He thought, "If Esau comes and attacks the first group, the other may be able to escape."

9 Then Jacob prayed, "God of my grandfather Abraham and God of my father Isaac, hear me! You told me, LORD, to go back to my land and to my relatives, and you would make everything go well for me. 10 I am not worth all the kindness and faithfulness that you have shown me, your servant. I crossed the Jordan with nothing but a walking stick, and now I have come back with these two groups. 11 Save me, I pray, from my brother Esau. I am afraid — afraid that he is coming to attack us and destroy us all, even the women and children. 12 Remember that you promised to make everything go well for me and to give me more descendants than anyone could count, as many as the grains of sand along the seashore."

32.2 MAHANAIM: *This name in Hebrew means "two camps".*
See also: 32.12: Gen 22.17

13–15 After spending the night there, Jacob chose from his livestock as a present for his brother Esau: 200 female goats and twenty males, 200 female sheep and twenty males, 30 milk camels with their young, 40 cows and ten bulls, twenty female donkeys and ten males. 16 He divided them into herds and put one of his servants in charge of each herd. He said to them, "Go ahead of me, and leave a space between each herd and the one behind it." 17 He ordered the first servant, "When my brother Esau meets you and asks, 'Who is your master? Where are you going? Who owns these animals in front of you?' 18 you must answer, 'They belong to your servant Jacob. He sends them as a present to his master Esau. Jacob himself is just behind us.' " 19 He gave the same order to the second, the third, and to all the others who were in charge of the herds: "This is what you must say to Esau when you meet him. 20 You must say, 'Yes, your servant Jacob is just behind us.' " Jacob was thinking, "I will win him over with the gifts, and when I meet him, perhaps he will forgive me." 21 He sent the gifts on ahead of him and spent that night in camp.

Jacob Wrestles at Peniel

22 That same night Jacob got up, took his two wives, his two concubines, and his eleven children, and crossed the River Jabbok. 23 After he had sent them across, he also sent across all that he owned, 24 but he stayed behind, alone.

Then a man came and wrestled with him until just before daybreak. 25 When the man saw that he was not winning the struggle, he struck Jacob on the hip, and it was thrown out of joint. 26 The man said, "Let me go; daylight is coming."

"I won't, unless you bless me," Jacob answered.

27 "What is your name?" the man asked.

"Jacob," he answered.

28 The man said, "Your name will no longer be Jacob. You have struggled with God and with men, and you have won; so your name will be Israel."*

29 Jacob said, "Now tell me your name." "

But he answered, "Why do you want to know my name?" Then he blessed Jacob.

30 Jacob said, "I have seen God face to face, and I am still alive"; so he named the place Peniel.* 31 The sun rose as Jacob was leaving Peniel, and he was limping because of his hip. 32 Even today the descendants of Israel do not eat the muscle which is on the hip joint, because it was on this muscle that Jacob was struck.

Jacob Meets Esau

33 Jacob saw Esau coming with his 400 men, so he divided the children among Leah, Rachel, and the two concubines. 2 He put the concubines and their children first, then Leah and her children, and finally Rachel and Joseph at the rear. 3 Jacob went ahead of them and bowed down to the ground seven times as he approached his brother. 4 But Esau ran to meet him, threw his arms round him, and kissed him. They were both crying. 5 When Esau looked round and saw the women and the children, he asked, "Who are these people with you?"

"These, sir, are the children whom God has been good enough to give me," Jacob answered. 6 Then the concubines came up with their children and bowed down; 7 then Leah and her children came, and last of all Joseph and Rachel came and bowed down.

8 Esau asked, "What about that other group I met? What did that mean?"

Jacob answered, "It was to gain your favour."

9 But Esau said, "I have enough, my brother; keep what you have."

10 Jacob said, "No, please, if I have gained your favour, accept my gift. To see your face is for me like seeing the face of God, now that you have been so friendly to me. 11 Please accept this gift which I have brought for you; God has been kind to me and given me everything I need." Jacob kept on urging him until he accepted.

12 Esau said, "Let's prepare to leave. I will go ahead of you."

13 Jacob answered, "You know that the children are weak, and I must think of the

32.28 ISRAEL: *This name sounds like the Hebrew for "he struggles with God" or "God struggles".*
See also: 32.24–26: Hos 12.3–4   **32.28:** Gen 35.10

32.30 PENIEL: *This name sounds like the Hebrew for "the face of God".*
See also: 32.29: Judg 13.17–18

Esau ... threw his arms round him (33.4)

sheep and cattle with their young. If they are driven hard for even one day, the whole herd will die. ¹⁴ Please go on ahead of me, and I will follow slowly, going as fast as I can with the livestock and the children until I catch up with you in Edom."

¹⁵ Esau said, "Then let me leave some of my men with you."

But Jacob answered, "There is no need for that for I only want to gain your favour."* ¹⁶ So that day Esau started on his way back to Edom. ¹⁷ But Jacob went to Sukkoth, where he built a house for himself and shelters for his livestock. That is why the place was named Sukkoth.*

¹⁸ On his return from Mesopotamia Jacob arrived safely at the city of Shechem in the land of Canaan and set up his camp in a field near the city. ¹⁹ He bought that part of the field from the descendants of Hamor father of Shechem for a hundred pieces of silver. ²⁰ He put up an altar there and named it after El, the God of Israel.

33.15 for I only want to gain your favour; *or* if it's all right with you.
33.17 SUKKOTH: *This name in Hebrew means "shelters".*

See also: 33.19: Josh 24.32; Jn 4.5

The Rape of Dinah

34 One day Dinah, the daughter of Jacob and Leah, went to visit some of the Canaanite women. ² When Shechem son of Hamor the Hivite, who was chief of that region, saw her, he took her and raped her. ³ But he found the young woman so attractive that he fell in love with her and tried to win her affection.* ⁴ He said to his father, "I want you to get this woman for me as my wife."

⁵ Jacob learnt that his daughter had been disgraced, but because his sons were out in the fields with his livestock, he did nothing until they came back. ⁶ Shechem's father Hamor went out to talk with Jacob, ⁷ just as Jacob's sons were coming in from the fields. When they heard about it, they were shocked and furious that Shechem had done such a thing and had insulted the people of Israel by raping Jacob's daughter. ⁸ Hamor said to him, "My son Shechem has fallen in love with your daughter; please let him marry her. ⁹ Let us make an agreement that there will be intermarriage between our people and yours. ¹⁰ Then you may stay here in our country with us; you may live anywhere you wish, trade freely, and own property."

34.3 tried to win her affection; *or* comforted her.

11 Then Shechem said to Dinah's father and brothers, "Do me this favour, and I will give you whatever you want. 12 Tell me what presents you want, and set the payment for the bride as high as you wish; I will give you whatever you ask, if you will only let me marry her."

13 Because Shechem had disgraced their sister Dinah, Jacob's sons answered Shechem and his father Hamor in a deceitful way. 14 They said to him, "We cannot let our sister marry a man who is not circumcised; that would be a disgrace for us. 15 We can agree only on the condition that you become like us by circumcising all your males. 16 Then we will agree to intermarriage. We will settle among you and become one people with you. 17 But if you will not accept our terms and be circumcised, we will take her and leave."

18 These terms seemed fair to Hamor and his son Shechem, 19 and the young man lost no time in doing what was suggested, because he was in love with Jacob's daughter. He was the most important member of his family.

20 Hamor and his son Shechem went to the meeting place at the city gate and spoke to the people of the town: 21 "These men are friendly; let them live in the land with us and travel freely. The land is large enough for them also. Let us marry their daughters and give them ours in marriage. 22 But these men will agree to live among us and be one people with us only on condition that we circumcise all our males, as they are circumcised. 23 Won't all their livestock and everything else they own be ours? So let us agree that they can live among us." 24 All the citizens of the city agreed with what Hamor and Shechem proposed, and all the males were circumcised.

25 Three days later, when the men were still sore from their circumcision, two of Jacob's sons, Simeon and Levi, the brothers of Dinah, took their swords, went into the city without arousing suspicion, and killed all the men, 26 including Hamor and his son Shechem. Then they took Dinah from Shechem's house and left. 27 After the slaughter Jacob's other sons looted the town to take revenge for their sister's disgrace. 28 They took the flocks, the cattle, the donkeys, and everything else in the city and in the fields. 29 They took everything of value, captured all the women and children, and carried off everything in the houses.

30 Jacob said to Simeon and Levi, "You have brought trouble on me; now the Canaanites, the Perizzites, and everybody else in the land will hate me. I haven't many men; if they all band together against me and attack me, our whole family will be destroyed."

31 But they answered, "We cannot let our sister be treated like a common whore."

God Blesses Jacob at Bethel

35 God said to Jacob, "Go to Bethel at once, and live there. Build an altar there to me, the God who appeared to you when you were running away from your brother Esau."

2 So Jacob said to his family and to all who were with him, "Get rid of the foreign gods that you have; purify yourselves and put on clean clothes. 3 We are going to leave here and go to Bethel, where I will build an altar to the God who helped me in the time of my trouble and who has been with me everywhere I have gone." 4 So they gave Jacob all the foreign gods that they had and also the earrings that they were wearing. He buried them beneath the oak tree near Shechem.

5 When Jacob and his sons started to leave, great fear fell on the people of the nearby towns, and they did not pursue them. 6 Jacob came with all his people to Luz, which is now known as Bethel, in the land of Canaan. 7 He built an altar there and named the place after the God of Bethel, because God had revealed himself to him there when he was running away from his brother. 8 Rebecca's nurse Deborah died and was buried beneath the oak south of Bethel. So it was named "Oak of Weeping".

9 When Jacob returned from Mesopotamia, God appeared to him again and blessed him. 10 God said to him, "Your name is Jacob, but from now on it will be Israel." So God named him Israel. 11 And God said to him, "I am

See also: 35.1: Gen 28.11–17   **35.10:** Gen 32.28
35.11–12: Gen 17.4–8

Almighty God. Have many children. Nations will be descended from you, and you will be the ancestor of kings. 12 I will give you the land which I gave to Abraham and to Isaac, and I will also give it to your descendants after you." 13 Then God left him. 14 There, where God had spoken to him, Jacob set up a memorial stone and consecrated it by pouring wine and olive oil on it. 15 He named the place Bethel.

The Death of Rachel
16 Jacob and his family left Bethel, and when they were still some distance from Ephrath, the time came for Rachel to have her baby, and she was having difficult labour. 17 When her labour pains were at their worst, the midwife said to her, "Don't be afraid, Rachel; it's another boy." 18 But she was dying, and as she breathed her last, she named her son Benoni,* but his father named him Benjamin.*

19 When Rachel died, she was buried beside the road to Ephrath, now known as Bethlehem. 20 Jacob set up a memorial stone there, and it still marks Rachel's grave to this day. 21 Jacob moved on and set up his camp on the other side of the tower of Eder.

The Sons of Jacob
(1 Chr 2.1–2)
22 While Jacob was living in that land, Reuben had sexual intercourse with Bilhah, one of his father's concubines; Jacob heard about it and was furious.*

Jacob had twelve sons. 23 The sons of Leah were Reuben (Jacob's eldest son), Simeon, Levi, Judah, Issachar, and Zebulun. 24 The sons of Rachel were Joseph and Benjamin. 25 The sons of Rachel's slave Bilhah were Dan and Naphtali. 26 The sons of Leah's slave Zilpah were Gad and Asher. These sons were born in Mesopotamia.

The Death of Isaac
27 Jacob went to his father Isaac at Mamre, near Hebron, where Abraham and

Isaac had lived. 28 Isaac lived to be 180 years old 29 and died at a ripe old age; and his sons Esau and Jacob buried him.

The Descendants of Esau
(1 Chr 1.34–37)

36 These are the descendants of Esau, also called Edom. 2 Esau married Canaanite women: Adah, the daughter of Elon the Hittite; Oholibamah, the daughter of Anah son* of Zibeon the Hivite; 3 and Basemath, the daughter of Ishmael and sister of Nebaioth. 4 Adah bore Eliphaz; Basemath bore Reuel; 5 and Oholibamah bore Jeush, Jalam, and Korah. All these sons were born to Esau in the land of Canaan.

6 Then Esau took his wives, his sons, his daughters, and all the people of his house, together with all his livestock and all the possessions he had acquired in the land of Canaan, and went away from his brother Jacob to another land. 7 He left because the land where he and Jacob were living was not able to support them; they had too much livestock and could no longer stay together. 8 So Esau lived in the hill country of Edom.

9 These are the descendants of Esau, the ancestor of the Edomites. 10–13 Esau's wife Adah bore him one son, Eliphaz, and Eliphaz had five sons: Teman, Omar, Zepho, Gatam, and Kenaz. And by another wife, Timna, he had one more son, Amalek.

Esau's wife Basemath bore him one son, Reuel, and Reuel had four sons: Nahath, Zerah, Shammah, and Mizzah.

14 Esau's wife Oholibamah, the daughter of Anah son* of Zibeon, bore him three sons: Jeush, Jalam, and Korah.

15 These are the tribes descended from Esau. Esau's first son Eliphaz was the ancestor of the following tribes: Teman, Omar, Zepho, Kenaz, 16 Korah, Gatam, and Amalek. These were all descendants of Esau's wife Adah.

17 Esau's son Reuel was the ancestor of the following tribes: Nahath, Zerah, Shammah, and Mizzah. These were all descendants of Esau's wife Basemath.

35.18 BENONI: *This name in Hebrew means "son of my sorrow".*
35.18 BENJAMIN: *This name in Hebrew means "son who will be fortunate".*
35.22 *One ancient translation* and was furious; *Hebrew does not have these words.*

See also: 35.14–15: Gen 28.18–19
35.22: Gen 49.4   35.27: Gen 13.18

36.2, 36.14 *Some ancient translations* son; *Hebrew* daughter; *or* granddaughter.

See also: 36.2: Gen 26.34   36.3: Gen 28.9

[18] The following tribes were descended from Esau by his wife Oholibamah, the daughter of Anah: Jeush, Jalam, and Korah. [19] All these tribes were descended from Esau.

The Descendants of Seir
(1 Chr 1.38–42)

[20–21] The original inhabitants of the land of Edom were divided into tribes which traced their ancestry to the following descendants of Seir, a Horite: Lotan, Shobal, Zibeon, Anah, Dishon, Ezer, and Dishan.

[22] Lotan was the ancestor of the clans of Hori and Heman. (Lotan had a sister named Timna.)

[23] Shobal was the ancestor of the clans of Alvan, Manahath, Ebal, Shepho, and Onam.

[24] Zibeon had two sons, Aiah and Anah. (This is the Anah who found the hot springs in the wilderness when he was taking care of his father's donkeys.) [25–26] Anah was the father of Dishon, who was the ancestor of the clans of Hemdan, Eshban, Ithran, and Cheran. Anah also had a daughter named Oholibamah.

[27] Ezer was the ancestor of the clans of Bilhan, Zaavan, and Akan.

[28] Dishan was the ancestor of the clans of Uz and Aran.

[29–30] These are the Horite tribes in the land of Edom: Lotan, Shobal, Zibeon, Anah, Dishon, Ezer, and Dishan.

The Kings of Edom
(1 Chr 1.43–54)

[31–39] Before there were any kings in Israel, the following kings ruled over the land of Edom in succession:
Bela son of Beor from Dinhabah
Jobab son of Zerah from Bozrah
Husham from the region of Teman
Hadad son of Bedad from Avith (he defeated the Midianites in a battle in the country of Moab)
Samlah from Masrekah
Shaul from Rehoboth-on-the-River
Baal Hanan son of Achbor
Hadad from Pau (his wife was Mehetabel, the daughter of Matred and granddaughter of Mezahab)

[40–43] Esau was the ancestor of the following Edomite tribes: Timna, Alvah, Jetheth, Oholibamah, Elah, Pinon, Kenaz, Teman, Mibzar, Magdiel, and Iram. The area where each of these tribes lived was known by the name of the tribe.

Joseph and his Brothers

37 Jacob continued to live in the land of Canaan, where his father had lived, [2] and this is the story of Jacob's family.

Joseph, a young man of seventeen, took care of the sheep and goats with his brothers, the sons of Bilhah and Zilpah, his father's concubines. He brought bad reports to his father about what his brothers were doing.

[3] Jacob loved Joseph more than all his other sons, because he had been born to him when he was old. He made a long robe with full sleeves* for him. [4] When his brothers saw that their father loved Joseph more than he loved them, they hated their brother so much that they would not speak to him in a friendly manner.

[5] One night Joseph had a dream, and when he told his brothers about it, they hated him even more. [6] He said, "Listen to the dream I had. [7] We were all in the field tying up sheaves of wheat, when my sheaf got up and stood up straight. Yours formed a circle round mine and bowed down to it."

[8] "Do you think you are going to be a king and rule over us?" his brothers asked. So they hated him even more because of his dreams and because of what he said about them.

[9] Then Joseph had another dream and said to his brothers, "I had another dream, in which I saw the sun, the moon, and eleven stars bowing down to me."

[10] He also told the dream to his father, and his father scolded him: "What kind of a dream is that? Do you think that your mother, your brothers, and I are going to come and bow down to you?" [11] Joseph's brothers were jealous of him, but his father kept thinking about the whole matter.

Joseph is Sold and Taken to Egypt

[12] One day when Joseph's brothers had gone to Shechem to take care of their father's flock, [13] Jacob said to Joseph, "I want you to go to Shechem, where your brothers are taking care of the flock."

Joseph answered, "I am ready."

37.3, 37.23 robe with full sleeves; *or* decorated robe.
See also: 37.11: Acts 7.9

14 His father said, "Go and see if your brothers are safe and if the flock is all right; then come back and tell me." So his father sent him on his way from the Valley of Hebron.

Joseph arrived at Shechem 15 and was wandering about in the country when a man saw him and asked him, "What are you looking for?"

16 "I am looking for my brothers, who are taking care of their flock," he answered. "Can you tell me where they are?"

17 The man said, "They have already left. I heard them say that they were going to Dothan." So Joseph went after his brothers and found them at Dothan.

18 They saw him in the distance, and before he reached them, they plotted against him and decided to kill him. 19 They said to one another, "Here comes that dreamer. 20 Come on now, let's kill him and throw his body into one of the dry wells. We can say that a wild animal killed him. Then we will see what becomes of his dreams."

21 Reuben heard them and tried to save Joseph. "Let's not kill him," he said. 22 "Just throw him into this well in the wilderness, but don't hurt him." He said this, planning to save him from them and send him back to his father. 23 When Joseph came up to his brothers, they ripped off his long robe with full sleeves.* 24 Then they took him and threw him into the well, which was dry.

25 While they were eating, they suddenly saw a group of Ishmaelites travelling from Gilead to Egypt. Their camels were loaded with spices and resins. 26 Judah said to his brothers, "What will we gain by killing our brother and covering up the murder? 27 Let's sell him to these Ishmaelites. Then we won't have to hurt him; after all, he is our brother, our own flesh and blood." His brothers agreed, 28 and when some Midianite traders came by, the brothers* pulled Joseph out of the well and sold him for twenty pieces of silver to the Ishmaelites, who took him to Egypt.

29 When Reuben came back to the well and found that Joseph was not there,

he tore his clothes in sorrow. 30 He returned to his brothers and said, "The boy is not there! What am I going to do?"

31 Then they killed a goat and dipped Joseph's robe in its blood. 32 They took the robe to their father and said, "We found this. Does it belong to your son?"

33 He recognized it and said, "Yes, it is his! Some wild animal has killed him. My son Joseph has been torn to pieces!" 34 Jacob tore his clothes in sorrow and put on sackcloth. He mourned for his son a long time. 35 All his sons and daughters came to comfort him, but he refused to be comforted and said, "I will go down to the world of the dead still mourning for my son." So he continued to mourn for his son Joseph.

36 Meanwhile, in Egypt, the Midianites had sold Joseph to Potiphar, one of the king's officers, who was the captain of the palace guard.

Judah and Tamar

38 About that time Judah left his brothers and went to stay with a man named Hirah, who was from the town of Adullam. 2 There Judah met a young Canaanite woman whose father was named Shua. He married her, 3 and she bore him a son, whom he named Er. 4 She became pregnant again and bore another son and named him Onan. 5 Again she had a son and named him Shelah. Judah was at Achzib when the boy was born.

6 For his first son Er, Judah got a wife whose name was Tamar. 7 Er's conduct was evil, and it displeased the LORD, so the LORD killed him. 8 Then Judah said to Er's brother Onan, "Go and sleep with your brother's widow. Fulfil your obligation to her as her husband's brother, so that your brother may have descendants." 9 But Onan knew that the children would not belong to him, so whenever he had intercourse with his brother's widow, he let the semen spill on the ground, so that there would be no children for his brother. 10 What he did displeased the LORD, and the LORD killed him also. 11 Then Judah said to his daughter-in-law Tamar, "Return to your father's house and remain a widow until my son Shelah grows up." He said this because he was afraid that Shelah would be killed, as his brothers had been. So Tamar went back home.

37.23, 37.3 robe with full sleeves; or decorated robe.
37.28 the brothers; Hebrew they.
See also: 37.28: Acts 7.9

12 After some time Judah's wife died. When he had finished the time of mourning, he and his friend Hirah of Adullam went to Timnah, where his sheep were being sheared. 13 Someone told Tamar that her father-in-law was going to Timnah to shear his sheep. 14 So she changed from the widow's clothes she had been wearing, covered her face with a veil, and sat down at the entrance to Enaim, a town on the road to Timnah. As she well knew, Judah's youngest son Shelah had now grown up, and yet she had not been given to him in marriage.

15 When Judah saw her, he thought that she was a prostitute, because she had her face covered. 16 He went over to her at the side of the road and said, "All right, how much do you charge?" (He did not know that she was his daughter-in-law.)

She said, "What will you give me?"

17 He answered, "I will send you a young goat from my flock."

She said, "All right, if you will give me something to keep as a pledge until you send the goat."

18 "What shall I give you as a pledge?" he asked.

She answered, "Your seal with its cord and the stick you are carrying." He gave them to her. Then they had intercourse, and she became pregnant. 19 Tamar went home, took off her veil, and put her widow's clothes back on.

20 Judah sent his friend Hirah to take the goat and get back from the woman the articles he had pledged, but Hirah could not find her. 21 He asked some men at Enaim, "Where is the prostitute who was here by the road?"

"There has never been a prostitute here," they answered.

22 He returned to Judah and said, "I couldn't find her. The men of the place said that there had never been a prostitute there."

23 Judah said, "Let her keep the things. We don't want people to laugh at us. I did try to pay her, but you couldn't find her."

24 About three months later someone said to Judah, "Your daughter-in-law Tamar has been acting like a whore, and now she is pregnant."

Judah ordered, "Take her out and burn her to death."

25 As she was being taken out, she sent word to her father-in-law: "I am pregnant by the man who owns these things. Look at them and see whose they are — this seal with its cord and this stick."

26 Judah recognized them and said, "She is in the right. I have failed in my obligation to her — I should have given her to my son Shelah in marriage." And Judah never had intercourse with her again.

27 When the time came for her to give birth, it was discovered that she was going to have twins. 28 While she was in labour, one of them put out an arm; the midwife caught it, tied a red thread round it, and said, "This one was born first." 29 But he pulled his arm back, and his brother was born first. Then the midwife said, "So this is how you break your way out!" So he was named Perez.* 30 Then his brother was born with the red thread on his arm, and he was named Zerah.*

Joseph and Potiphar's Wife

39 Now the Ishmaelites had taken Joseph to Egypt and sold him to Potiphar, one of the king's officers, who was the captain of the palace guard. 2 The Lord was with Joseph and made him successful. He lived in the house of his Egyptian master, 3 who saw that the Lord was with Joseph and had made him successful in everything he did. 4 Potiphar was pleased with him and made him his personal servant; so he put him in charge of his house and everything he owned. 5 From then on, because of Joseph the Lord blessed the household of the Egyptian and everything that he had in his house and in his fields. 6 Potiphar handed over everything he had to the care of Joseph and did not concern himself with anything except the food he ate.

Joseph was well-built and good-looking, 7 and after a while his master's wife began to desire Joseph and asked him to go to bed with her. 8 He refused and said to her, "Look, my master does not have to concern himself with anything in the house, because I am here. He has put me in

---

38.29 PEREZ: *This name in Hebrew means "breaking out".*
38.30 ZERAH: *This name sounds like a Hebrew word for the red brightness of dawn.*
See also: 39.2: Acts 7.9

charge of everything he has. 9 I have as much authority in this house as he has, and he has not kept back anything from me except you. How then could I do such an immoral thing and sin against God?" 10 Although she asked Joseph day after day, he would not go to bed with her.

11 But one day when Joseph went into the house to do his work, none of the house servants was there. 12 She caught him by his robe and said, "Come to bed with me." But he escaped and ran outside, leaving his robe in her hand. 13 When she saw that he had left his robe and had run out of the house, 14 she called to her house servants and said, "Look at this! This Hebrew that my husband brought to the house is insulting us. He came into my room and tried to rape me, but I screamed as loud as I could. 15 When he heard me scream, he ran outside, leaving his robe beside me."

16 She kept his robe with her until Joseph's master came home. 17 Then she told him the same story: "That Hebrew slave that you brought here came into my room and insulted me. 18 But when I screamed, he ran outside, leaving his robe beside me."

19 Joseph's master was furious 20 and had Joseph arrested and put in the prison where the king's prisoners were kept, and there he stayed. 21 But the LORD was with Joseph and blessed him, so that the jailer was pleased with him. 22 He put Joseph in charge of all the other prisoners and made him responsible for everything that was done in the prison. 23 The jailer did not have to look after anything for which Joseph was responsible, because the LORD was with Joseph and made him succeed in everything he did.

Joseph Interprets the Prisoners' Dreams

40 Some time later the king of Egypt's wine steward and his chief baker offended the king. 2 He was angry with these two officials 3 and put *them in prison* in the house of the captain of the guard, in the same place where Joseph was being kept. 4 They spent a long time in prison, and the captain assigned Joseph as their servant.

See also: 39.21: Acts 7.9

5 One night there in prison the wine steward and the chief baker each had a dream, and the dreams had different meanings. 6 When Joseph came to them in the morning, he saw that they were upset. 7 He asked them, "Why do you look so worried today?"

8 They answered, "Each of us had a dream, and there is no one here to explain what the dreams mean."

"It is God who gives the ability to interpret dreams," Joseph said. "Tell me your dreams."

9 So the wine steward said, "In my dream there was a grapevine in front of me 10 with three branches on it. As soon as the leaves came out, the blossoms appeared, and the grapes ripened. 11 I was holding the king's cup; so I took the grapes and squeezed them into the cup and gave it to him."

12 Joseph said, "This is what it means: the three branches are three days. 13 In three days the king will release you, pardon you, and restore you to your position. You will give him his cup as you did before when you were his wine steward. 14 But please remember me when everything is going well for you, and please be kind enough to mention me to the king and help me to get out of this prison. 15 After all, I was kidnapped from the land of the Hebrews, and even here in Egypt I didn't do anything to deserve being put in prison."

16 When the chief baker saw that the interpretation of the wine steward's dream was favourable, he said to Joseph, "I had a dream too; I was carrying three bread baskets on my head. 17 In the top basket there were all kinds of pastries for the king, and the birds were eating them."

18 Joseph answered, "This is what it means: the three baskets are three days. 19 In three days the king will release you — and have your head cut off! Then he will hang your body on a pole, and the birds will eat your flesh."

20 On his birthday three days later the king gave a banquet for all his officials; he released his wine steward and his chief baker and brought them before his officials. 21 He restored the wine steward to his former position, 22 but he executed the chief baker. It all happened just as Joseph had said. 23 But the wine steward never gave Joseph another thought — he forgot all about him.

Joseph Interprets the King's Dreams

41 After two years had passed, the king of Egypt dreamt that he was standing by the River Nile, 2 when seven cows, fat and sleek, came up out of the river and began to feed on the grass. 3 Then seven other cows came up; they were thin and bony. They came and stood by the other cows on the river bank, 4 and the thin cows ate up the fat cows. Then the king woke up. 5 He fell asleep again and had another dream. Seven ears of corn, full and ripe, were growing on one stalk. 6 Then seven other ears of corn sprouted, thin and scorched by the desert wind, 7 and the thin ears of corn swallowed the full ones. The king woke up and realized that he had been dreaming. 8 In the morning he was worried, so he sent for all the magicians and wise men of Egypt. He told them his dreams, but no one could explain them to him.

9 Then the wine steward said to the king, "I must confess today that I have done wrong. 10 You were angry with the chief baker and me, and you put us in prison in the house of the captain of the guard. 11 One night each of us had a dream, and the dreams had different meanings. 12 A young Hebrew was there with us, a slave of the captain of the guard. We told him our dreams, and he interpreted them for us. 13 Things turned out just as he said: you restored me to my position, but you executed the baker."

14 The king sent for Joseph, and he was immediately brought from the prison. After he had shaved and changed his clothes, he came into the king's presence. 15 The king said to him, "I have had a dream, and no one can explain it. I have been told that you can interpret dreams."

16 Joseph answered, "I cannot, Your Majesty, but God will give a favourable interpretation."

17 The king said, "I dreamt that I was standing on the bank of the Nile, 18 when seven cows, fat and sleek, came up out of the river and began feeding on the grass. 19 Then seven other cows came up which were thin and bony. They were the poorest cows I have ever seen anywhere in Egypt.

20 The thin cows ate up the fat ones, 21 but no one would have known it, because they looked just as bad as before. Then I woke up. 22 I also dreamt that I saw seven ears of corn which were full and ripe, growing on one stalk. 23 Then seven ears of corn sprouted, thin and scorched by the desert wind, 24 and the thin ears of corn swallowed the full ones. I told the dreams to the magicians, but none of them could explain them to me."

25 Joseph said to the king, "The two dreams mean the same thing; God has told you what he is going to do. 26 The seven fat cows are seven years, and the seven full ears of corn are also seven years; they have the same meaning. 27 The seven thin cows which came up later and the seven thin ears of corn scorched by the desert wind are seven years of famine. 28 It is just as I told you — God has shown you what he is going to do. 29 There will be seven years of great plenty in all the land of Egypt. 30 After that, there will be seven years of famine, and all the good years will be forgotten, because the famine will ruin the country. 31 The time of plenty will be entirely forgotten, because the famine which follows will be so terrible. 32 The repetition of your dream means that the matter is fixed by God and that he will make it happen in the near future.

33 "Now you should choose some man with wisdom and insight and put him in charge of the country. 34 You must also appoint other officials and take a fifth of the crops during the seven years of plenty. 35 Order them to collect all the food during the good years that are coming, and give them authority to store up corn in the cities and guard it. 36 The food will be a reserve supply for the country during the seven years of famine which are going to come on Egypt. In this way the people will not starve."

Joseph is Made Governor over Egypt

37 The king and his officials approved this plan, 38 and he said to them, "We will never find a better man than Joseph, a man who has God's spirit in him." 39 The king said to Joseph, "God has shown you all this, so it is obvious that you have

See also: 41.8: Dan 2.2

greater wisdom and insight than anyone else. 40 I will put you in charge of my country, and all my people will obey your orders. Your authority will be second only to mine. 41 I now appoint you governor over all Egypt." 42 The king removed from his finger the ring engraved with the royal seal and put it on Joseph's finger. He put a fine linen robe on him, and placed a gold chain round his neck. 43 He gave him the second royal chariot to ride in, and his guard of honour went ahead of him and cried out, "Make way! Make way!" And so Joseph was appointed governor over all Egypt. 44 The king said to him, "I am the king — and no one in all Egypt shall so much as lift a hand or a foot without your permission." 45–46 He gave Joseph the Egyptian name Zaphenath Paneah, and he gave him a wife, Asenath, the daughter of Potiphera, a priest in the city of Heliopolis.

Joseph was 30 years old when he began to serve the king of Egypt. He left the king's court and travelled all over the land. 47 During the seven years of plenty the land produced abundant crops, 48 all of which Joseph collected and stored in the cities. In each city he stored the food from the fields around it. 49 There was so much corn that Joseph stopped measuring it — it was like the sand of the sea.

50 Before the years of famine came, Joseph had two sons by Asenath. 51 He said, "God has made me forget all my sufferings and all my father's family"; so he named his first son Manasseh.* 52 He also said, "God has given me children in the land of my trouble"; so he named his second son Ephraim.*

53 The seven years of plenty that the land of Egypt had enjoyed came to an end, 54 and the seven years of famine began, just as Joseph had said. There was famine in every other country, but there was food throughout Egypt. 55 When the Egyptians began to be hungry, they cried out to the king for food. So he ordered them to go to Joseph and do what he told them. 56 The famine grew worse and spread over the

whole country, so Joseph opened all the storehouses and sold corn to the Egyptians. 57 People came to Egypt from all over the world to buy corn from Joseph, because the famine was severe everywhere.

Joseph's Brothers Go to Egypt to Buy Corn

42 When Jacob learnt that there was corn in Egypt, he said to his sons, "Why don't you do something? 2 I hear that there is corn in Egypt; go there and buy some to keep us from starving to death." 3 So Joseph's ten half-brothers went to buy corn in Egypt, 4 but Jacob did not send Joseph's full-brother Benjamin with them, because he was afraid that something might happen to him.

5 The sons of Jacob came with others to buy corn, because there was famine in the land of Canaan. 6 Joseph, as governor of the land of Egypt, was selling corn to people from all over the world. So Joseph's brothers came and bowed down before him with their faces to the ground. 7 When Joseph saw his brothers, he recognized them, but he acted as if he did not know them. He asked them harshly, "Where do you come from?"

"We have come from Canaan to buy food," they answered.

8 Although Joseph recognized his brothers, they did not recognize him. 9 He remembered the dreams he had dreamt about them and said, "You are spies; you have come to find out where our country is weak."

10 "No, sir," they answered. "We have come as your slaves, to buy food. 11 We are all brothers. We are not spies, sir, we are honest men."

12 Joseph said to them, "No! You have come to find out where our country is weak."

13 They said, "We were twelve brothers in all, sir, sons of the same man in the land of Canaan. One brother is dead, and the youngest is now with our father."

14 "It is just as I said," Joseph answered. *"You are spies. 15 This is how you will be* tested: I swear by the name of the king that you will never leave unless your youngest brother comes here. 16 One of you must go

---

41.51 MANASSEH: *This name sounds like the Hebrew for "cause to forget".*
41.52 EPHRAIM: *This name sounds like the Hebrew for "give children".*

See also: **41.40:** Acts 7.10   **41.42:** Dan 5.29
41.54: Acts 7.11   **41.55:** Jn 2.5

See also: **42.2:** Acts 7.12   **42.9:** Gen 37.5–10

and get him. The rest of you will be kept under guard until the truth of what you say can be tested. Otherwise, as sure as the king lives, you are spies." 17 Then he put them in prison for three days.

18 On the third day Joseph said to them, "I am a God-fearing man, and I will spare your lives on one condition. 19 To prove that you are honest, one of you will stay in the prison where you have been kept; the rest of you may go and take back to your starving families the corn that you have bought. 20 Then you must bring your youngest brother to me. This will prove that you have been telling the truth, and I will not put you to death."

They agreed to this 21 and said to one another, "Yes, now we are suffering the consequences of what we did to our brother; we saw the great trouble he was in when he begged for help, but we would not listen. That is why we are in this trouble now."

22 Reuben said, "I told you not to harm the boy, but you wouldn't listen. And now we are being paid back for his death." 23 Joseph understood what they said, but they did not know it, because they had been speaking to him through an interpreter. 24 Joseph left them and began to cry. When he was able to speak again, he came back, picked out Simeon, and had him tied up in front of them.

Joseph's Brothers Return to Canaan

25 Joseph gave orders to fill his brothers' packs with corn, to put each man's money back in his sack, and to give them food for the journey. This was done. 26 The brothers loaded their donkeys with the corn they had bought, and then they left. 27 At the place where they spent the night, one of them opened his sack to feed his donkey and found his money at the top of the sack. 28 "My money has been returned to me," he called to his brothers. "Here it is in my sack!" Their hearts sank, and in fear they asked one another, "What has God done to us?"

29 When they came to their father Jacob in Canaan, they told him all that had happened to them: 30 "The governor of Egypt

spoke harshly to us and accused us of spying against his country. 31 'We are not spies,' we answered, 'we are honest men. 32 We were twelve brothers in all, sons of the same father. One brother is dead, and the youngest is still in Canaan with our father.' 33 The man answered, 'This is how I will find out if you are honest men: one of you will stay with me; the rest will take corn for your starving families and leave. 34 Bring your youngest brother to me. Then I will know that you are not spies, but honest men; I will give your brother back to you, and you can stay here and trade.' "

35 Then when they emptied out their sacks, every one of them found his bag of money; and when they saw the money, they and their father Jacob were afraid. 36 Their father said to them, "Do you want to make me lose all my children? Joseph is gone; Simeon is gone; and now you want to take away Benjamin. I am the one who suffers!"

37 Reuben said to his father, "If I do not bring Benjamin back to you, you can kill my two sons. Put him in my care, and I will bring him back."

38 But Jacob said, "My son cannot go with you; his brother is dead, and he is the only one left. Something might happen to him on the way. I am an old man, and the sorrow you would cause me would kill me."

Joseph's Brothers Return to Egypt with Benjamin

43 The famine in Canaan got worse, 2 and when the family of Jacob had eaten all the corn which had been brought from Egypt, Jacob said to his sons, "Go back and buy a little food for us."

3 Judah said to him, "The man sternly warned us that we would not be admitted to his presence unless we had our brother with us. 4 If you are willing to send our brother with us, we will go and buy food for you. 5 If you are not willing, we will not go, because the man told us we would not be admitted to his presence unless our brother was with us."

6 Jacob said, "Why did you cause me so much trouble by telling the man that you had another brother?"

7 They answered, "The man kept asking about us and our family, 'Is your father

See also: 42.22: Gen 37.21–22

still living? Have you got another brother?' We had to answer his questions. How could we know that he would tell us to bring our brother with us?"

8 Judah said to his father, "Send the boy with me, and we will leave at once. Then none of us will starve to death. 9 I will pledge my own life, and you can hold me responsible for him. If I do not bring him back to you safe and sound, I will always bear the blame. 10 If we had not waited so long, we could have been there and back twice by now."

11 Their father said to them, "If that is how it has to be, then take the best products of the land in your packs as a present for the governor: a little resin, a little honey, spices, pistachio nuts, and almonds. 12 Take with you also twice as much money, because you must take back the money that was returned in the top of your sacks. Maybe it was a mistake. 13 Take your brother and return at once. 14 May Almighty God cause the man to have pity on you, so that he will give Benjamin and your other brother back to you. As for me, if I must lose my children, I must lose them."

15 So the brothers took the gifts and twice as much money, and set out for Egypt with Benjamin. There they presented themselves to Joseph. 16 When Joseph saw Benjamin with them, he said to the servant in charge of his house, "Take these men to my house. They are going to eat with me at noon, so kill an animal and prepare it." 17 The servant did as he was commanded and took the brothers to Joseph's house.

18 As they were being brought to the house, they were afraid and thought, "We are being brought here because of the money that was returned in our sacks the first time. They will suddenly attack us, take our donkeys, and make us his slaves." 19 So at the door of the house, they said to the servant in charge, 20 "If you please, sir, we came here once before to buy food. 21 When we set up camp on the way home, we opened our sacks, and each man found his money in the top of his sack — every bit of it. We have brought it back to you. 22 We have also brought some more money with us to buy more food. We do not know who put our money back in our sacks."

23 The servant said, "Don't worry. Don't be afraid. Your God, the God of your father, must have put the money in your sacks for you. I received your payment." Then he brought Simeon to them.

24 The servant took the brothers into the house. He gave them water so that they could wash their feet, and he fed their donkeys. 25 They got their gifts ready to present to Joseph when he arrived at noon, because they had been told that they were to eat with him. 26 When Joseph got home, they took the gifts into the house to him and bowed down to the ground before him. 27 He asked about their health and then said, "You told me about your old father — how is he? Is he still alive and well?"

28 They answered, "Your humble servant, our father, is still alive and well." And they knelt and bowed down before him.

29 When Joseph saw his brother Benjamin, he said, "So this is your youngest brother, the one you told me about. God bless you, my son." 30 Then Joseph left suddenly, because his heart was full of tender feelings for his brother. He was about to break down, so he went to his room and cried. 31 After he had washed his face, he came out, and controlling himself, he ordered the meal to be served. 32 Joseph was served at one table and his brothers at another. The Egyptians who were eating there were served separately, because they considered it beneath their dignity to eat with Hebrews. 33 The brothers had been seated at table, facing Joseph, in the order of their age from the eldest to the youngest. When they saw how they had been seated, they looked at one another in amazement. 34 Food was served to them from Joseph's table, and Benjamin was served five times as much as the rest of them. So they ate and drank with Joseph until they were drunk.

The Missing Cup

44 Joseph commanded the servant in charge of his house, "Fill the men's sacks with as much food as they can carry, and put each man's money in the top of his sack. 2 Put my silver cup in the top of the youngest brother's sack, together with the money for his corn." He did as he was told. 3 Early in the morning the brothers were

sent on their way with their donkeys. 4 When they had gone only a short distance from the city, Joseph said to the servant in charge of his house, "Hurry after those men. When you catch up with them, ask them, 'Why have you paid back evil for good? 5 Why did you steal my master's silver cup?* It is the one he drinks from, the one he uses for divination. You have committed a serious crime!' "

6 When the servant caught up with them, he repeated these words. 7 They answered him, "What do you mean, sir, by talking like this? We swear that we have done no such thing. 8 You know that we brought back to you from the land of Canaan the money we found in the top of our sacks. Why then should we steal silver or gold from your master's house? 9 Sir, if any one of us is found to have it, he will be put to death, and the rest of us will become your slaves."

10 He said, "I agree; but only the one who has taken the cup will become my slave, and the rest of you can go free." 11 So they quickly lowered their sacks to the ground, and each man opened his sack. 12 Joseph's servant searched carefully, beginning with the eldest and ending with the youngest, and the cup was found in Benjamin's sack. 13 The brothers tore their clothes in sorrow, loaded their donkeys, and returned to the city.

14 When Judah and his brothers came to Joseph's house, he was still there. They bowed down before him, 15 and Joseph said, "What have you done? Didn't you know that a man in my position could find you out by practising divination?"

16 "What can we say to you, sir?" Judah answered. "How can we argue? How can we clear ourselves? God has uncovered our guilt. All of us are now your slaves and not just the one with whom the cup was found."

17 Joseph said, "Oh, no! I would never do that! Only the one who had the cup will be my slave. The rest of you may go back safe and sound to your father."

Judah Pleads for Benjamin

18 Judah went up to Joseph and said, "Please, sir, allow me to speak with you

freely. Don't be angry with me; you are like the king himself. 19 Sir, you asked us, 'Have you got a father or another brother?' 20 We answered, 'We have a father who is old and a younger brother, born to him in his old age. The boy's brother is dead, and he is the only one of his mother's children still alive; his father loves him very much.' 21 Sir, you told us to bring him here, so that you could see him, 22 and we answered that the boy could not leave his father; if he did, his father would die. 23 Then you said, 'You will not be admitted to my presence again unless your youngest brother comes with you.'

24 "When we went back to our father, we told him what you had said. 25 Then he told us to return and buy a little food. 26 We answered, 'We cannot go; we will not be admitted to the man's presence unless our youngest brother is with us. We can go only if our youngest brother goes also.' 27 Our father said to us, 'You know that my wife Rachel bore me only two sons. 28 One of them has already left me. He must have been torn to pieces by wild animals, because I have not seen him since he left. 29 If you take this one from me now and something happens to him, the sorrow you would cause me would kill me, old as I am.'

30-31 "And now, sir," Judah continued, "if I go back to my father without the boy, as soon as he sees that the boy is not with me, he will die. His life is wrapped up with the life of the boy, and he is so old that the sorrow we would cause him would kill him. 32 What is more, I pledged my life to my father for the boy. I told him that if I did not bring the boy back to him, I would bear the blame all my life. 33 And now, sir, I will stay here as your slave in place of the boy; let him go back with his brothers. 34 How can I go back to my father if the boy is not with me? I cannot bear to see this disaster come upon my father."

Joseph Tells his Brothers Who he Is

45 Joseph was no longer able to control his feelings in front of his servants, so he ordered them all to leave the room. No one else was with him when Joseph told his brothers who he was. 2 He cried with such loud sobs that the

---

44.5 *One ancient translation* Why did you steal my master's silver cup?; *Hebrew does not have these words.*

See also: 45.1: Acts 7.13

Egyptians heard it, and the news was taken to the king's palace. 3 Joseph said to his brothers, "I am Joseph. Is my father still alive?" But when his brothers heard this, they were so terrified that they could not answer. 4 Then Joseph said to them, "Please come closer." They did, and he said, "I am your brother Joseph, whom you sold into Egypt. 5 Now do not be upset or blame yourselves because you sold me here. It was really God who sent me ahead of you to save people's lives. 6 This is only the second year of famine in the land; there will be five more years in which there will be neither ploughing nor reaping. 7 God sent me ahead of you to rescue you in this amazing way and to make sure that you and your descendants survive. 8 So it was not really you who sent me here, but God. He has made me the king's highest official. I am in charge of his whole country; I am the ruler of all Egypt.

9 "Now hurry back to my father and tell him that this is what his son Joseph says: 'God has made me ruler of all Egypt; come to me without delay. 10 You can live in the region of Goshen, where you can be near me — you, your children, your grandchildren, your sheep, your goats, your cattle, and everything else that you have. 11 If you are in Goshen, I can take care of you. There will still be five years of famine; and I do not want you, your family, and your livestock to starve.' "

12 Joseph continued, "Now all of you, and you too, Benjamin, can see that I am really Joseph. 13 Tell my father how powerful I am here in Egypt and tell him about everything that you have seen. Then hurry and bring him here."

14 He threw his arms round his brother Benjamin and began to cry; Benjamin also cried as he hugged him. 15 Then, still weeping, he embraced each of his brothers and kissed them. After that, his brothers began to talk with him.

16 When the news reached the palace that Joseph's brothers had come, the king and his officials were pleased. 17 He said to Joseph, "Tell your brothers to load their animals and to return to the land of Canaan. 18 Let them get their father and their families and come back here. I will give them the best land in Egypt, and they will

have more than enough to live on. 19 Tell them also to take wagons with them from Egypt for their wives and small children and to bring their father with them. 20 They are not to worry about leaving their possessions behind; the best in the whole land of Egypt will be theirs."

21 Jacob's sons did as they were told. Joseph gave them wagons, as the king had ordered, and food for the journey. 22 He also gave each of them a change of clothes, but he gave Benjamin 300 pieces of silver and five changes of clothes. 23 He sent his father ten donkeys loaded with the best Egyptian goods and ten donkeys loaded with corn, bread, and other food for the journey. 24 He sent his brothers off and as they left, he said to them, "Don't quarrel on the way."

25 They left Egypt and went back home to their father Jacob in Canaan. 26 "Joseph is still alive!" they told him. "He is the ruler of all Egypt!" Jacob was stunned and could not believe them.

27 But when they told him all that Joseph had said to them, and when he saw the wagons which Joseph had sent to take him to Egypt, he recovered from the shock. 28 "My son Joseph is still alive!" he said. "This is all I could ask for! I must go and see him before I die."

Jacob and his Family Go to Egypt

46 Jacob packed up all he had and went to Beersheba, where he offered sacrifices to the God of his father Isaac. 2 God spoke to him in a vision at night and called, "Jacob, Jacob!"

"Yes, here I am," he answered.

3 "I am God, the God of your father," he said. "Do not be afraid to go to Egypt; I will make your descendants a great nation there. 4 I will go with you to Egypt, and I will bring your descendants back to this land. Joseph will be with you when you die."

5 Jacob set out from Beersheba. His sons put him, their small children, and their wives in the wagons which the king of Egypt had sent. 6 They took their livestock and the possessions they had acquired in Canaan and went to Egypt. Jacob took all his descendants with him: 7 his sons, his grandsons, his daughters, and his granddaughters.

See also: **45.9–11:** Acts 7.14

See also: **46.6:** Acts 7.15

8 The members of Jacob's family who went to Egypt with him were his eldest son Reuben 9 and Reuben's sons: Hanoch, Pallu, Hezron, and Carmi. 10 Simeon and his sons: Jemuel, Jamin, Ohad, Jachin, Zohar, and Shaul, the son of a Canaanite woman. 11 Levi and his sons: Gershon, Kohath, and Merari. 12 Judah and his sons: Shelah, Perez, and Zerah. (Judah's other sons, Er and Onan, had died in Canaan.) Perez' sons were Hezron and Hamul. 13 Issachar and his sons: Tola, Puah, Jashub, and Shimron. 14 Zebulun and his sons: Sered, Elon, and Jahleel. 15 These are the sons that Leah had borne to Jacob in Mesopotamia, besides his daughter Dinah. In all, his descendants by Leah numbered 33.

16 Gad and his sons: Zephon, Haggi, Shuni, Ezbon, Eri, Arod, and Areli. 17 Asher and his sons: Imnah, Ishvah, Ishvi, Beriah, and their sister Serah. Beriah's sons were Heber and Malchiel. 18 These sixteen are the descendants of Jacob by Zilpah, the slave woman whom Laban gave to his daughter Leah.

19 Jacob's wife Rachel bore him two sons: Joseph and Benjamin. 20 In Egypt Joseph had two sons, Manasseh and Ephraim, by Asenath, the daughter of Potiphera, a priest in Heliopolis. 21 Benjamin's sons were Bela, Becher, Ashbel, Gera, Naaman, Ehi, Rosh, Muppim, Huppim, and Ard. 22 These fourteen are the descendants of Jacob by Rachel.

23 Dan and his son Hushim. 24 Naphtali and his sons: Jahzeel, Guni, Jezer, and Shillem. 25 These seven are the descendants of Jacob by Bilhah, the slave woman whom Laban gave to his daughter Rachel.

26 The total number of the direct descendants of Jacob who went to Egypt was 66, not including his sons' wives. 27 Two sons were born to Joseph in Egypt, bringing to 70 the total number of Jacob's family who went there.

Jacob and his Family in Egypt

28 Jacob sent Judah ahead to ask Joseph to meet them in Goshen. When they arrived, 29 Joseph got in his chariot and went to Goshen to meet his father. When they met, Joseph threw his arms round his father's neck and cried for a long time. 30 Jacob said to Joseph, "I am ready to die, now that I have seen you and know that you are still alive."

31 Then Joseph said to his brothers and the rest of his father's family, "I must go and tell the king that my brothers and all my father's family, who were living in Canaan, have come to me. 32 I will tell him that you are shepherds and take care of livestock and that you have brought your flocks and herds and everything else that belongs to you. 33 When the king calls for you and asks what your occupation is, 34 be sure to tell him that you have taken care of livestock all your lives, just as your ancestors did. In this way he will let you live in the region of Goshen." Joseph said this because Egyptians will have nothing to do with shepherds.

47 So Joseph took five of his brothers and went to the king. He said, "My father and my brothers have come from Canaan with their flocks, their herds, and all that they own. They are now in the region of Goshen." 2 He then presented his brothers to the king. 3 The king asked them, "What is your occupation?"

"We are shepherds, sir, just as our ancestors were," they answered. 4 "We have come to live in this country, because in the land of Canaan the famine is so severe that there is no pasture for our flocks. Please give us permission to live in the region of Goshen." 5 The king said to Joseph, "Now that your father and your brothers have arrived, 6 the land of Egypt is theirs. Let them settle in the region of Goshen, the best part of the land. And if there are any capable men among them, put them in charge of my own livestock."

7 Then Joseph brought his father Jacob and presented him to the king. Jacob gave the king his blessing, 8 and the king asked him, "How old are you?"

9 Jacob answered, "My life of wandering has lasted a hundred and thirty years. Those years have been few and difficult, unlike the long years of my ancestors in their wanderings." 10 Jacob gave the king a farewell blessing and left. 11 Then Joseph settled his father and his brothers in Egypt, giving them property in the best of the land near the city of Rameses, as the king had commanded. 12 Joseph provided food for his father, his brothers, and all the rest of his father's family, including the very youngest.

See also: 46.20: Gen 41.50–52   **46.27:** Acts 7.14

The Famine

13 The famine was so severe that there was no food anywhere, and the people of Egypt and Canaan became weak with hunger. 14 As they bought corn, Joseph collected all the money and took it to the palace. 15 When all the money in Egypt and Canaan was spent, the Egyptians came to Joseph and said, "Give us food! Don't let us die. Do something! Our money is all gone."

16 Joseph answered, "Bring your livestock; I will give you food in exchange for it if your money is all gone." 17 So they brought their livestock to Joseph, and he gave them food in exchange for their horses, sheep, goats, cattle, and donkeys. That year he supplied them with food in exchange for all their livestock.

18 The following year they came to him and said, "We will not hide the fact from you, sir, that our money is all gone and our livestock belongs to you. There is nothing left to give you except our bodies and our lands. 19 Don't let us die. Do something! Don't let our fields be deserted. Buy us and our land in exchange for food. We will be the king's slaves, and he will own our land. Give us corn to keep us alive and seed to sow in our fields."

20 Joseph bought all the land in Egypt for the king. Every Egyptian was forced to sell his land, because the famine was so severe; and all the land became the king's property. 21 Joseph made slaves of the people from one end of Egypt to the other. 22 The only land he did not buy was the land that belonged to the priests. They did not have to sell their lands, because the king gave them an allowance to live on. 23 Joseph said to the people, "You see, I have now bought you and your lands for the king. Here is seed for you to sow in your fields. 24 At the time of harvest you must give a fifth to the king. You can use the rest for seed and for food for yourselves and your families."

25 They answered, "You have saved our lives; you have been good to us, sir, and we will be the king's slaves." 26 So Joseph made it a law for the land of Egypt that a fifth of the harvest should belong to the king. This law still remains in force today. Only the lands of the priests did not become the king's property.

Jacob's Last Request

27 The Israelites lived in Egypt in the region of Goshen, where they became rich and had many children. 28 Jacob lived in Egypt for seventeen years, until he was 147 years old. 29 When the time drew near for him to die, he called for his son Joseph and said to him, "Place your hand between my thighs* and make a solemn vow that you will not bury me in Egypt. 30 I want to be buried where my fathers are; carry me out of Egypt and bury me where they are buried."

Joseph answered, "I will do as you say."

31 Jacob said, "Make a vow that you will." Joseph made the vow, and Jacob gave thanks there on his bed.

Jacob Blesses Ephraim and Manasseh

48 Some time later Joseph was told that his father was ill. So he took his two sons, Manasseh and Ephraim, and went to see Jacob. 2 When Jacob was told that his son Joseph had come to see him, he gathered his strength and sat up in bed. 3 Jacob said to Joseph, "Almighty God appeared to me at Luz in the land of Canaan and blessed me. 4 He said to me, 'I will give you many children, so that your descendants will become many nations; I will give this land to your descendants as their possession for ever.' "

5 Jacob continued, "Joseph, your two sons, who were born to you in Egypt before I came here, belong to me; Ephraim and Manasseh are just as much my sons as Reuben and Simeon. 6 If you have any more sons, they will not be considered mine; the inheritance they get will come through Ephraim and Manasseh. 7 I am doing this because of your mother Rachel. To my great sorrow she died in the land of Canaan, not far from Ephrath, as I was returning from Mesopotamia. I buried her there beside the road to Ephrath." (Ephrath is now known as Bethlehem.)

8 When Jacob saw Joseph's sons, he asked, "Who are these boys?"

9 *Joseph answered, "These are my sons,* whom God has given me here in Egypt."

47.29 PLACE... THIGHS: *See 24.2.*
See also: 47.29–30: Gen 49.29–32, 50.6
48.3–4: Gen 28.13–14   **48.7:** Gen 35.16–19

Jacob said, "Bring them to me so that I may bless them." [10] Jacob's eyesight was failing because of his age, and he could not see very well. Joseph brought the boys to him, and he hugged them and kissed them. [11] Jacob said to Joseph, "I never expected to see you again, and now God has even let me see your children." [12] Then Joseph took them from Jacob's lap and bowed down before him with his face to the ground.

May God ... bless these boys! (48.15)

[13] Joseph put Ephraim at Jacob's left and Manasseh at his right. [14] But Jacob crossed his hands, and put his right hand on the head of Ephraim, even though he was the younger, and his left hand on the head of Manasseh, who was the elder. [15] Then he blessed Joseph: *

"May the God whom my fathers
    Abraham and Isaac served bless
    these boys!
May God, who has led me to this
    very day, bless them!
[16] May the angel, who has rescued me
    from all harm, bless them!
May my name and the name of my
    fathers Abraham and Isaac live
    on through these boys!
May they have many children, many
    descendants!"

[17] Joseph was upset when he saw that his father had put his right hand on Ephraim's head; so he took his father's hand to move it from Ephraim's head to the head of Manasseh. [18] He said to his father, "Not that way, father. This is the elder boy; put your right hand on his head."

[19] His father refused, saying, "I know, my son, I know. Manasseh's descendants will also become a great people. But his younger brother will be greater than he, and his descendants will become great nations."

[20] So he blessed them that day, saying, "The Israelites will use your names when they pronounce blessings. They will say, 'May God make you like Ephraim and Manasseh.' " In this way Jacob put Ephraim before Manasseh.

[21] Then Jacob said to Joseph, "As you see, I am about to die, but God will be with you and will take you back to the land of your ancestors. [22] It is to you and not to your brothers that I am giving Shechem, that fertile region which I took from the Amorites with my sword and my bow."

The Last Words of Jacob

49 Jacob called for his sons and said, "Gather round, and I will tell you what will happen to you in the future:

[2] "Come together and listen, sons of
        Jacob.
    Listen to your father Israel.

[3] "Reuben, my firstborn, you are my
        strength
    And the first child of my manhood,
    The proudest and strongest of all
        my sons.
[4] You are like a raging flood,
    But you will not be the most
        important,
    For you slept with my concubine
    And dishonoured your father's bed.

[5] "Simeon and Levi are brothers.
    They use their weapons to commit
        violence.
[6] I will not join in their secret talks,
    Nor will I take part in their meetings,
    For they killed men in anger
    And they crippled bulls for sport.
[7] A curse be on their anger, because
        it is so fierce,

48.15 JOSEPH: *In blessing Ephraim and Manasseh, Jacob was in fact blessing Joseph.*

See also: 48.20: Heb 11.21

And on their fury, because it is so
    cruel.
I will scatter them throughout the
    land of Israel.
I will disperse them among its people.

8 "Judah, your brothers will praise you.
You hold your enemies by the neck.
Your brothers will bow down
    before you.
9 Judah is like a lion,
Killing his victim and returning to
    his den,
Stretching out and lying down.
No one dares disturb him.
10 Judah will hold the royal sceptre,
And his descendants will always rule.
Nations will bring him tribute*
And bow in obedience before him.
11 He ties his young donkey to a
    grapevine,
To the very best of the vines.
He washes his clothes in blood-red
    wine.
12 His eyes are bloodshot from
    drinking wine,
His teeth white from drinking milk.*

13 "Zebulun will live beside the sea.
His shore will be a haven for ships.
His territory will reach as far as Sidon.

14 "Issachar is no better than a donkey
That lies stretched out between its
    saddlebags.
15 But he sees that the resting place is
    good
And that the land is delightful.
So he bends his back to carry the load
And is forced to work as a slave.

16 "Dan will be a ruler for his people.
They will be like the other tribes of
    Israel.
17 Dan will be a snake at the side of
    the road,
A poisonous snake beside the path,
That strikes at the horse's heel,
So that the rider is thrown off
    backwards.

18 "I wait for your deliverance, LORD.

19 "Gad will be attacked by a band of
    robbers,
But he will turn and pursue them.

20 "Asher's land will produce rich food.
He will provide food fit for a king.

21 "Naphtali is a deer that runs free,
Who bears lovely fawns.*

22 "Joseph is like a wild donkey by a
    spring,
A wild colt on a hillside.*
23 His enemies attack him fiercely
And pursue him with their bows
    and arrows.
24 But his bow remains steady,
And his arms are made strong*
By the power of the Mighty God of
    Jacob,
By the Shepherd, the Protector of
    Israel.
25 It is your father's God who helps you,
The Almighty God who blesses you
With blessings of rain from above
And of deep waters from beneath
    the ground,
Blessings of many cattle and children,
26 Blessings of corn and flowers,*
Blessings of ancient mountains,*
Delightful things from everlasting
    hills.
May these blessings rest on the
    head of Joseph,
On the brow of the one set apart
    from his brothers.

27 "Benjamin is like a vicious wolf.
Morning and evening he kills and
    devours."

28 These are the twelve tribes of Israel,
and this is what their father said as he spoke
a suitable word of farewell to each son.

49.10 *Probable text* Nations… tribute; *Hebrew unclear.*
49.12 His eyes… milk; *or* His eyes are darker than
wine, his teeth are whiter than milk.
See also: 49.9: Num 24.9; Rev 5.5

49.21 Naphtali… fawns; *or* Naphtali is a spreading
tree that puts out lovely branches.
49.22 Joseph…, hillside; or Joseph is like a tree by a
spring, a fruitful tree that spreads over a wall.
49.24 But… strong; *or* But their bows were broken
and splintered, the muscles of their arms torn apart.
49.26 *Probable text* corn and flowers; *Hebrew* your
fathers are mightier than.
49.26 *One ancient translation* ancient mountains;
Hebrew my ancestors to.

The Death and Burial of Jacob

29 Then Jacob commanded his sons, "Now that I am going to join my people in death, bury me with my fathers in the cave that is in the field of Ephron the Hittite, 30 at Machpelah, east of Mamre, in the land of Canaan. Abraham bought this cave and field from Ephron for a burial ground. 31 That is where they buried Abraham and his wife Sarah; that is where they buried Isaac and his wife Rebecca; and that is where I buried Leah. 32 The field and the cave in it were bought from the Hittites. Bury me there." 33 When Jacob had finished giving instructions to his sons, he lay down again and died.

50 Joseph threw himself on his father, crying and kissing his face. 2 Then Joseph gave orders to embalm his father's body. 3 It took 40 days, the normal time for embalming. The Egyptians mourned for him 70 days.

4 When the time of mourning was over, Joseph said to the king's officials, "Please take this message to the king: 5 'When my father was about to die, he made me promise him that I would bury him in the tomb which he had prepared in the land of Canaan. So please let me go and bury my father, and then I will come back.' "

6 The king answered, "Go and bury your father, as you promised you would."

7 So Joseph went to bury his father. All the king's officials, the senior men of his court, and all the leading men of Egypt went with Joseph. 8 His family, his brothers, and the rest of his father's family all went with him. Only their small children and their sheep, goats, and cattle stayed in the region of Goshen. 9 Men in chariots and men on horseback also went with him; it was a huge group.

10 When they came to the threshing place at Atad east of the Jordan, they mourned loudly for a long time, and Joseph performed mourning ceremonies for seven days. 11 When the citizens of Canaan saw those people mourning at Atad, they said, "What a solemn ceremony of mourning the Egyptians are holding!" That is why the place was named Abel Mizraim.*

12 So Jacob's sons did as he had commanded them; 13 they carried his body to Canaan and buried it in the cave at Machpelah, east of Mamre, in the field which Abraham had bought from Ephron the Hittite for a burial ground. 14 After Joseph had buried his father, he returned to Egypt with his brothers and all who had gone with him for the funeral.

Joseph Reassures his Brothers

15 After the death of their father, Joseph's brothers said, "What if Joseph still hates us and plans to pay us back for all the harm we did to him?" 16 So they sent a message to Joseph: "Before our father died, 17 he told us to ask you, 'Please forgive the crime your brothers committed when they wronged you.' Now please forgive the wrong that we, the servants of your father's God, have done." Joseph cried when he received this message.

18 Then his brothers themselves came and bowed down before him. "Here we are before you as your slaves," they said.

19 But Joseph said to them, "Don't be afraid; I can't put myself in the place of God. 20 You plotted evil against me, but God turned it into good, in order to preserve the lives of many people who are alive today because of what happened. 21 You have nothing to fear. I will take care of you and your children." So he reassured them with kind words that touched their hearts.

The Death of Joseph

22 Joseph continued to live in Egypt with his father's family; he was 110 years old when he died. 23 He lived to see Ephraim's children and grandchildren. He also lived to receive the children of Machir son of Manasseh into the family. 24 He said to his brothers, "I am about to die, but God will certainly take care of you and lead you out of this land to the land he solemnly promised to Abraham, Isaac, and Jacob." 25 Then Joseph asked his people to make a vow. "Promise me," he said, "that when God leads you to that land, you will take my body with you." 26 So Joseph died in Egypt at the age of 110. They embalmed his body and put it in a coffin.

50.11 ABEL MIZRAIM: *This name sounds like the Hebrew for "mourning of the Egyptians".*

See also: 49.30: Gen 23.3–20 **49.31:** Gen 25.9–10, 35.29 **49.33:** Acts 7.15 **50.5:** Gen 47.29–31

See also: 50.13: Acts 7.16 **50.25:** Ex 13.19; Josh 24.32; Heb 11.22

EXODUS

INTRODUCTION

The name *Exodus* means "departure", and refers to the most important event in Israel's history, which is described in this book — the departure of the people of Israel from Egypt, where they had been slaves. The book has four main parts: (1) The freeing of the Hebrews from slavery; (2) Their journey to Mount Sinai; (3) God's covenant with his people at Sinai, which gave them moral, civil, and religious laws to live by; (4) The building and furnishing of a place of worship for Israel, and laws regarding the priests and the worship of God.

Above all, this book describes what God did, as he liberated his enslaved people and formed them into a nation with hope for the future.

The central human figure in the book is Moses, the man whom God chose to lead his people from Egypt. The most widely known part of the book is the list of the Ten Commandments (20.1–17).

Outline of Contents

The Israelites are Treated Cruelly in Egypt

1 The sons of Jacob who went to Egypt with him, each with his family, were 2 Reuben, Simeon, Levi, Judah, 3 Issachar, Zebulun, Benjamin, 4 Dan, Naphtali, Gad, and Asher. 5 The total number of these people directly descended from Jacob was 70.* His son Joseph was already in Egypt. 6 In the course of time Joseph, his brothers, and all the rest of that generation died, 7 but their descendants, the Israelites, had many children and became so numerous and strong that Egypt was filled with them.

8 Then, a new king, who knew nothing about Joseph, came to power in Egypt. 9 He said to his people, "These Israelites *are so numerous and strong that they are* a threat to us. 10 In case of war they might join our enemies in order to fight

against us, and might escape from* the country. We must find some way to keep them from becoming even more numerous." 11 So the Egyptians put slave-drivers over them to crush their spirits with hard labour. The Israelites built the cities of Pithom and Rameses to serve as supply centres for the king. 12 But the more the Egyptians oppressed the Israelites, the more they increased in number and the further they spread through the land. The Egyptians came to fear the Israelites 13–14 and made their lives miserable by forcing them into cruel slavery. They made them work on their building projects and in their fields, and they had no mercy on them.

15 Then the king of Egypt spoke to Shiphrah and Puah, the two midwives who *helped the Hebrew women.* 16 "When you help the Hebrew women give birth," he said to them, "kill the baby if it is a boy; but if it is a girl, let it live." 17 But the midwives

---

1.5 *One ancient translation* 75 *(see Acts 7.14).*
See also: 1.1–4: Gen 46.8–27   **1.7:** Acts 7.17
1.8: Acts 7.18   **1.10:** Acts 7.19

1.10 *escape from; or* take control of.

feared God and so did not obey the king; instead, they let the boys live. 18 So the king sent for the midwives and asked them, "Why are you doing this? Why are you letting the boys live?"

19 They answered, "The Hebrew women are not like Egyptian women; they give birth easily, and their babies are born before either of us gets there." 20–21 Because the midwives feared God, he was good to them and gave them families of their own. And the Israelites continued to increase and become strong. 22 Finally the king issued a command to all his people: "Take every newborn Hebrew boy and throw him into the Nile, but let all the girls live."

The Birth of Moses

2 During this time a man from the tribe of Levi married a woman of his own tribe, 2 and she bore him a son. When she saw what a fine baby he was, she hid him for three months. 3 But when she could not hide him any longer, she took a basket made of reeds and covered it with tar to make it watertight. She put the baby in it and then placed it in the tall grass at the edge of the river. 4 The baby's sister stood some distance away to see what would happen to him.

The king's daughter ... noticed the basket (2.5)

5 The king's daughter came down to the river to bathe, while her servants walked along the bank. Suddenly she noticed the basket in the tall grass and sent a slave woman to get it. 6 The princess opened it and saw a baby boy. He was crying, and she felt sorry for him. "This is one of the Hebrew babies," she said.

7 Then his sister asked her, "Shall I go and call a Hebrew woman to act as a wet nurse?"

8 "Please do," she answered. So the girl went and brought the baby's own mother. 9 The princess told the woman, "Take this baby and nurse him for me, and I will pay you." So she took the baby and nursed him. 10 Later, when the child was old enough, she took him to the king's daughter, who adopted him as her own son. She said to herself, "I pulled him out of the water, and so I name him Moses."*

Moses Escapes to Midian

11 When Moses had grown up, he went out to visit his people, the Hebrews, and he saw how they were forced to do hard labour. He even saw an Egyptian kill a Hebrew, one of Moses' own people. 12 Moses looked all round, and when he saw that no one was watching, he killed the Egyptian and hid his body in the sand. 13 The next day he went back and saw two Hebrew men fighting. He said to the one who was in the wrong, "Why are you beating up a fellow-Hebrew?"

14 The man answered, "Who made you our ruler and judge? Are you going to kill me just as you killed that Egyptian?" Then Moses was afraid and said to himself, "People have found out what I have done." 15–16 When the king heard about what had happened, he tried to have Moses killed, but Moses fled and went to live in the land of Midian.

One day, when Moses was sitting by a well, seven daughters of Jethro, the priest of Midian, came to draw water and fill the troughs for their father's sheep and goats. 17 But some shepherds drove Jethro's daughters away. Then Moses went to their rescue and watered their animals for them. 18 When they returned to their father, he asked, "Why have you come back so early today?"

2.10 MOSES: *This name sounds like the Hebrew for "pull out".*

See also: **2.10**: Acts 7.21   **2.11**: Heb 11.24
2.11–14: Acts 7.23–28   **2.15**: Acts 7.29; Heb 11.27

See also: **1.22**: Acts 7.19   **2.2**: Acts 7.20; Heb 11.23

19 "An Egyptian rescued us from the shepherds," they answered, "and he even drew water for us and watered our animals."

20 "Where is he?" he asked his daughters. "Why did you leave the man out there? Go and invite him to eat with us."

21 So Moses agreed to live there, and Jethro gave him his daughter Zipporah in marriage, 22 who bore him a son. Moses said to himself, "I am a foreigner in this land, and so I name him Gershom."*

23 Years later the king of Egypt died, but the Israelites were still groaning under their slavery and cried out for help. Their cry went up to God, 24 who heard their groaning and remembered his covenant with Abraham, Isaac, and Jacob. 25 He saw the slavery of the Israelites and was concerned for them.*

God Calls Moses

3 One day while Moses was taking care of the sheep and goats of his father-in-law Jethro, the priest of Midian, he led the flock across the desert and came to Sinai, the holy mountain. 2 There the angel of the LORD appeared to him as a flame coming from the middle of a bush. Moses saw that the bush was on fire but that it was not burning up. 3 "This is strange," he thought. "Why isn't the bush burning up? I will go closer and see."

4 When the LORD saw that Moses was coming closer, he called to him from the middle of the bush and said, "Moses! Moses!"

He answered, "Yes, here I am."

5 God said, "Do not come any closer. Take off your sandals, because you are standing on holy ground. 6 I am the God of your ancestors, the God of Abraham, Isaac, and Jacob." So Moses covered his face, because he was afraid to look at God.

7 Then the LORD said, "I have seen how cruelly my people are being treated in Egypt; I have heard them cry out to be rescued from their slave-drivers. I know all about their sufferings, 8 and so I have

come down to rescue them from the Egyptians and to bring them out of Egypt to a spacious land, one which is rich and fertile and in which the Canaanites, the Hittites, the Amorites, the Perizzites, the Hivites, and the Jebusites now live. 9 I have indeed heard the cry of my people, and I see how the Egyptians are oppressing them. 10 Now I am sending you to the king of Egypt so that you can lead my people out of his country."

I AM … This is my name for ever   (3.14–15)

11 But Moses said to God, "I am nobody. How can I go to the king and bring the Israelites out of Egypt?"

12 God answered, "I will be with you, and when you bring the people out of Egypt, you will worship me on this mountain. That will be the proof that I have sent you."

13 But Moses replied, "When I go to the Israelites and say to them, 'The God of your ancestors sent me to you,' they will ask me, 'What is his name?' So what can I tell them?"

14 God said, "I am who I am. This is what you must say to them: 'The one who is called I AM* has sent me to you.' 15 Tell the

---

2.22 GERSHOM: *This name sounds like the Hebrew for "foreigner".*
2.25 was concerned for them; *one ancient translation* revealed himself to them.
See also: **2.24:** Gen 15.13–14   **3.2–10:** Acts 7.30–34

3.14 I am who I am… I AM; *or* I will be who I will be… I WILL BE. *"I am" sounds like the Hebrew name Yahweh, traditionally transliterated as Jehovah. This name is represented in this translation by "the LORD" in capital letters, following a usage which is widespread in English versions.*
See also: **3.13:** Ex 6.2–3   **3.14:** Rev 1.4,8

Israelites that I, the LORD, the God of their ancestors, the God of Abraham, Isaac, and Jacob, have sent you to them. This is my name for ever; this is what all future generations are to call me. 16 Go and gather the leaders of Israel together and tell them that I, the LORD, the God of their ancestors, the God of Abraham, Isaac, and Jacob, appeared to you. Tell them that I have come to them and have seen what the Egyptians are doing to them. 17 I have decided that I will bring them out of Egypt, where they are being treated cruelly, and will take them to a rich and fertile land — the land of the Canaanites, the Hittites, the Amorites, the Perizzites, the Hivites, and the Jebusites.

18 "My people will listen to what you say to them. Then you must go with the leaders of Israel to the king of Egypt and say to him, 'The LORD, the God of the Hebrews, has revealed himself to us. Now allow us to travel for three days into the desert to offer sacrifices to the LORD, our God.' 19 I know that the king of Egypt will not let you go unless he is forced to do so. 20 But I will use my power and will punish Egypt by doing terrifying things there. After that he will let you go.

21 "I will make the Egyptians respect you so that when my people leave, they will not go empty-handed. 22 Every Israelite woman will go to her Egyptian neighbours and to any Egyptian woman living in her house and will ask for clothing and for gold and silver jewellery. The Israelites will put these things on their sons and daughters and carry away the wealth of the Egyptians."

God Gives Moses Miraculous Power

4 Then Moses answered the LORD, "But suppose the Israelites do not believe me and will not listen to what I say. What shall I do if they say that you did not appear to me?"

2 So the LORD asked him, "What are you holding?"

"A stick," he answered.

3 The LORD said, "Throw it on the ground." When Moses threw it down, it turned into a snake, and he ran away from it. 4 Then the

To prove … that the LORD … has appeared to you (4.5)

LORD said to Moses, "Bend down and pick it up by the tail." So Moses bent down and caught it, and it became a stick again. 5 The LORD said, "Do this to prove to the Israelites that the LORD, the God of their ancestors, the God of Abraham, Isaac, and Jacob, has appeared to you."

6 The LORD spoke to Moses again, "Put your hand inside your robe." Moses obeyed; and when he took his hand out, it was diseased, covered with white spots, like snow. 7 Then the LORD said, "Put your hand inside your robe again." He did so, and when he took it out this time, it was healthy, just like the rest of his body. 8 The LORD said, "If they will not believe you or be convinced by the first miracle, then this one will convince them. 9 If in spite of these two miracles they still will not believe you, and if they refuse to listen to what you say, take some water from the Nile and pour it on the ground. The water will turn into blood."

10 But Moses said, "No, LORD, don't send me. I have never been a good speaker, and I haven't become one since you began to speak to me. I am a poor speaker, slow and hesitant."

11 The LORD said to him, "Who gives man his mouth? Who makes him deaf or dumb? Who gives him sight or makes him blind? It is I, the LORD. 12 Now, go! I will help you to speak, and I will tell you what to say."

13 But Moses answered, "No, Lord, please send someone else."

14 At this the LORD became angry with Moses and said, "What about your brother Aaron, the Levite? I know that he can speak well. In fact, he is now coming to meet you and will be glad to see you. 15 You can speak to him and tell him what to say. I will help both of you to speak, and I will tell you both what to do. 16 He will be your spokesman and speak to the people for you. Then you will be like God, telling him what to say. 17 Take this stick with you; for with it you will perform miracles."

See also: 3.21–22: Ex 12.35–36

Moses Returns to Egypt

18 Then Moses went back to Jethro, his father-in-law, and said to him, "Please let me go back to my relatives in Egypt to see if they are still alive." Jethro agreed and said goodbye to him.

19 While Moses was still in Midian, the LORD said to him, "Go back to Egypt, for all those who wanted to kill you are dead." 20 So Moses took his wife and his sons, put them on a donkey, and set out with them for Egypt, carrying the stick that God had told him to take.

21 Again the LORD said to Moses, "Now that you are going back to Egypt, be sure to perform before the king all the miracles which I have given you the power to do. But I will make the king stubborn, and he will not let the people go. 22 Then you must tell him that I, the LORD, say, 'Israel is my firstborn son. 23 I told you to let my son go, so that he might worship me, but you refused. Now I am going to kill your firstborn son.'"

24 At a camping place on the way to Egypt, the LORD met Moses and tried to kill him. 25-26 Then Zipporah, his wife, took a sharp stone, cut off the foreskin of her son, and touched Moses' feet* with it. Because of the rite of circumcision she said to Moses, "You are a husband of blood to me." And so the LORD spared Moses' life.

27 Meanwhile the LORD had said to Aaron, "Go into the desert to meet Moses." So he went to meet him at the holy mountain; and when he met him, he kissed him. 28 Then Moses told Aaron everything that the LORD had said when he told him to return to Egypt; he also told him about the miracles which the LORD had ordered him to perform. 29 So Moses and Aaron went to Egypt and gathered all the Israelite leaders together. 30 Aaron told them everything that the LORD had said to Moses, and then Moses performed all the miracles in front of the people. 31 They believed, and when they heard that the LORD had come to them and had seen how they were being treated cruelly, they bowed down and worshipped.

4.25-26 FEET: This reference to "feet" is thought by some to be a euphemism for the genitals.
See also: 4.23: Ex 12.29

Moses and Aaron before the King of Egypt

5 Then Moses and Aaron went to the king of Egypt and said, "The LORD, the God of Israel, says, 'Let my people go, so that they can hold a festival in the desert to honour me.'"

2 "Who is the LORD?" the king demanded. "Why should I listen to him and let Israel go? I do not know the LORD; and I will not let Israel go."

3 Moses and Aaron replied, "The God of the Hebrews has revealed himself to us. Allow us to travel for three days into the desert to offer sacrifices to the LORD our God. If we don't do so, he will kill us with disease or by war."

4 The king said to Moses and Aaron, "What do you mean by making the people neglect their work? Get those slaves back to work! 5 You people have become more numerous than the Egyptians. And now you want to stop working!"

6 That same day the king commanded the Egyptian slave-drivers and the Israelite foremen: 7 "Stop giving the people straw for making bricks. Make them go and find it for themselves. 8 But still require them to make the same number of bricks as before, not one brick less. They haven't enough work to do, and that is why they keep asking me to let them go and offer sacrifices to their God! 9 Make these people work harder and keep them busy, so that they won't have time to listen to a pack of lies."

10 The slave-drivers and the Israelite foremen went out and said to the Israelites, "The king has said that he will not supply you with any more straw. 11 He says that you must go and get it for yourselves wherever you can find it, but you must still make the same number of bricks." 12 So the people went all over Egypt looking for straw. 13 The slave-drivers kept trying to force them to make the same number of bricks every day as they had made when they were given straw. 14 The Egyptian slave-drivers beat the Israelite foremen, *whom they had put in charge of the work.* They demanded, "Why aren't you people making the same number of bricks as you made before?"

15 Then the foremen went to the king and complained, "Why do you do this to us,

Your Majesty? 16 We are given no straw, but we are still ordered to make bricks! And now we are being beaten. It is your people that are at fault."

17 The king answered, "You are lazy and don't want to work, and that is why you ask me to let you go and offer sacrifices to the Lord. 18 Now get back to work! You will not be given any straw, but you must still make the same number of bricks."

19 The foremen realized that they were in trouble when they were told that they had to make the same number of bricks every day as they had made before.

20 As they were leaving, they met Moses and Aaron, who were waiting for them. 21 They said to Moses and Aaron, "The Lord has seen what you have done and will punish you for making the king and his officers hate us. You have given them an excuse to kill us."

Moses Complains to the Lord

22 Then Moses turned to the Lord again and said, "Lord, why do you ill-treat your people? Why did you send me here? 23 Ever since I went to the king to speak for you, he has treated them cruelly. And you have done nothing to help them!"

6 Then the Lord said to Moses, "Now you are going to see what I will do to the king. I will force him to let my people go. In fact, I will force him to drive them out of his land."

God Calls Moses

2 God spoke to Moses and said, "I am the Lord. 3 I appeared to Abraham, to Isaac, and to Jacob as Almighty God, but I did not make myself known to them by my holy name, the Lord.* 4 I also made my covenant with them, promising to give them the land of Canaan, the land in which they had lived as foreigners. 5 Now I have heard the groaning of the Israelites, whom the Egyptians have enslaved, and I have remembered my covenant. 6 So tell the Israelites that I say to them, 'I am the Lord; I will rescue you and set you free from your slavery to the Egyptians. I will raise my mighty arm to bring terrible punishment upon them, and I will save you. 7 I will make you my

own people, and I will be your God. You will know that I am the Lord your God when I set you free from slavery in Egypt. 8 I will bring you to the land that I solemnly promised to give to Abraham, Isaac, and Jacob; and I will give it to you as your own possession. I am the Lord.' " 9 Moses told this to the Israelites, but they would not listen to him, because their spirit had been broken by their cruel slavery.

10 Then the Lord said to Moses, 11 "Go and tell the king of Egypt that he must let the Israelites leave his land."

12 But Moses replied, "Even the Israelites will not listen to me, so why should the king? I am such a poor speaker."

13 The Lord commanded Moses and Aaron: "Tell the Israelites and the king of Egypt that I have ordered you to lead the Israelites out of Egypt."

The Family Record of Moses and Aaron

14 Reuben, Jacob's firstborn, had four sons: Hanoch, Pallu, Hezron, and Carmi; they were the ancestors of the clans that bear their names. 15 Simeon had six sons: Jemuel, Jamin, Ohad, Jachin, Zohar, and Shaul, the son of a Canaanite woman; they were the ancestors of the clans that bear their names. 16 Levi had three sons: Gershon, Kohath, and Merari; they were the ancestors of the clans that bear their names. Levi lived 137 years. 17 Gershon had two sons: Libni and Shimei, and they had many descendants. 18 Kohath had four sons: Amram, Izhar, Hebron, and Uzziel. Kohath lived 133 years. 19 Merari had two sons: Mahli and Mushi. These are the clans of Levi with their descendants.

20 Amram married his father's sister Jochebed, who bore him Aaron and Moses. Amram lived 137 years. 21 Izhar had three sons: Korah, Nepheg, and Zichri. 22 Uzziel also had three sons: Mishael, Elzaphan, and Sithri.

23 Aaron married Elisheba, the daughter of Amminadab and sister of Nahshon; she bore him Nadab, Abihu, Eleazar, and Ithamar. 24 Korah had three sons: Assir, Elkanah, and Abiasaph; they were the ancestors of the divisions of the clan of Korah. 25 Eleazar,

6.3 THE LORD: *See 3.14.*
See also: 6.2–3: Gen 17.1, 28.3, 35.11; Ex 3.13–15

See also: 6.16–19: Num 3.17–20, 26.57–58; 1 Chr 6.16–19

Aaron's son, married one of Putiel's daughters, who bore him Phinehas. These were the heads of the families and the clans of the tribe of Levi.

26 Aaron and Moses were the ones to whom the LORD said, "Lead the tribes of Israel out of Egypt." 27 They were the men who told the king of Egypt to free the Israelites.

The LORD's Command to Moses and Aaron

28 When the LORD spoke to Moses in the land of Egypt, 29 he said, "I am the LORD. Tell the king of Egypt everything I tell you."

30 But Moses answered, "You know that I am such a poor speaker; why should the king listen to me?"

7 The LORD said, "I am going to make you like God to the king, and your brother Aaron will speak to him as your prophet. 2 Tell Aaron everything I command you, and he will tell the king to let the Israelites leave his country. 3–4 But I will make the king stubborn, and he will not listen to you, no matter how many terrifying things I do in Egypt. Then I will bring severe punishment on Egypt and lead the tribes of my people out of the land. 5 The Egyptians will then know that I am the LORD, when I raise my hand against them and bring the Israelites out of their country." 6 Moses and Aaron did what the LORD commanded. 7 At the time when they spoke to the king, Moses was 80 years old, and Aaron was 83.

Aaron's Stick

8 The LORD said to Moses and Aaron, 9 "If the king demands that you prove yourselves by performing a miracle, tell Aaron to take his stick and throw it down in front of the king, and it will turn into a snake." 10 So Moses and Aaron went to the king and did as the LORD had commanded. Aaron threw his stick down in front of the king and his officers, and it turned into a snake. 11 Then the king called for his wise men and magicians, and by their magic they did the same thing. 12 They threw down their sticks, and the sticks turned into snakes. But Aaron's stick swallowed theirs. 13 The king, however,

remained stubborn and, just as the LORD had said, the king would not listen to Moses and Aaron.

Disasters Strike Egypt

Blood

14 Then the LORD said to Moses, "The king is very stubborn and refuses to let the people go. 15 So go and meet him in the morning when he goes down to the Nile. Take with you the stick that was turned into a snake, and wait for him on the bank of the river. 16 Then say to the king, 'The LORD, the God of the Hebrews, sent me to tell you to let his people go, so that they can worship him in the desert. But until now you have not listened. 17 Now, Your Majesty, the LORD says that you will find out who he is by what he is going to do. Look, I am going to strike the surface of the river with this stick, and the water will be turned into blood. 18 The fish will die, and the river will stink so much that the Egyptians will not be able to drink from it.' "

19 The LORD said to Moses, "Tell Aaron to take his stick and hold it out over all the rivers, canals, and pools in Egypt. The water will become blood, and all over the land there will be blood, even in the wooden tubs and stone jars."

20 Then Moses and Aaron did as the LORD commanded. In the presence of the king and his officers, Aaron raised his stick and struck the surface of the river, and all the water in it was turned into blood. 21 The fish in the river died, and it smelt so bad that the Egyptians could not drink from it. There was blood everywhere in Egypt. 22 Then the king's magicians did the same thing by means of their magic, and the king was as stubborn as ever. Just as the LORD had said, the king refused to listen to Moses and Aaron. 23 Instead, he turned and went back to his palace without paying any attention even to this. 24 All the Egyptians dug along the bank of the river for drinking water, *because they were not able to drink water* from the river.

25 Seven days passed after the LORD struck the river.

See also: 7.3: Acts 7.36

See also: 7.17: Rev 16.4

Frogs

8 Then the Lord said to Moses, "Go to the king and tell him that the Lord says, 'Let my people go, so that they can worship me. 2 If you refuse, I will punish your country by covering it with frogs. 3 The Nile will be so full of frogs that they will leave it and go into your palace, your bedroom, your bed, the houses of your officials and your people, and even into your ovens and baking pans. 4 They will jump up on you, your people, and all your officials.' "

They will jump up on you   (8.4)

5 The Lord said to Moses, "Tell Aaron to hold out his stick over the rivers, the canals, and the pools, and make frogs come up and cover the land of Egypt." 6 So Aaron held it out over all the water, and the frogs came out and covered the land. 7 But the magicians used magic, and they too made frogs come up on the land.

8 The king called for Moses and Aaron and said, "Pray to the Lord to take away these frogs, and I will let your people go, so that they can offer sacrifices to the Lord."

9 Moses replied, "I will be glad to pray for you. Just set the time when I am to pray for you, your officers, and your people. Then you will be rid of the frogs, and there will be none left except in the Nile."

10 The king answered, "Pray for me tomorrow."

Moses said, "I will do as you ask, and then you will know that there is no other god like the Lord, our God. 11 You, your officials, and your people will be rid of the frogs, and there will be none left except in the Nile." 12 Then Moses and Aaron left

the king, and Moses prayed to the Lord to take away the frogs which he had brought on the king. 13 The Lord did as Moses asked, and the frogs in the houses, the courtyards, and the fields died. 14 The Egyptians piled them up in great heaps, until the land stank with them. 15 When the king saw that the frogs were dead, he became stubborn again and, just as the Lord had said, the king would not listen to Moses and Aaron.

Gnats

16 The Lord said to Moses, "Tell Aaron to strike the ground with his stick, and all over the land of Egypt the dust will change into gnats." 17 So Aaron struck the ground with his stick, and all the dust in Egypt was turned into gnats, which covered the people and the animals. 18 The magicians tried to use their magic to make gnats appear, but they failed. There were gnats everywhere, 19 and the magicians said to the king, "God has done this!" But the king was stubborn and, just as the Lord had said, the king would not listen to Moses and Aaron.

Flies

20 The Lord said to Moses, "Early tomorrow morning go and meet the king as he goes to the river, and tell him that the Lord says, 'Let my people go, so that they can worship me. 21 I warn you that if you refuse, I will punish you by sending flies on you, your officials, and your people. The houses of the Egyptians will be full of flies, and the ground will be covered with them. 22 But I will spare the region of Goshen, where my people live, so that there will be no flies there. I will do this so that you will know that I, the Lord, am at work in this land. 23 I will make a distinction* between my people and your people. This miracle will take place tomorrow.' " 24 The Lord sent great swarms of flies into the king's palace and the houses of his officials. The whole land of Egypt was brought to ruin by the flies.

25 Then the king called for Moses and Aaron and said, "Go and offer sacrifices to your God here in this country."

8.23 *Some ancient translations* a distinction; *Hebrew* redemption.
See also: 8.19: Lk 11.20

26 "It would not be right to do that," Moses answered, "because the Egyptians would be offended by our sacrificing the animals that we offer to the LORD our God. If we use these animals and offend the Egyptians by sacrificing them where they can see us, they will stone us to death. 27 We must travel three days into the desert to offer sacrifices to the LORD our God, just as he commanded us."

28 The king said, "I will let you go to sacrifice to the LORD, your God, in the desert, if you do not go very far. Pray for me."

29 Moses answered, "As soon as I leave, I will pray to the LORD that tomorrow the flies will leave you, your officials, and your people. But you must not deceive us again and prevent the people from going to sacrifice to the LORD."

30 Moses left the king and prayed to the LORD, 31 and the LORD did as Moses asked. The flies left the king, his officials, and his people; not one fly remained. 32 But even this time the king became stubborn, and again he would not let the people go.

Death of the Animals

9 The LORD said to Moses, "Go to the king and tell him that the LORD, the God of the Hebrews, says, 'Let my people go, so that they may worship me. 2 If you again refuse to let them go, 3 I will punish you by sending a terrible disease on all your animals — your horses, donkeys, camels, cattle, sheep, and goats. 4 I will make a distinction between the animals of the Israelites and those of the Egyptians, and no animal that belongs to the Israelites will die. 5 I, the LORD, have set tomorrow as the time when I will do this.' "

6 The next day the LORD did as he had said, and all the animals of the Egyptians died, but not one of the animals of the Israelites died. 7 The king asked what had happened and was told that none of the animals of the Israelites had died. But he was stubborn and would not let the people go.

Boils

8 Then the LORD said to Moses and Aaron, "Take a few handfuls of ashes from a furnace; Moses shall throw them into the air in front of the king. 9 They will spread out like fine dust over all the land of Egypt, and everywhere they will produce boils that become open sores on the people and the animals." 10 So they got some ashes and stood before the king; Moses threw them into the air, and they produced boils that became open sores on the people and the animals. 11 The magicians were not able to appear before Moses, because they were covered with boils, like all the other Egyptians. 12 But the LORD made the king stubborn and, just as the LORD had said, the king would not listen to Moses and Aaron.

Hail

13 The LORD then said to Moses, "Early tomorrow morning meet with the king and tell him that the LORD, the God of the Hebrews, says, 'Let my people go, so that they may worship me. 14 This time I will punish not only your officials and your people, but I will punish you as well, so that you may know that there is no one like me in all the world. 15 If I had raised my hand to strike you and your people with disease, you would have been completely destroyed. 16 But to show you my power I have let you live so that my fame might spread over the whole world. 17 Yet you are still arrogant and refuse to let my people go. 18 This time tomorrow I will cause a heavy hailstorm, such as Egypt has never known in all its history. 19 Now give orders for your livestock and everything else you have in the open to be put under shelter. Hail will fall on the people and animals left outside unprotected, and they will all die.' " 20 Some of the king's officials were afraid because of what the LORD had said, and they brought their slaves and animals indoors for shelter. 21 Others, however, paid no attention to the LORD's warning and left their slaves and animals out in the open.

22 Then the LORD said to Moses, "Raise your hand towards the sky, and hail will fall over the whole land of Egypt — on the people, the animals, and all the plants in the fields." 23 So Moses raised his stick towards the sky, and the LORD sent thunder and hail, and lightning struck the ground. The LORD sent 24 a heavy hailstorm, with lightning flashing to and fro. It was the

See also: 9.10: Rev 16.2   **9.16:** Rom 9.17
9.24: Rev 8.7, 16.21

worst storm that Egypt had ever known in all its history. 25 All over Egypt the hail struck down everything in the open, including all the people and all the animals. It beat down all the plants in the fields and broke all the trees. 26 The region of Goshen, where the Israelites lived, was the only place where there was no hail.

27 The king sent for Moses and Aaron and said, "This time I have sinned; the LORD is in the right, and my people and I are in the wrong. 28 Pray to the LORD! We have had enough of this thunder and hail! I promise to let you go; you don't have to stay here any longer."

29 Moses said to him, "As soon as I go out of the city, I will lift up my hands in prayer to the LORD. The thunder will stop, and there will be no more hail, so that you may know that the earth belongs to the LORD. 30 But I know that you and your officials do not yet fear the LORD God."

31 The flax and the barley were ruined, because the barley was ripe, and the flax was budding. 32 But none of the wheat was ruined, because it ripens later.

33 Moses left the king, went out of the city, and lifted up his hands in prayer to the LORD. The thunder, the hail, and the rain all stopped. 34 When the king saw what had happened, he sinned again. He and his officials remained as stubborn as ever 35 and, just as the LORD had foretold through Moses, the king would not let the Israelites go.

Locusts

10 Then the LORD said to Moses, "Go and see the king. I have made him and his officials stubborn, in order that I may perform these miracles among them 2 and in order that you may be able to tell your children and grandchildren how I made fools of the Egyptians when I performed the miracles. All of you will know that I am the LORD."

3 So Moses and Aaron went to the king and said to him, "The LORD, the God of the Hebrews, says 'How much longer will you refuse to submit to me? Let my people go, so that they may worship me. 4 If you keep on refusing, then I will bring locusts into your country tomorrow. 5 There will be so many that they will completely cover the ground. They will eat everything that the hail did not destroy, even the trees that are left. 6 They will fill your palaces and the houses of all your officials and all your people. They will be worse than anything your ancestors ever saw.' " Then Moses turned and left.

7 The king's officials said to him, "How long is this man going to give us trouble? Let the Israelite men go, so that they can worship the LORD their God. Don't you realize that Egypt is ruined?"

8 So Moses and Aaron were brought back to the king, and he said to them, "You may go and worship the LORD your God. But exactly who will go?"

9 Moses answered, "We will all go, including our children and our old people. We will take our sons and daughters, our sheep and goats, and our cattle, because we must hold a festival to honour the LORD."

10 The king said, "I swear by the LORD that I will never let you take your women and children! It is clear that you are plotting to revolt. 11 No! Only the men may go and worship the LORD if that is what you want." With that, Moses and Aaron were driven out of the king's presence.

12 Then the LORD said to Moses, "Raise your hand over the land of Egypt to bring the locusts. They will come and eat everything that grows, everything that has survived the hail." 13 So Moses raised his stick, and the LORD caused a wind from the east to blow on the land all that day and all that night. By morning it had brought the locusts. 14 They came in swarms and settled over the whole country. It was the largest swarm of locusts that had ever been seen or that ever would be seen again. 15 They covered the ground until it was black with them; they ate everything that the hail had left, including all the fruit on the trees. Not a green thing was left on any tree or plant in all the land of Egypt.

16 Then the king hurriedly called Moses and Aaron and said, "I have sinned against the LORD your God and against you. 17 Now forgive my sin this once and pray to the LORD your God to take away this fatal punishment from me." 18 Moses left the king and prayed to the LORD. 19 And the LORD

See also: 10.14–15: Rev 9.2–3

changed the east wind into a very strong west wind, which picked up the locusts and blew them into the Gulf of Suez.* Not one locust was left in all Egypt. 20 But the LORD made the king stubborn, and he did not let the Israelites go.

Darkness

21 The LORD then said to Moses, "Raise your hand towards the sky, and a darkness thick enough to be felt will cover the land of Egypt." 22 Moses raised his hand towards the sky, and there was total darkness throughout Egypt for three days. 23 The Egyptians could not see each other, and no one left his house during that time. But the Israelites had light where they were living.

24 The king called Moses and said, "You may go and worship the LORD; even your women and children may go with you. But your sheep, goats, and cattle must stay here."

25 Moses answered, "Then you would have to provide us with animals for sacrifices and burnt offerings to offer to the LORD our God. 26 No, we will take our animals with us; not one will be left behind. We ourselves must select the animals with which to worship the LORD our God. And until we get there, we will not know what animals to sacrifice to him."

27 The LORD made the king stubborn, and he would not let them go. 28 He said to Moses, "Get out of my sight! Don't let me ever see you again! On the day I do, you will die!"

29 "You are right," Moses answered. "You will never see me again."

Moses Announces the Death of the Firstborn

11 Then the LORD said to Moses, "I will send only one more punishment on the king of Egypt and his people. After that he will let you leave. In fact, he will drive all of you out of here. 2 Now speak to the people of Israel and tell all of them to ask their neighbours for gold and silver jewellery." 3 The LORD made the Egyptians respect the Israelites. Indeed, the officials and all the people considered Moses to be a very great man.

4 Moses then said to the king, "The LORD says, 'At about midnight I will go through Egypt, 5 and every firstborn son in Egypt will die, from the king's son, who is heir to the throne, to the son of the slave woman who grinds corn. The firstborn of all the cattle will die also. 6 There will be loud crying all over Egypt, such as there has never been before or ever will be again. 7 But not even a dog will bark at the Israelites or their animals. Then you will know that I, the LORD, make a distinction between the Egyptians and the Israelites.' " 8 Moses concluded by saying, "All your officials will come to me and bow down before me, and they will beg me to take all my people and go away. After that, I will leave." Then in great anger Moses left the king.

9 The LORD had said to Moses, "The king will continue to refuse to listen to you, in order that I may do more of my miracles in Egypt." 10 Moses and Aaron performed all these miracles before the king, but the LORD made him stubborn, and he would not let the Israelites leave his country.

The Passover

12 The LORD spoke to Moses and Aaron in Egypt: 2 "This month is to be the first month of the year for you. 3 Give these instructions to the whole community of Israel: on the tenth day of this month each man must choose either a lamb or a young goat for his household. 4 If his family is too small to eat a whole animal, he and his next-door neighbour may share an animal, in proportion to the number of people and the amount that each person can eat. 5 You may choose either a sheep or a goat, but it must be a one-year-old male without any defects. 6 Then, on the evening of the fourteenth day of the month, the whole community of Israel will kill the animals. 7 The people are to take some of the blood and put it on the doorposts and above the doors of the houses in which the animals are to be eaten. 8 That night the meat is to be roasted, and eaten with bitter herbs and with bread made without yeast. 9 Do not eat any of it raw or boiled, but eat it roasted whole, including the head, the legs, and the internal organs. 10 You must not leave

10.19 GULF OF SUEZ: *See Red Sea in 13.18.*
See also: 10.22: Ps 105.28; Rev 16.10

See also: 12.1–13: Lev 23.5; Num 9.1–5, 28.16; Deut 16.1–2

any of it until morning; if any is left over, it must be burnt. 11 You are to eat it quickly, for you are to be dressed for travel, with your sandals on your feet and your stick in your hand. It is the Passover Festival to honour me, the LORD.

12 "On that night I will go through the land of Egypt, killing every firstborn male, both human and animal, and punishing all the gods of Egypt. I am the LORD. 13 The blood on the doorposts will be a sign to mark the houses in which you live. When I see the blood, I will pass over you and will not harm you when I punish the Egyptians. 14 You must celebrate this day as a religious festival to remind you of what I, the LORD, have done. Celebrate it for all time to come."

The Festival of Unleavened Bread

15 The LORD said, "For seven days you must not eat any bread made with yeast — eat only unleavened bread. On the first day you are to get rid of all the yeast in your houses, for if anyone during those seven days eats bread made with yeast, he shall no longer be considered one of my people. 16 On the first day and again on the seventh day you are to meet for worship. No work is to be done on those days, but you may prepare food. 17 Keep this festival, because it was on this day that I brought your tribes out of Egypt. For all time to come you must celebrate this day as a festival. 18 From the evening of the fourteenth day of the first month to the evening of the twenty-first day, you must not eat any bread made with yeast. 19–20 For seven days no yeast must be found in your houses, for if anyone, native-born or foreign, eats bread made with yeast, he shall no longer be considered one of my people."

The First Passover

21 Moses called for all the leaders of Israel and said to them, "Each of you is to choose a lamb or a young goat and kill it, so that your families can celebrate Passover. 22 Take a sprig of hyssop, dip it in the bowl containing* the animal's blood, and

wipe the blood on the doorposts and the beam above the door of your house. Not one of you is to leave the house until morning. 23 When the LORD goes through Egypt to kill the Egyptians, he will see the blood on the beams and the doorposts and will not let the Angel of Death enter your houses and kill you. 24 You and your children must obey these rules for ever. 25 When you enter the land that the LORD has promised to give you, you must perform this ritual. 26 When your children ask you, 'What does this ritual mean?' 27 you will answer, 'It is the sacrifice of Passover to honour the LORD, because he passed over the houses of the Israelites in Egypt. He killed the Egyptians, but spared us.'"

The Israelites knelt down and worshipped. 28 Then they went and did what the LORD had commanded Moses and Aaron.

The Death of the Firstborn

29 At midnight the LORD killed all the firstborn sons in Egypt, from the king's son, who was heir to the throne, to the son of the prisoner in the dungeon; all the firstborn of the animals were also killed. 30 That night, the king, his officials, and all the other Egyptians were awakened. There was loud crying throughout Egypt, because there was not one home in which there was not a dead son. 31 That same night the king sent for Moses and Aaron and said, "Get out, you and your Israelites! Leave my country; go and worship the LORD, as you asked. 32 Take your sheep, goats, and cattle, and leave. Also pray for a blessing on me."

33 The Egyptians urged the people to hurry and leave the country; they said, "We will all be dead if you don't leave." 34 So the people filled their baking pans with unleavened dough, wrapped them in clothing, and carried them on their shoulders. 35 The Israelites had done as Moses had said, and had asked the Egyptians for gold and silver jewellery and for clothing. 36 The LORD made the Egyptians respect the people and give them what they asked for. In this way the Israelites carried away the wealth of the Egyptians.

12.22 dip it in the bowl containing; *or* put it on the threshold covered with.

See also: 12.14–20: Ex 23.15, 34.18; Lev 23.6–8; Num 28.17–25; Deut 16.3–8

See also: 12.23: Heb 11.28 **12.29:** Ex 4.22–32 **12.35–36:** Ex 3.21–22

The people filled their baking pans with unleavened dough   (12.34)

The Israelites Leave Egypt

37 The Israelites set out on foot from Rameses for Sukkoth. There were about six hundred thousand men, not counting women and children. 38 A large number of other people and many sheep, goats, and cattle also went with them. 39 They baked unleavened bread from the dough that they had brought out of Egypt, for they had been driven out of Egypt so suddenly that they did not have time to get their food ready or to prepare leavened dough.

40 The Israelites had lived in Egypt for 430 years. 41 On the day the 430 years ended, all the tribes of the LORD's people left Egypt. 42 It was a night when the LORD kept watch to bring them out of Egypt; this same night is dedicated to the LORD for all time to come as a night when the Israelites must keep watch.

Regulations about Passover

43 The LORD said to Moses and Aaron, "These are the Passover regulations: no foreigner shall eat the Passover meal, 44 but any slave that you have bought may eat it if you circumcise him first. 45 No temporary resident or hired worker may eat it. 46 The whole meal must be eaten in the house in which it was prepared; it must not be taken outside. And do not break any of the animal's bones. 47 The whole community of Israel must celebrate this festival, 48 but no *uncircumcised* man may eat it. If a foreigner has settled among you and wants to celebrate Passover to honour the LORD, you must first circumcise all the males of

his household. He is then to be treated like a native-born Israelite and may join in the festival. 49 The same regulations apply to native-born Israelites and to foreigners who settle among you." 50 All the Israelites obeyed and did what the LORD had commanded Moses and Aaron. 51 On that day the LORD brought the Israelite tribes out of Egypt.

Dedication of the Firstborn

13 The LORD said to Moses, 2 "Dedicate all the firstborn males to me, for every firstborn male Israelite and every firstborn male animal belongs to me."

The Festival of Unleavened Bread

3 Moses said to the people, "Remember this day — the day on which you left Egypt, the place where you were slaves. This is the day the LORD brought you out by his great power. No leavened bread is to be eaten. 4 You are leaving Egypt on this day in the first month, the month of Abib. 5 The LORD solemnly promised your ancestors to give you the land of the Canaanites, the Hittites, the Amorites, the Hivites, and the Jebusites. When he brings you into that rich and fertile land, you must celebrate this festival in the first month of every year. 6 For seven days you must eat unleavened bread and on the seventh day there is to be a festival to honour the LORD. 7 For seven days you must not eat any bread made with yeast; there must *be no yeast or leavened bread anywhere in* your land. 8 When the festival begins, explain to your sons that you do all this because of what the LORD did for you when

---

See also: 12.40: Gen 15.13; Gal 3.17
12.46: Num 9.12; Jn 19.36

See also: 13.2: Num 3.13; Lk 2.23

you left Egypt. 9 This observance will be a reminder, like something tied on your hand or on your forehead; it will remind you to continue to recite and study the Law of the LORD, because the LORD brought you out of Egypt by his great power. 10 Celebrate this festival at the appointed time each year.

The Firstborn

11 "The LORD will bring you into the land of the Canaanites, which he solemnly promised to you and your ancestors. When he gives it to you, 12 you must offer every firstborn male to the LORD. Every firstborn male of your animals belongs to the LORD, 13 but you must buy back from him every firstborn male donkey by offering a lamb in its place. If you do not want to buy back the donkey, break its neck. You must buy back every firstborn male child of yours. 14 In the future, when your son asks what this observance means, you will answer him, 'By using great power the LORD brought us out of Egypt, the place where we were slaves. 15 When the king of Egypt was stubborn and refused to let us go, the LORD killed every firstborn male in the land of Egypt, both human and animal. That is why we sacrifice every firstborn male animal to the LORD, but buy back our firstborn sons. 16 This observance will be a reminder, like something tied on our hands or on our foreheads; it will remind us that the LORD brought us out of Egypt by his great power.' "

The Pillar of Cloud and the Pillar of Fire

17 When the king of Egypt let the people go, God did not take them by the road that goes up the coast to Philistia, although it was the shortest way. God thought, "I do not want the people to change their minds and return to Egypt when they see that they are going to have to fight." 18 Instead, he led them in a roundabout way through the desert towards the Red Sea.* The Israelites were armed for battle.

19 Moses took the body of Joseph with him, as Joseph had made the Israelites solemnly promise to do. Joseph had said, "When God rescues you, you must carry my body with you from this place."

20 The Israelites left Sukkoth and camped at Etham on the edge of the desert. 21 During the day the LORD went in front of them in a pillar of cloud to show them the way, and during the night he went in front of them in a pillar of fire to give them light, so that they could travel night and day. 22 The pillar of cloud was always in front of the people during the day, and the pillar of fire at night.

Crossing the Red Sea

14 Then the LORD said to Moses, 2 "Tell the Israelites to turn back and camp in front of Pi Hahiroth, between Migdol and the Red Sea, near Baal Zephon. 3 The king will think that the Israelites are wandering about in the country and are closed in by the desert. 4 I will make him stubborn, and he will pursue you, and my victory over the king and his army will bring me honour. Then the Egyptians will know that I am the LORD." The Israelites did as they were told.

5 When the king of Egypt was told that the people had escaped, he and his officials changed their minds and said, "What have we done? We have let the Israelites escape, and we have lost them as our slaves!" 6 The king got his war chariot and his army ready. 7 He set out with all his chariots, including the 600 finest, commanded by their officers. 8 The LORD made the king stubborn, and he pursued the Israelites, who were leaving triumphantly.* 9 The Egyptian army, with all the horses, chariots, and drivers, pursued them and caught up with them where they were camped by the Red Sea near Pi Hahiroth and Baal Zephon.

10 When the Israelites saw the king and his army marching against them, they were terrified and cried out to the LORD for help. 11 They said to Moses, "Weren't there any graves in Egypt? Did you have to bring us out here in the desert to die? Look what you have done by bringing us

---

13.18 RED SEA: *(in Hebrew literally "Sea of Reeds") evidently referred to (1) a series of lakes and marshes between the head of the Gulf of Suez and the Mediterranean, the region generally regarded as the site of the events described in Exodus 13, and was also used to designate (2) the Gulf of Suez, and (3) the Gulf of Aqaba.*
See also: **13.12**: Ex 34.19–20; Lk 2.23

14.8 triumphantly; *or* under the protection of the LORD.
See also: **13.19**: Gen 50.25; Josh 24.32

The Egyptians will know that I am the LORD   *(14.18)*

out of Egypt! ¹² Didn't we tell you before we left that this would happen? We told you to leave us alone and let us go on being slaves of the Egyptians. It would be better to be slaves there than to die here in the desert."

¹³ Moses answered, "Don't be afraid! Stand your ground, and you will see what the LORD will do to save you today; you will never see these Egyptians again. ¹⁴ The LORD will fight for you, and there is no need for you to do anything."

¹⁵ The LORD said to Moses, "Why are you crying out for help? Tell the people to move forward. ¹⁶ Lift up your stick and hold it out over the sea. The water will divide, and the Israelites will be able to walk through the sea on dry ground. ¹⁷ I will make the Egyptians so stubborn that they will go in after them, and I will gain honour by my victory over the king, his army, his chariots, and his drivers. ¹⁸ When I defeat them, the Egyptians will know that I am the LORD."

19 The angel of God, who had been in front of the army of Israel, moved and went to the rear. The pillar of cloud also moved until it was 20 between the Egyptians and the Israelites. The cloud made it dark for the Egyptians, but gave light to the people of Israel,* and so the armies could not come near each other all night.

21 Moses held out his hand over the sea, and the LORD drove the sea back with a strong east wind. It blew all night and turned the sea into dry land. The water was divided, 22 and the Israelites went through the sea on dry ground, with walls of water on both sides. 23 The Egyptians pursued them and went after them into the sea with all their horses, chariots, and drivers. 24 Just before dawn the LORD looked down from the pillar of fire and cloud at the Egyptian army and threw them into a panic. 25 He made the wheels of their chariots get stuck, so that they moved with great difficulty. The Egyptians said, "The LORD is fighting for the Israelites against us. Let's get out of here!"

26 The LORD said to Moses, "Hold out your hand over the sea, and the water will come back over the Egyptians and their chariots and drivers." 27 So Moses held out his hand over the sea, and at daybreak the water returned to its normal level. The Egyptians tried to escape from the water, but the LORD threw them into the sea. 28 The water returned and covered the chariots, the drivers, and all the Egyptian army that had followed the Israelites into the sea; not one of them was left. 29 But the Israelites walked through the sea on dry ground, with walls of water on both sides.

30 On that day the LORD saved the people of Israel from the Egyptians, and the Israelites saw them lying dead on the seashore. 31 When the Israelites saw the great power with which the LORD had defeated the Egyptians, they stood in awe of the LORD; and they had faith in the LORD and in his servant Moses.

The Song of Moses

15 Then Moses and the Israelites sang this song to the LORD:

"I will sing to the LORD, because he
     has won a glorious victory;
he has thrown the horses and their
     riders into the sea.
2 The LORD is my strong defender;
     he is the one who has saved me.
He is my God, and I will praise him,
     my father's God, and I will sing
     about his greatness.
3 The LORD is a warrior;
     the LORD is his name.

4 "He threw Egypt's army and its
     chariots into the sea;
the best of its officers were
     drowned in the Red Sea.
5 The deep sea covered them;
     they sank to the bottom like a
     stone.

6 "Your right hand, LORD, is awesome
     in power;
it breaks the enemy in pieces.
7 In majestic triumph you overthrow
     your foes;
your anger blazes out and burns
     them up like straw.
8 You blew on the sea and the water
     piled up high;
it stood up straight like a wall;
the deepest part of the sea
     became solid.
9 The enemy said, 'I will pursue them
     and catch them;
I will divide their wealth and take
     all I want;
I will draw my sword and take all
     they have.'
10 But one breath from you, LORD, and
     the Egyptians were drowned;
they sank like lead in the terrible
     water.

11 "LORD, who among the gods is like
     you?
Who is like you, wonderful in
     holiness?
Who can work miracles and
     mighty acts like yours?

14.20 *Probable text* The cloud... Israel; *Hebrew unclear.*
See also: 14.22: 1 Cor 10.1–2; Heb 11.29

See also: 15.1: Rev 15.3   **15.2:** Ps 118.14; Is 12.2

12 You stretched out your right hand,
and the earth swallowed our
enemies.
13 Faithful to your promise, you led the
people you had rescued;
by your strength you guided them
to your sacred land.
14 The nations have heard, and they
tremble with fear;
the Philistines are seized with terror.
15 The leaders of Edom are terrified;
Moab's mighty men are trembling;
the people of Canaan lose their
courage.
16 Terror and dread fall upon them.
They see your strength, O LORD,
and stand helpless with fear
until your people have marched
past —
the people you set free from slavery.
17 You bring them in and plant them
on your mountain,
the place that you, LORD, have
chosen for your home,
the Temple that you yourself have
built.
18 You, LORD, will be king for ever and
ever."

The Song of Miriam

19 The Israelites walked through the sea
on dry ground. But when the Egyptian
chariots with their horses and drivers went
into the sea, the LORD brought the water
back, and it covered them.
20 The prophet Miriam, Aaron's sister,
took her tambourine, and all the women
followed her, playing tambourines and
dancing. 21 Miriam sang for them:
"Sing to the LORD, because he has
won a glorious victory;
he has thrown the horses and their
riders into the sea."

Bitter Water

22 Then Moses led the people of Israel
away from the Red Sea into the desert of
Shur. For three days they walked through
the desert, but found no water. 23 Then they
came to a place called Marah, but the water
there was so bitter that they could not drink
it. That is why it was named Marah.* 24 The
people complained to Moses and asked,

"What are we going to drink?" 25 Moses
prayed earnestly to the LORD, and the LORD
showed him a piece of wood, which he
threw into the water; and the water became
fit to drink.
There the LORD gave them laws to live by,
and there he also tested them. 26 He said,
"If you will obey me completely by doing
what I consider right and by keeping my
commands, I will not punish you with any
of the diseases that I brought on the Egyptians. I am the LORD, the one who heals
you."
27 Next they came to Elim, where there
were twelve springs and 70 palm trees;
there they camped by the water.

The Manna and the Quails

16 The whole Israelite community set
out from Elim, and on the fifteenth
day of the second month after they had
left Egypt, they came to the desert of Sin,
which is between Elim and Sinai. 2 There in
the desert they all complained to Moses
and Aaron 3 and said to them, "We wish
that the LORD had killed us in Egypt. There
we could at least sit down and eat meat
and as much other food as we wanted. But
you have brought us out into this desert to
starve us all to death."
4 The LORD said to Moses, "Now I am
going to make food rain down from the sky
for all of you. The people must go out every
day and gather enough for that day. In this
way I can test them to find out if they will
follow my instructions. 5 On the sixth day
they are to bring in twice as much as usual
and prepare it."
6 So Moses and Aaron said to all the Israelites, "This evening you will know that it
was the LORD who brought you out of
Egypt. 7 In the morning you will see the
dazzling light of the LORD's presence.
He has heard your complaints against
him — yes, against him, because we are
only carrying out his instructions." 8 Then
Moses said, "It is the LORD who will give
you meat to eat in the evening and as
much bread as you want in the morning,
because *he has heard how much you have*
complained against him. When you complain against us, you are really complaining against the LORD."

15.23 MARAH: *This name in Hebrew means "bitter".*

See also: 16.4: Jn 6.31

9 Moses said to Aaron, "Tell the whole community to come and stand before the Lord, because he has heard their complaints." 10 As Aaron spoke to the whole community, they turned towards the desert, and suddenly the dazzling light of the Lord appeared in a cloud. 11 The Lord said to Moses, 12 "I have heard the complaints of the Israelites. Tell them that at twilight they will have meat to eat, and in the morning they will have all the bread they want. Then they will know that I, the Lord, am their God."

13 In the evening a large flock of quails flew in, enough to cover the camp, and in the morning there was dew all round the camp. 14 When the dew evaporated, there was something thin and flaky on the surface of the desert. It was as delicate as frost. 15 When the Israelites saw it, they didn't know what it was and asked each other, "What is it?"

Moses said to them, "This is the food that the Lord has given you to eat. 16 The Lord has commanded that each of you is to gather as much of it as he needs, two litres for each member of his household."

The food that the Lord has given you to eat (16.15)

17 The Israelites did this, some gathering more, others less. 18 When they measured it, those who gathered much did not have too much, and those who gathered less did not have too little. Each had gathered just what he needed. 19 Moses said to them, "No one is to keep any of it for tomorrow."

20 But some of them did not listen to Moses and saved part of it. The next morning it was full of worms and smelt rotten, and Moses was angry with them. 21 Every morning each one gathered as much as he needed; and when the sun grew hot, what was left on the ground melted.

22 On the sixth day they gathered twice as much food, four litres for each person. All the leaders of the community came and told Moses about it, 23 and he said to them, "The Lord has commanded that tomorrow is a holy day of rest, dedicated to him. Bake today what you want to bake and boil what you want to boil. Whatever is left should be put aside and kept for tomorrow." 24 As Moses had commanded, they kept what was left until the next day; it did not spoil or get worms in it. 25 Moses said, "Eat this today, because today is the Sabbath, a day of rest dedicated to the Lord, and you will not find any food outside the camp. 26 You must gather food for six days, but on the seventh day, the day of rest, there will be none."

27 On the seventh day some of the people went out to gather food, but they did not find any. 28 Then the Lord said to Moses, "How much longer will you people refuse to obey my commands? 29 Remember that I, the Lord, have given you a day of rest, and that is why on the sixth day I will always give you enough food for two days. Everyone is to stay where he is on the seventh day and not leave his home." 30 So the people did no work on the seventh day.

31 The people of Israel called the food manna.* It was like a small white seed, and tasted like biscuits made with honey. 32 Moses said, "The Lord has commanded us to save some manna, to be kept for our descendants, so that they can see the food which he gave us to eat in the desert when he brought us out of Egypt." 33 Moses said to Aaron, "Take a jar, put two litres of manna in it, and place it in the Lord's presence to be kept for our descendants." 34 As the Lord had commanded Moses, Aaron put it in front of the Covenant Box, so that it could be kept. 35 The Israelites ate

---

16.31 MANNA: *This word sounds like the Hebrew for "what is it?" (see verse 15).*

See also: **16.23:** Ex 20.8–11   **16.31:** Num 11.7–8
16.33: Heb 9.4   **16.35:** Josh 5.12

See also: **16.15:** 1 Cor 10.3   **16.18:** 2 Cor 8.15

manna for the next 40 years, until they reached the land of Canaan, where they settled. 36 (The standard dry measure then in use equalled 20 litres.)

Water from the Rock
(Num 20.1–13)

17 The whole Israelite community left the desert of Sin, moving from one place to another at the command of the LORD. They made camp at Rephidim, but there was no water there to drink. 2 They complained to Moses and said, "Give us water to drink."

Moses answered, "Why are you complaining? Why are you putting the LORD to the test?"

3 But the people were very thirsty and continued to complain to Moses. They said, "Why did you bring us out of Egypt? To kill us and our children and our livestock with thirst?"

4 Moses prayed earnestly to the LORD and said, "What can I do with these people? They are almost ready to stone me."

5 The LORD said to Moses, "Take some of the leaders of Israel with you, and go on ahead of the people. Take along the stick with which you struck the Nile. 6 I will stand before you on a rock at Mount Sinai. Strike the rock, and water will come out of it for the people to drink." Moses did so in the presence of the leaders of Israel.

7 The place was named Massah and Meribah,* because the Israelites complained and put the LORD to the test when they asked, "Is the LORD with us or not?"

War with the Amalekites

8 The Amalekites came and attacked the Israelites at Rephidim. 9 Moses said to Joshua, "Pick out some men to go and fight the Amalekites tomorrow. I will stand on top of the hill holding the stick that God told me to carry." 10 Joshua did as Moses commanded him and went out to fight the Amalekites, while Moses, Aaron, and Hur went up to the top of the hill. 11 As long as *Moses held up his arms, the Israelites won,* but when he put his arms down, the Amalekites started winning. 12 When Moses' arms grew tired, Aaron and Hur

They ... held ... his arms ... steady until the sun went down   (17.12)

brought a stone for him to sit on, while they stood beside him and held up his arms, holding them steady until the sun went down. 13 In this way Joshua totally defeated the Amalekites.

14 Then the LORD said to Moses, "Write an account of this victory, so that it will be remembered. Tell Joshua that I will completely destroy the Amalekites." 15 Moses built an altar and named it "The LORD is my Banner". 16 He said, "Hold high the banner of the LORD!* The LORD will continue to fight against the Amalekites for ever!"

Jethro Visits Moses

18 Moses' father-in-law Jethro, the priest of Midian, heard about everything that God had done for Moses and the people of Israel when he led them out of Egypt. 2 So he came to Moses, bringing with him Moses' wife Zipporah, who had been left behind, 3 and Gershom and Eliezer, her two sons. (Moses had said, "I have been a foreigner in a strange land"; so he had named one son Gershom.* 4 He had also said, "The God of my father helped me and saved me from being killed by the king of Egypt"; so he had named the other son Eliezer.*) 5 Jethro came with Moses' wife and her two sons into the desert where Moses was camped at the holy mountain. 6 He had sent word to Moses that they were coming, 7 so Moses went out to meet him, bowed before him, and kissed him. They asked about each other's health and then went

---

17.7 MASSAH... MERIBAH: *These names in Hebrew mean "testing" and "complaining".*

17.16 *Probable text Hold... LORD; Hebrew unclear.*
18.3 GERSHOM: *This name sounds like the Hebrew for "foreigner".*
18.4 ELIEZER: *This name sounds like the Hebrew for "God helps me".*

See also: 17.14: Deut 25.17–19; 1 Sam 15.2–9
18.2–3: Ex 2.21–22   18.3: Acts 7.29

into Moses' tent. 8 Moses told Jethro everything that the LORD had done to the king and the people of Egypt in order to rescue the Israelites. He also told him about the hardships the people had faced on the way and how the LORD had saved them. 9 When Jethro heard all this, he was happy 10 and said, "Praise the LORD, who saved you from the king and the people of Egypt! Praise the LORD, who saved his people from slavery! 11 Now I know that the LORD is greater than all the gods, because he did this when the Egyptians treated the Israelites with such contempt." 12 Then Jethro brought an offering to be burnt whole and other sacrifices to be offered to God; and Aaron and all the leaders of Israel went with him to eat the sacred meal as an act of worship.

The Appointment of Judges
(Deut 1.9–18)

13 The next day Moses was settling disputes among the people, and he was kept busy from morning till night. 14 When Jethro saw everything that Moses had to do, he asked, "What is all this that you are doing for the people? Why are you doing this all alone, with people standing here from morning till night to consult you?"

15 Moses answered, "I must do this because the people come to me to learn God's will. 16 When two people have a dispute, they come to me, and I decide which one of them is right, and I tell them God's commands and laws."

17 Then Jethro said, "You are not doing it the right way. 18 You will wear yourself out and these people as well. This is too much for you to do alone. 19 Now let me give you some good advice, and God will be with you. It is right for you to represent the people before God and bring their disputes to him. 20 You should teach them God's commands and explain to them how they should live and what they should do. 21 But in addition, you should choose some capable men and appoint them as leaders of the people: leaders of thousands, hundreds, fifties, and tens. They must be God-fearing men who can be trusted and who cannot be bribed. 22 Let them serve as judges for the people on a permanent basis. They can bring all the difficult cases to you, but they themselves can decide all the smaller disputes.

That will make it easier for you, as they share your burden. 23 If you do this, as God commands, you will not wear yourself out, and all these people can go home with their disputes settled."

24 Moses took Jethro's advice 25 and chose capable men from among all the Israelites. He appointed them as leaders of thousands, hundreds, fifties, and tens. 26 They served as judges for the people on a permanent basis, bringing the difficult cases to Moses but deciding the smaller disputes themselves.

27 Then Moses said goodbye to Jethro, and Jethro went back home.

The Israelites at Mount Sinai

19 1–2 The people of Israel left Rephidim, and on the first day of the third month after they had left Egypt they came to the desert of Sinai. There they set up camp at the foot of Mount Sinai, 3 and Moses went up the mountain to meet with God.

The LORD called to him from the mountain and told him to say to the Israelites, Jacob's descendants: 4 "You saw what I, the LORD, did to the Egyptians and how I carried you as an eagle carries her young on her wings, and brought you here to me. 5 Now, if you will obey me and keep my covenant, you will be my own people. The whole earth is mine, but you will be my chosen people, 6 a people dedicated to me alone, and you will serve me as priests." 7 So Moses went down and called the leaders of the people together and told them everything that the LORD had commanded him. 8 Then all the people answered together, "We will do everything that the LORD has said," and Moses reported this to the LORD.

9 The LORD said to Moses, "I will come to you in a thick cloud, so that the people will hear me speaking with you and will believe you from now on."

Moses told the LORD what the people had answered, 10 and the LORD said to him, "Go to the people and tell them to spend today and tomorrow purifying themselves for worship. They must wash their clothes 11 and be ready the day after tomorrow.

See also: 19.5: Deut 4.20, 7.6, 14.2, 26.18; Tit 2.14
19.5–6: 1 Pet 2.9   **19.6:** Rev 1.6, 5.10

On that day I will come down on Mount Sinai, where all the people can see me. 12 Mark a boundary round the mountain that the people must not cross, and tell them not to go up the mountain or even get near it. If anyone sets foot on it, he is to be put to death; 13 he must either be stoned or shot with arrows, without anyone touching him. This applies to both men and animals; they must be put to death. But when the trumpet is blown, then the people are to go up to the mountain."

14 Then Moses came down the mountain and told the people to get ready for worship. So they washed their clothes, 15 and Moses said to them, "Be ready by the day after tomorrow and don't have sexual intercourse in the meantime."

16 On the morning of the third day there was thunder and lightning, a thick cloud appeared on the mountain, and a very loud trumpet blast was heard. All the people in the camp trembled with fear. 17 Moses led them out of the camp to meet God, and they stood at the foot of the mountain. 18 The whole of Mount Sinai was covered with smoke, because the LORD had come down on it in fire. The smoke went up like the smoke of a furnace, and all the people trembled violently. 19 The sound of the trumpet became louder and louder. Moses spoke, and God answered him with thunder. 20 The LORD came down on the top of Mount Sinai and called Moses to the top of the mountain. Moses went up 21 and the LORD said to him, "Go down and warn the people not to cross the boundary to come and look at me; if they do, many of them will die. 22 Even the priests who come near me must purify themselves, or I will punish them."

23 Moses said to the LORD, "The people cannot come up, because you commanded us to consider the mountain sacred and to mark a boundary round it."

24 The LORD replied, "Go down and bring Aaron back with you. But the priests and the people must not cross the boundary to come up to me, or I will punish them." 25 Moses then went down to the people and told them what the LORD had said.

See also: 19.12–13: Heb 12.18–20   19.16: Rev 4.5
19.16–18: Deut 4.11–12

The Ten Commandments
(Deut 5.1–21)

20 God spoke, and these were his words: 2 "I am the LORD your God who brought you out of Egypt, where you were slaves.

3 "Worship no god but me.

4 "Do not make for yourselves images of anything in heaven or on earth or in the water under the earth. 5 Do not bow down to any idol or worship it, because I am the LORD your God and I tolerate no rivals. I bring punishment on those who hate me and on their descendants down to the third and fourth generation. 6 But I show my love to thousands of generations* of those who love me and obey my laws.

7 "Do not use my name for evil purposes, for I, the LORD your God, will punish anyone who misuses my name.

8 "Observe the Sabbath and keep it holy. 9 You have six days in which to do your work, 10 but the seventh day is a day of rest dedicated to me. On that day no one is to work — neither you, your children, your slaves, your animals, nor the foreigners who live in your country. 11 In six days I, the LORD, made the earth, the sky, the sea, and everything in them, but on the seventh day I rested. That is why I, the LORD, blessed the Sabbath and made it holy.

12 "Respect your father and your mother, so that you may live a long time in the land that I am giving you.

13 "Do not commit murder.

14 "Do not commit adultery.

15 "Do not steal.

16 "Do not accuse anyone falsely.

17 "Do not desire another man's house; do not desire his wife, his slaves, his cattle, his donkeys, or anything else that he owns."

20.6 thousands of generations; or thousands.

See also: 20.4–5: Ex 34.17; Lev 19.4, 26.1;
Deut 4.15–18, 27.15   20.5–6: Ex 34.6–7;
Num 14.18; Deut 7.9–10   20.7: Lev 19.12
20.8: Ex 16.23–30, 31.12–14   20.9–10: Ex 23.12,
31.15, 34.21, 35.2; Lev 23.3   20.11: Gen 2.1–3;
Ex 31.17   20.12: Deut 27.16; Mt 15.4, 19.19;
Mk 7.10, 10.19; Lk 18.20; Eph 6.2, 3
20.13: Gen 9.6; Lev 24.17; Mt 5.21, 19.18; Mk 10.19;
Lk 18.20; Rom 13.9; Jas 2.11   20.14: Lev 20.10;
Mt 5.27, 19.18; Mk 10.19; Lk 18.20; Rom 13.9;
Jas 2.11   20.15: Lev 19.11; Mt 19.18; Mk 10.19;
Lk 18.20; Rom 13.9   20.16: Ex 23.1; Mt 19.18;
Mk 10.19; Lk 18.20   20.17: Rom 7.7, 13.9

The People's Fear

(Deut 5.22–33)

18 When the people heard the thunder and the trumpet blast and saw the lightning and the smoking mountain, they trembled with fear and stood a long way off. 19 They said to Moses, "If you speak to us, we will listen; but we are afraid that if God speaks to us, we will die." 20 Moses replied, "Don't be afraid; God has only come to test you and make you keep on obeying him, so that you will not sin." 21 But the people continued to stand a long way off, and only Moses went near the dark cloud where God was.

Laws about Altars

22 The LORD commanded Moses to say to the Israelites: "You have seen how I, the LORD, have spoken to you from heaven. 23 Do not make for yourselves gods of silver or gold to be worshipped in addition to me. 24 Make an altar of earth for me, and on it sacrifice your sheep and your cattle as offerings to be completely burnt and as fellowship offerings. In every place that I set aside for you to worship me, I will come to you and bless you. 25 If you make an altar of stone for me, do not build it out of cut stones, because when you use a chisel on stones, you make them unfit for my use. 26 Do not build an altar for me with steps leading up to it; if you do, you will expose yourselves as you go up the steps.

The Treatment of Slaves

(Deut 15.12–18)

21 "Give the Israelites the following laws: 2 If you buy a Hebrew slave, he shall serve you for six years. In the seventh year he is to be set free without having to pay anything. 3 If he was unmarried when he became your slave, he is not to take a wife with him when he leaves; but if he was married when he became your slave, he may take his wife with him. 4 If his master gave him a wife and she bore him sons or daughters, the woman and her children belong to the master, and the man shall leave by himself. 5 But if the slave declares that he loves his master, his wife, and his children and does not want to be set free, 6 then his

master shall take him to the place of worship. There he is to make him stand against the door or the door-post and pierce his ear. Then he will be his slave for life.

7 "If a man sells his daughter as a slave, she is not to be set free, as male slaves are. 8 If she is sold to someone who intends to make her his wife, but he doesn't like her, then she is to be sold back to her father; her master cannot sell her to foreigners, because he has treated her unfairly. 9 If a man buys a female slave to give to his son, he is to treat her like a daughter. 10 If a man takes a second wife, he must continue to give his first wife the same amount of food and clothing and the same rights that she had before. 11 If he does not fulfil these duties to her, he must set her free and not receive any payment.

Laws about Violent Acts

12 "Whoever hits someone and kills him is to be put to death. 13 But if it was an accident and he did not mean to kill him, he can escape to a place which I will choose for you, and there he will be safe. 14 But when anyone gets angry and deliberately kills someone else, he is to be put to death, even if he has run to my altar for safety.

15 "Whoever hits his father or his mother is to be put to death.

16 "Whoever kidnaps someone, either to sell him or to keep him as a slave, is to be put to death.

17 "Whoever curses his father or his mother is to be put to death.

18–19 "If there is a fight and one person hits another with a stone or with their fist, but does not kill them, they are not to be punished. If the one who was hit has to stay in bed, but later is able to get up and walk outside with the help of a stick, the one who hit them is to pay for their lost time and take care of them until they get well.

20 "If a slave owner takes a stick and beats his slave, whether male or female, and the slave dies on the spot, the slave owner is to be punished. 21 But if the slave does not die for a day or two, the master is not to be punished. The loss of his property is punishment enough.

See also: 20.18–19: Heb 12.18–19
20.25: Deut 27.5–7; Josh 8.31   **21.2–6:** Lev 25.39–46

See also: 21.12: Lev 24.17   **21.13:** Num 35.10–34; Deut 19.1–13; Josh 20.1–9   **21.16:** Deut 24.7
21.17: Lev 20.9; Mt 15.4; Mk 7.10

22 "If some men are fighting and hurt a pregnant woman so that she loses her child, but she is not injured in any other way, the one who hurt her is to be fined whatever amount the woman's husband demands, subject to the approval of the judges. 23 But if the woman herself is injured, the punishment shall be life for life, 24 eye for eye, tooth for tooth, hand for hand, foot for foot, 25 burn for burn, wound for wound, bruise for bruise.

26 "If someone hits his male or female slave in the eye and puts it out, he is to free the slave as payment for the eye. 27 If he knocks out a tooth, he is to free the slave as payment for the tooth.

The Responsibility of Owners

28 "If a bull gores someone to death, it is to be stoned, and its flesh shall not be eaten; but its owner is not to be punished. 29 But if the bull had been in the habit of attacking people and its owner had been warned, but did not keep it penned up — then if it gores someone to death, it is to be stoned, and its owner is to be put to death also. 30 However, if the owner is allowed to pay a fine to save his life, he must pay the full amount required. 31 If the bull kills a boy or a girl, the same rule applies. 32 If the bull kills a male or female slave, its owner shall pay the owner of the slave thirty pieces of silver, and the bull shall be stoned to death.

33 "If someone takes the cover off a pit or if he digs one and does not cover it, and a bull or a donkey falls into it, 34 he must pay for the animal. He is to pay the money to the owner and may keep the dead animal. 35 If someone's bull kills someone else's bull, the two of them shall sell the live bull and divide the money; they shall also divide up the meat from the dead animal. 36 But if it was known that the bull had been in the habit of attacking and its owner did not keep it penned up, he must make good the loss by giving the other man a live bull, but he may keep the dead animal.

Laws about Repayment

22 "If someone steals a cow or a sheep and kills it or sells it, he must pay five cows for one cow and four sheep for one sheep. 2–4 He must pay for what he

stole. If he owns nothing, he shall be sold as a slave to pay for what he has stolen. If the stolen animal, whether a cow, a donkey, or a sheep, is found alive in his possession, he shall pay two for one.

"If a thief is caught breaking into a house at night and is killed, the one who killed him is not guilty of murder. But if it happens during the day, he is guilty of murder.

5 "If someone lets his animals graze in a field or a vineyard and they stray away and eat up the crops* growing in someone else's field, he must make good the loss with the crops from his own fields or vineyards.

They … eat up the crops growing in someone else's field (22.5)

6 "If someone starts a fire in his own field and it spreads through the weeds to someone else's field and burns up corn that is growing or that has been cut and stacked, the one who started the fire is to pay for the damage.

7 "If anyone agrees to keep someone else's money or other valuables for him and they are stolen from his house, the thief, if found, shall repay double. 8 But if the thief is not found, the one who was keeping the valuables is to be brought to the place of worship and there he must take an oath that he has not stolen the other one's property.

9 "In every case of a dispute about property, whether it involves cattle, donkeys, sheep, clothing, or any other lost object, the two people claiming the property shall be taken to the place of worship. The one whom God declares to be guilty shall pay double to the other one.

10 "If someone agrees to keep a neighbour's donkey, cow, sheep, or other animal for him, and the animal dies or is

---

See also: 21.24: Lev 24.19–20; Deut 19.21; Mt 5.38

22.5 If… crops; or If someone burns off a field or a vineyard, and lets the fire get out of control and burn up the crops.

injured or is carried off in a raid, and if there was no witness, 11 the man must go to the place of worship and take an oath that he has not stolen the other man's animal. If the animal was not stolen, the owner shall accept the loss, and the other man need not repay him; 12 but if the animal was stolen, the man must repay the owner. 13 If it was killed by wild animals, the man is to bring the remains as evidence; he need not pay for what has been killed by wild animals.

14 "If anyone borrows an animal from someone else and it is injured or dies when its owner is not present, he must pay for it. 15 But if that happens when the owner is present, he need not repay. If it is a hired animal, the loss is covered by the hiring charge.

Moral and Religious Laws

16 "If a man seduces a virgin who is not engaged, he must pay the bride price for her and marry her. 17 But if her father refuses to let him marry her, he must pay the father a sum of money equal to the bride price for a virgin.

18 "Put to death any woman who practises magic.

19 "Put to death any man who has sexual relations with an animal.

20 "Condemn to death anyone who offers sacrifices to any god except to me, the LORD.

21 "Do not ill-treat or oppress a foreigner; remember that you were foreigners in Egypt. 22 Do not ill-treat any widow or orphan. 23 If you do, I, the LORD, will answer them when they cry out to me for help, 24 and I will be angry and kill you in war. Your wives will become widows, and your children will be fatherless.

25 "If you lend money to any of my people who are poor, do not act like a moneylender and require him to pay interest. 26 If you take someone's cloak as a pledge that he will pay you, you must give it back to him before the sun sets, 27 because it is the only covering he has to keep him warm. What else can he sleep in?

When he cries out to me for help, I will answer him because I am merciful.

28 "Do not speak evil of God,* and do not curse a leader of your people.

29 "Give me the offerings from your corn, your wine, and your olive oil when they are due.

"Give me your firstborn sons. 30 Give me the firstborn of your cattle and your sheep. Let the firstborn male stay with its mother for seven days, and on the eighth day offer it to me.

31 "You are my people, so you must not eat the meat of any animal that has been killed by wild animals; instead, give it to the dogs.

Justice and Fairness

23 "Do not spread false rumours, and do not help a guilty person by giving false evidence. 2 Do not follow the majority when they do wrong or when they give evidence that perverts justice. 3 Do not show partiality to a poor person at his trial.

4 "If you happen to see your enemy's cow or donkey running loose, take it back to him. 5 If his donkey has fallen under its load, help him get the donkey to its feet again; don't just walk off.

6 "Do not deny justice to a poor person when he appears in court. 7 Do not make false accusations, and do not put an innocent person to death, for I will condemn anyone who does such an evil thing. 8 Do not accept a bribe, for a bribe makes people blind to what is right and ruins the cause of those who are innocent.

9 "Do not ill-treat a foreigner; you know how it feels to be a foreigner, because you were foreigners in Egypt.

The Seventh Year and the Seventh Day

10 "For six years sow your field and gather in what it produces. 11 But in the seventh year let it rest, and do not harvest anything that grows on it. The poor may

---

22.28 God; *or* the judges.

See also: 22.16–17: Deut 22.28–29
22.18: Deut 18.10, 11　**22.19:** Lev 18.23, 20.15–16;
Deut 27.21　**22.20:** Deut 17.2–7
22.21–22: Ex 23.9; Lev 19.33–34; Deut 24.17–18,
27.19　**22.25:** Lev 25.35–38; Deut 15.7–11,
23.19–20　**22.26–27:** Deut 24.10–13

See also: 22.28: Acts 23.5　**22.31:** Lev 17.15
23.1: Ex 20.16; Lev 19.11–12; Deut 5.20
23.3: Lev 19.15　**23.4–5:** Deut 22.1–4
23.6–8: Lev 19.15; Deut 16.19　**23.9:** Ex 22.21;
Lev 19.33–34; Deut 24.17–18, 27.19
23.10–11: Lev 25.1–7

eat what grows there, and the wild animals can have what is left. Do the same with your vineyards and your olive trees.

12 "Work six days a week, but do no work on the seventh day, so that your slaves and the foreigners who work for you and even your animals can rest.

13 "Listen to everything that I, the Lord, have said to you. Do not pray to other gods; do not even mention their names.

The Three Great Festivals
(Ex 34.18–26; Deut 16.1–17)

14 "Celebrate three festivals a year to honour me. 15 In the month of Abib, the month in which you left Egypt, celebrate the Festival of Unleavened Bread in the way that I commanded you. Do not eat any bread made with yeast during the seven days of this festival. Never come to worship me without bringing an offering.

16 "Celebrate the Harvest Festival when you begin to harvest your crops.

"Celebrate the Festival of Shelters in the autumn, when you gather the fruit from your vineyards and orchards. 17 Every year at these three festivals all your men must come to worship me, the Lord your God.

18 "Do not offer bread made with yeast when you sacrifice an animal to me. The fat of animals sacrificed to me during these festivals is not to be left until the following morning.

19 "Each year bring to the house of the Lord your God the first corn that you harvest.

"Do not cook a young sheep or goat in its mother's milk.

Promises and Instructions

20 "I will send an angel ahead of you to protect you as you travel and to bring you to the place which I have prepared. 21 Pay attention to him and obey him. Do not rebel against him, for I have sent him, and he will not pardon such rebellion. 22 But if you obey him and do everything I command, I will fight against all your enemies. 23 My angel will go ahead of you and take you into the

land of the Amorites, the Hittites, the Perizzites, the Canaanites, the Hivites, and the Jebusites, and I will destroy them. 24 Do not bow down to their gods or worship them, and do not adopt their religious practices. Destroy their gods and break down their sacred stone pillars. 25 If you worship me, the Lord your God, I will bless you with food and water and take away all your illnesses. 26 In your land no woman will have a miscarriage or be without children. I will give you long lives.

27 "I will make the people who oppose you afraid of me; I will bring confusion among the people against whom you fight, and I will make all your enemies turn and run from you. 28 I will throw your enemies into a panic;* I will drive out the Hivites, the Canaanites, and the Hittites as you advance. 29 I will not drive them out within one year; if I did, the land would become deserted, and the wild animals would be too many for you. 30 Instead, I will drive them out little by little, until there are enough of you to take possession of the land. 31 I will make the borders of your land extend from the Gulf of Aqaba to the Mediterranean Sea and from the desert to the Euphrates River. I will give you power over the inhabitants of the land, and you will drive them out as you advance. 32 Do not make any agreement with them or with their gods. 33 Do not let those people live in your country; if you do, they will make you sin against me. If you worship their gods, it will be a fatal trap for you."

The Covenant is Sealed

24 The Lord said to Moses, "Come up the mountain to me, you and Aaron, Nadab, Abihu, and 70 of the leaders of Israel; and while you are still some distance away, bow down in worship. 2 You alone, and none of the others, are to come near me. The people are not even to come up the mountain."

3 Moses went and told the people all the Lord's commands and all the ordinances, and all the people answered together, *"We will do everything that the Lord has said."* 4 Moses wrote down all the Lord's commands. Early the next morning he built

See also: 23.12: Ex 20.9–11, 31.15, 34.21, 35.2; Lev 23.3; Deut 5.13–14 23.15: Ex 12.14–20; Lev 23.6–8; Num 28.17–25 23.16: Lev 23.15–21, 39–43; Num 28.26–31 23.19: Ex 34.26; Deut 14.21, 26.2

23.28 I will… panic; *or* I will send hornets among your enemies.

an altar at the foot of the mountain and set up twelve stones, one for each of the twelve tribes of Israel. 5 Then he sent young men, and they burnt sacrifices to the LORD and sacrificed some cattle as fellowship offerings. 6 Moses took half the blood of the animals and put it in bowls; and the other half he threw against the altar. 7 Then he took the book of the covenant, in which the LORD's commands were written, and read it aloud to the people. They said, "We will obey the LORD and do everything that he has commanded."

8 Then Moses took the blood in the bowls and threw it on the people. He said, "This is the blood that seals the covenant which the LORD made with you when he gave all these commands."

9 Moses, Aaron, Nadab, Abihu, and 70 of the leaders of Israel went up the mountain 10 and they saw the God of Israel. Beneath his feet was what looked like a pavement of sapphire, as blue as the sky. 11 God did not harm these leading men of Israel; they saw God, and then they ate and drank together.

Moses on Mount Sinai

12 The LORD said to Moses, "Come up the mountain, and while you are here, I will give you two stone tablets which contain all the laws that I have written for the instruction of the people." 13 Moses and his helper Joshua got ready, and Moses began* to go up the holy mountain. 14 Moses said to the leaders, "Wait here in the camp for us until we come back. Aaron and Hur are here with you; and so whoever has a dispute to settle can go to them."

15 Moses went up Mount Sinai, and a cloud covered it. 16–17 The dazzling light of the LORD's presence came down on the mountain. To the Israelites the light looked like a fire burning on top of the mountain. The cloud covered the mountain for six days, and on the seventh day the LORD called to Moses from the cloud. 18 Moses went on up the mountain into the cloud. There he stayed for 40 days and nights.

Offerings for the Sacred Tent
(Ex 35.4–9)

25 The Lord said to Moses, 2 "Tell the Israelites to make an offering to me. Receive whatever offerings anyone wishes to give. 3 These offerings are to be: gold, silver, and bronze; 4 fine linen; blue, purple, and red wool; cloth made of goats' hair; 5 rams' skin dyed red; fine leather; acacia wood; 6 oil for the lamps; spices for the anointing oil and for the sweet-smelling incense; 7 carnelians and other jewels to be set in the ephod* of the High Priest and in his breastpiece. 8 The people must make a sacred tent for me, so that I may live among them. 9 Make it and all its furnishings according to the plan that I will show you.

The Covenant Box
(Ex 37.1–9)

10 "Make a box out of acacia wood, 110 centimetres long, 66 centimetres wide, and 66 centimetres high. 11 Cover it with pure gold inside and out and put a gold border all round it. 12 Make four carrying rings of gold for it and attach them to its four legs, with two rings on each side. 13 Make carrying poles of acacia wood and cover them with gold 14 and put them through the rings on each side of the box. 15 The poles are to be left in the rings and must not be taken out. 16 Then put in the box the two stone tablets that I will give you, on which the commandments are written.

17 "Make a lid of pure gold, 110 centimetres long and 66 centimetres wide. 18 Make two winged creatures* of hammered gold, 19 one for each end of the lid. Make them so that they form one piece with the lid. 20 The winged creatures are to face each other across the lid, and their outspread wings are to cover it. 21 Put the two stone tablets inside the box and put the lid on top of it. 22 I will meet you there, and from above the lid between the two winged creatures I will give you all my laws for the people of Israel.

24.13 Moses began; *one ancient translation* they began.

See also: 24.8: Mt 26.28; Mk 14.24; Lk 22.20; 1 Cor 11.25; Heb 9.19–20, 10.29   **24.18:** Deut 9.9

25.7 EPHOD: *In most contexts the term ephod refers to a type of garment, in certain respects resembling a waistcoat. It was made of costly and colourful cloth and to it was attached a kind of pouch containing the Urim and Thummim, two objects used in determining God's will.*

25.18 WINGED CREATURES: *See Word List.*

See also: 25.17: Heb 9.5

The Table for the Bread Offered to God

(Ex 37.10–16)

23 "Make a table out of acacia wood, 88 centimetres long, 44 centimetres wide, and 66 centimetres high. 24 Cover it with pure gold and put a gold border round it. 25 Make a rim 75 millimetres wide round it and a gold border round the rim. 26 Make four carrying rings of gold for it and put them at the four corners, where the legs are. 27 The rings to hold the poles for carrying the table are to be placed near the rim. 28 Make the poles of acacia wood and cover them with gold. 29 Make plates, cups, jars, and bowls to be used for the wine offerings. All of these are to be made of pure gold. 30 The table is to be placed in front of the Covenant Box, and on the table there is always to be the sacred bread offered to me.

The Lampstand

(Ex 37.17–24)

31 "Make a lampstand of pure gold. Make its base and its shaft of hammered gold; its decorative flowers, including buds and petals, are to form one piece with it. 32 Six branches shall extend from its sides, three from each side. 33 Each of the six branches is to have three decorative flowers shaped like almond blossoms with buds and petals. 34 The shaft of the lampstand is to have four decorative flowers shaped like almond blossoms with buds and petals. 35 There is to be one bud below each of the three pairs of branches. 36 The buds, the branches, and the lampstand are to be a single piece of pure hammered gold. 37 Make seven lamps for the lampstand and set them up so that they shine towards the front. 38 Make its tongs and trays of pure gold. 39 Use 35 kilogrammes of pure gold to make the lampstand and all this equipment. 40 Take care to make them according to the plan that I showed you on the mountain.

The Tent of the Lord's Presence*

(Ex 36.8–38)

26 "Make the interior of the sacred Tent, the Tent of my presence, out of ten pieces of fine linen woven with blue,

purple, and red wool. Embroider them with figures of winged creatures. 2 Make each piece the same size, 12 metres long and 2 metres wide. 3 Sew five of them together in one set, and do the same with the other five. 4 Make loops of blue cloth on the edge of the outside piece in each set. 5 Put 50 loops on the first piece of the first set and 50 loops matching them on the last piece of the second set. 6 Make 50 gold hooks with which to join the two sets into one piece.

7 "Make a cover for the Tent out of eleven pieces of cloth made of goats' hair. 8 Make them all the same size, 13 metres long and 2 metres wide. 9 Sew five of them together in one set, and the other six in another set. Fold the sixth piece double over the front of the Tent. 10 Put 50 loops on the edge of the last piece of one set, and 50 loops on the edge of the other set. 11 Make 50 bronze hooks and put them in the loops to join the two sets so as to form one cover. 12 Hang the extra half-piece over the back of the Tent. 13 The extra 50 centimetres on each side of the length is to hang over the sides of the Tent to cover it.

14 "Make two more coverings, one of rams' skin dyed red and the other of fine leather, to serve as the outer cover.

15 "Make upright frames for the Tent out of acacia wood. 16 Each frame is to be 4 metres long and 66 centimetres wide, 17 with two matching projections, so that the frames can be joined together. All the frames are to have these projections. 18 Make twenty frames for the south side 19 and forty silver bases to go under them, two bases under each frame to hold its two projections. 20 Make twenty frames for the north side of the Tent 21 and forty silver bases, two under each frame. 22 For the back of the Tent on the west, make six frames, 23 and two frames for the corners. 24 These corner frames are to be joined at the bottom and connected all the way to the top. The two frames that form the two corners are to be made in this way. 25 So there will be eight frames with their sixteen silver bases, two under each frame.

26 "Make fifteen crossbars of acacia wood, five for the frames on one side of the Tent, 27 five for the frames on the other

---

Ch. 26 heading TENT OF THE LORD'S PRESENCE: *See Word List.*

See also: 25.30: Lev 24.5–8 **25.40:** Acts 7.44; Heb 8.5

The Tower of Babylon
OT 12

side, and five for the frames on the west end, at the back. 28 The middle crossbar, set halfway up the frames, is to extend from one end of the Tent to the other. 29 Cover the frames with gold and fit them with gold rings to hold the crossbars, which are also to be covered with gold. 30 Set up the Tent according to the plan that I showed you on the mountain.

31 "Make a curtain of fine linen woven with blue, purple, and red wool. Embroider it with figures of winged creatures. 32 Hang it on four posts of acacia wood covered with gold, fitted with hooks, and set in four silver bases. 33 Place the curtain under the row of hooks in the roof of the Tent, and behind the curtain put the Covenant Box containing the two stone tablets. The curtain will separate the Holy Place from the Most Holy Place. 34 Put the lid on the Covenant Box. 35 Outside the Most Holy Place put the table against the north side of the Tent and the lampstand against the south side.

36 "For the entrance of the Tent make a curtain of fine linen woven with blue, purple, and red wool and decorated with embroidery. 37 For this curtain make five posts of acacia wood covered with gold and fitted with gold hooks; make five bronze bases for these posts.

The Altar
(Ex 38.1–7)

27 "Make an altar out of acacia wood. It is to be square, 2.2 metres long and 2.2 metres wide, and it is to be 1.3 metres high. 2 Make projections at the top of the four corners. They are to form one piece with the altar, and the whole is to be covered with bronze. 3 Make pans for the greasy ashes, and make shovels, bowls, hooks, and firepans. All this equipment is to be made of bronze. 4 Make a bronze grating and put four bronze carrying rings on its corners. 5 Put the grating under the rim of the altar, so that it reaches halfway up the altar. 6 Make carrying poles of acacia wood, cover them with bronze, 7 and put them in the rings on each side of the altar when it is carried. 8 Make the altar out of boards and leave it hollow, according to the plan that I showed you on the mountain.

The Enclosure for the Tent of the Lord's Presence
(Ex 38.9–20)

9 "For the Tent of my presence make an enclosure out of fine linen curtains. On the south side the curtains are to be 44 metres long, 10 supported by twenty bronze posts in twenty bronze bases, with hooks and rods made of silver. 11 The same is to be done on the north side of the enclosure. 12 On the west side there are to be curtains 22 metres long, with ten posts and ten bases. 13 On the east side, where the entrance is, the enclosure is also to be 22 metres wide. 14–15 On each side of the entrance there are to be 6.6 metres of curtains, with three posts and three bases. 16 For the entrance itself there is to be a curtain 9 metres long made of fine linen woven with blue, purple, and red wool, and decorated with embroidery. It is to be supported by four posts in four bases. 17 All the posts round the enclosure are to be connected with silver rods, and their hooks are to be made of silver and their bases of bronze. 18 The enclosure is to be 44 metres long, 22 metres wide, and 2.2 metres high. The curtains are to be made of fine linen and the bases of bronze. 19 All the equipment that is used in the Tent and all the pegs for the Tent and for the enclosure are to be made of bronze.

Taking Care of the Lamp
(Lev 24.1–4)

20 "Command the people of Israel to bring you the best olive oil for the lamp, so that it can be lit each evening. 21 Aaron and his sons are to set up the lamp in the Tent of my presence outside the curtain which is in front of the Covenant Box. There in my presence it is to burn from evening until morning. This command is to be kept for ever by the Israelites and their descendants.

Garments for the Priests
(Ex 39.1–7)

28 "Summon your brother Aaron and his sons, Nadab, Abihu, Eleazar, and Ithamar. Separate them from the people of Israel, so that they may serve me as priests. 2 Make priestly garments for your brother Aaron, to provide him with dignity and beauty. 3 Call all the skilled workers to

See also: 26.33: Heb 6.19, 9.3–5

whom I have given ability, and tell them to make Aaron's clothes, so that he may be dedicated as a priest in my service. 4 Tell them to make a breastpiece, an ephod, a robe, an embroidered shirt, a turban, and a sash. They are to make these priestly garments for your brother Aaron and his sons, so that they can serve me as priests. 5 The skilled workers are to use blue, purple, and red wool, gold thread, and fine linen.

6 "They are to make the ephod of blue, purple, and red wool, gold thread, and fine linen, decorated with embroidery. 7 Two shoulder straps, by which it can be fastened, are to be attached to the sides. 8 A finely woven belt made of the same materials is to be attached to the ephod so as to form one piece with it. 9 Take two carnelian stones and engrave on them the names of the twelve sons of Jacob, 10 in the order of their birth, with six on one stone and six on the other. 11 Get a skilful jeweller to engrave on the two stones the names of the sons of Jacob, and mount the stones in gold settings. 12 Put them on the shoulder straps of the ephod to represent the twelve tribes of Israel. In this way Aaron will carry their names on his shoulders, so that I, the LORD, will always remember my people. 13 Make two gold settings 14 and two chains of pure gold twisted like cords, and attach them to the settings.

The Breastpiece
(Ex 39.8–21)

15 "Make a breastpiece for the High Priest to use in determining God's will. It is to be made of the same materials as the ephod and with similar embroidery. 16 It is to be square and folded double, 22 centimetres long and 22 centimetres wide. 17 Mount four rows of precious stones on it; in the first row mount a ruby, a topaz, and a garnet; 18 in the second row, an emerald, a sapphire, and a diamond; 19 in the third row, a turquoise, an agate, and an amethyst; 20 and in the fourth row, a beryl, a carnelian, and a jasper. These are to be mounted in gold settings. 21 Each of these twelve stones is to have engraved on it the name of one of the sons of Jacob, to represent the tribes of Israel. 22 For the breastpiece make chains of pure gold, twisted like cords. 23 Make two gold rings and attach them to the upper corners of the breastpiece, 24 and fasten the two gold cords to the two rings. 25 Fasten the other two ends of the cords to the two settings, and in this way attach them in front to the shoulder straps of the ephod. 26 Then make two rings of gold and attach them to the lower corners of the breastpiece on the inside edge next to the ephod. 27 Make two more gold rings and attach them to the lower part of the front of the two shoulder straps of the ephod near the seam and above the finely woven belt. 28 Tie the rings of the breastpiece to the rings of the ephod with a blue cord, so that the breastpiece rests above the belt and does not come loose.

29 "When Aaron enters the Holy Place, he will wear this breastpiece engraved with the names of the tribes of Israel, so that I, the LORD, will always remember my people. 30 Put the Urim and Thummim* in the breastpiece, so that Aaron will carry them when he comes into my holy presence. At such times he must always wear this breastpiece, so that he can determine my will for the people of Israel.

The Other Priestly Garments
(Ex 39.22–31)

31 "The robe that goes under the ephod is to be made entirely of blue wool. 32 It is to have a hole for the head, and this hole is to be reinforced with a woven binding to keep it from tearing. 33–34 All round its lower hem put pomegranates of blue, purple, and red wool, alternating with gold bells. 35 Aaron is to wear this robe when he serves as priest. When he comes into my presence in the Holy Place or when he leaves it, the sound of the bells will be heard, and he will not be killed.

36 "Make an ornament of pure gold and engrave on it 'Dedicated to the LORD'. 37 Tie it to the front of the turban with a blue cord. 38 Aaron is to wear it on his forehead, so that I, the LORD, will accept all the offerings that the Israelites dedicate to me, even if the people commit some error in offering them.

28.30 URIM AND THUMMIM: *Two objects used by the priest to determine God's will; it is not known precisely how they were used.*

See also: 28.30: Num 27.21; Deut 33.8; Ezra 2.63; Neh 7.65

39 "Weave Aaron's shirt of fine linen and make a turban of fine linen and also a sash decorated with embroidery.

40 "Make shirts, sashes, and caps for Aaron's sons, to provide them with dignity and beauty. 41 Put these clothes on your brother Aaron and his sons. Then ordain them and dedicate them by anointing them with olive oil, so that they may serve me as priests. 42 Make linen shorts for them, reaching from the waist to the thighs, so that they will not expose themselves. 43 Aaron and his sons must always wear them when they go into the Tent of my presence or approach the altar to serve as priests in the Holy Place, so that they will not be killed for exposing themselves. This is a permanent rule for Aaron and his descendants.

Instructions for Ordaining Aaron and his Sons as Priests
(Lev 8.1–36)

29 "This is what you are to do to Aaron and his sons to dedicate them as priests in my service. Take one young bull and two rams without any defects. 2 Use the best wheat flour, but no yeast, and make some bread with olive oil, some without it, and some in the form of biscuits brushed with oil. 3 Put them in a basket and offer them to me when you sacrifice the bull and the two rams.

4 "Bring Aaron and his sons to the entrance of the Tent of my presence, and tell them to take a ritual bath. 5 Then dress Aaron in the priestly garments — the shirt, the robe that goes under the ephod, the ephod, the breastpiece, and the belt. 6 Put the turban on him and tie on it the sacred sign of dedication engraved 'Dedicated to the LORD'. 7 Then take the anointing oil, pour it on his head, and anoint him.

8 "Bring his sons and put shirts on them; 9 put sashes round their waists and tie caps on their heads. That is how you are to ordain Aaron and his sons. They and their descendants are to serve me as priests for ever.

10 "Bring the bull to the front of the Tent of my presence and tell Aaron and his sons to put their hands on its head. 11 Kill the bull there in my holy presence at the entrance of the Tent. 12 Take some of the bull's blood and with your finger put it on the projections of the altar. Then pour out

the rest of the blood at the base of the altar. 13 Next, take all the fat which covers the internal organs, the best part of the liver, and the two kidneys with the fat on them and burn them on the altar as an offering to me. 14 But burn the bull's flesh, its skin, and its intestines outside the camp. This is an offering to take away the sins of the priests.

15 "Take one of the rams and tell Aaron and his sons to put their hands on its head. 16 Kill it, and take its blood and throw it against all four sides of the altar. 17 Cut the ram in pieces; wash its internal organs and its hind legs, and put them on top of the head and the other pieces. 18 Burn the whole ram on the altar as a food offering. The odour of this offering pleases me.

19 "Take the other ram — the ram used for dedication — and tell Aaron and his sons to put their hands on its head. 20 Kill it, and take some of its blood and put it on the lobes of the right ears of Aaron and his sons, on the thumbs of their right hands and on the big toes of their right feet. Throw the rest of the blood against all four sides of the altar. 21 Take some of the blood that is on the altar and some of the anointing oil, and sprinkle it on Aaron and his clothes and on his sons and their clothes. He, his sons, and their clothes will then be dedicated to me.

22 "Cut away the ram's fat, the fat tail, the fat covering the internal organs, the best part of the liver, the two kidneys with the fat on them, and the right thigh. 23 From the basket of bread which has been offered to me, take one loaf of each kind: one loaf made with olive oil and one made without it and one biscuit. 24 Put all this food in the hands of Aaron and his sons and tell them to dedicate it to me as a special gift. 25 Then take it from them and burn it on the altar, on top of the burnt offering, as a food offering to me. The odour of this offering pleases me.

26 "Take the breast of this ram and dedicate it to me as a special gift. This part of the animal will be yours.

27 "When a priest is ordained, the breast and the thigh of the ram being used for the ordination are to be dedicated to me as a special gift and set aside for the priests.

See also: 29.18: Eph 5.2; Phil 4.18

28 It is my unchanging decision that when my people make their fellowship offerings, the breast and the thigh of the animal belong to the priests. This is the people's gift to me, the LORD. 29 "Aaron's priestly garments are to be handed on to his sons after his death, for them to wear when they are ordained. 30 The son of Aaron who succeeds him as priest and who goes into the Tent of my presence to serve in the Holy Place is to wear these garments for seven days.

31 "Take the meat of the ram used for the ordination of Aaron and his sons and boil it in a holy place. 32 At the entrance of the Tent of my presence they are to eat it along with the bread left in the basket. 33 They shall eat what was used in the ritual of forgiveness at their ordination. Only priests may eat this food, because it is sacred. 34 If some of the meat or some of the bread is not eaten by morning, it is to be burnt; it is not to be eaten, for it is sacred.

35 "Perform the rites of ordination for Aaron and his sons for seven days exactly as I have commanded you. 36 Each day you must offer a bull as a sacrifice, so that sin may be forgiven. This will purify the altar. Then anoint it with olive oil to make it holy. 37 Do this every day for seven days. Then the altar will be completely holy, and anyone or anything that touches it will be harmed by the power of its holiness.*

The Daily Offerings
(Num 28.1–8)

38 "Every day for all time to come, sacrifice on the altar two one-year-old lambs. 39 Sacrifice one of the lambs in the morning and the other in the evening. 40 With the first lamb offer one kilogramme of fine wheat flour mixed with one litre of pure olive oil. Pour out one litre of wine as an offering. 41 Sacrifice the second lamb in the evening, and offer with it the same amounts of flour, olive oil, and wine as in the morning. This is a food offering to me, the LORD, and its odour pleases me. 42 For *all time to come, this burnt* offering is to be offered in my presence at the entrance of the Tent of my presence. That is where I will

meet my people and speak to you. 43 There I will meet the people of Israel, and the dazzling light of my presence will make the place holy. 44 I will make the Tent and the altar holy, and I will set Aaron and his sons apart to serve me as priests. 45 I will live among the people of Israel, and I will be their God. 46 They will know that I am the LORD their God who brought them out of Egypt so that I could live among them. I am the LORD their God.

The Altar for Burning Incense
(Ex 37.25–28)

30 "Make an altar out of acacia wood, for burning incense. 2 It is to be square, 45 centimetres long and 45 centimetres wide, and it is to be 90 centimetres high. Its projections at the four corners are to form one piece with it. 3 Cover its top, all four sides, and its projections with pure gold, and put a gold border round it. 4 Make two gold carrying rings for it and attach them below the border on two sides to hold the poles with which it is to be carried. 5 Make these poles of acacia wood and cover them with gold. 6 Put this altar outside the curtain which hangs in front of the Covenant Box. That is the place where I will meet you. 7 Every morning when Aaron comes to get the lamps ready, he is to burn sweet-smelling incense on it. 8 He must do the same when he lights the lamps in the evening. This offering of incense is to continue without interruption for all time to come. 9 Do not offer on this altar any forbidden incense, any animal-offering, or any grain offering, and do not pour out any wine offering on it. 10 Once a year Aaron is to perform the ritual for purifying the altar by putting on its four projections the blood of the animal sacrificed for sin. This is to be done every year for all time to come. This altar is to be completely holy, dedicated to me, the LORD."

The Tax for the Tent of the LORD's Presence

11 The LORD said to Moses, 12 "When you take a census of the people of Israel, each man is to pay me a price for his life, so that no disaster will come on him while the census is being taken. 13 Everyone included in

---

29.37 BE HARMED BY THE POWER OF ITS HOLINESS: *It was believed that ordinary people or things would be harmed by touching something holy.*

See also: 30.13: Ex 38.25–26; Mt 17.24

the census must pay the required amount of money, weighed according to the official standard. Everyone must pay this as an offering to me. 14 Everyone being counted in the census, that is, every man twenty years old or older, is to pay me this amount. 15 The rich man is not to pay more, nor the poor man less, when they pay this amount for their lives. 16 Collect this money from the people of Israel and spend it for the upkeep of the Tent of my presence. This tax will be the payment for their lives, and I will remember to protect them."

The Bronze Basin

17 The LORD said to Moses, 18 "Make a bronze basin with a bronze base. Place it between the Tent and the altar, and put water in it. 19 Aaron and his sons are to use the water to wash their hands and feet 20 before they go into the Tent or approach the altar to offer the food offering. Then they will not be killed. 21 They must wash their hands and feet, so that they will not die. This is a rule which they and their descendants are to observe for ever."

The Anointing Oil

22 The LORD said to Moses, 23 "Take the finest spices — 6 kilogrammes of liquid myrrh, 3 kilogrammes of sweet-smelling cinnamon, 3 kilogrammes of sweet-smelling cane, 24 and 6 kilogrammes of cassia (all weighed according to the official standard). Add 4 litres of olive oil, 25 and make a sacred anointing oil, mixed like perfume. 26 Use it to anoint the Tent of my presence, the Covenant Box, 27 the table and all its equipment, the lampstand and its equipment, the altar for burning incense, 28 the altar for burning offerings, together with all its equipment, and the washbasin with its base. 29 Dedicate these things in this way, and they will be completely holy, and anyone or anything that touches them will be harmed by the power of their holiness.* 30 Then anoint Aaron and his sons, and ordain them as priests in my service. 31 Say to the people of Israel, 'This holy anointing oil is to be used in my service for all time to come. 32 It must not be poured on ordinary men, and you must not use the same formula to make any

mixture like it. It is holy, and you must treat it as holy. 33 Whoever makes any like it or uses any of it on anyone who is not a priest will no longer be considered one of my people.' "

The Incense

34 The LORD said to Moses, "Take an equal part of each of the following sweet spices — stacte, onycha, galbanum, and pure frankincense. 35 Use them to make incense, mixed like perfume. Add salt to keep it pure and holy. 36 Beat part of it into a fine powder, take it into the Tent of my presence, and sprinkle it in front of the Covenant Box. Treat this incense as completely holy. 37 Do not use the same formula to make any incense like it for yourselves. Treat it as a holy thing dedicated to me. 38 If anyone makes any like it for use as perfume, he will no longer be considered one of my people."

Workers to make the Tent of the LORD's Presence
(Ex 35.30—36.1)

31 The LORD said to Moses, 2 "I have chosen Bezalel, the son of Uri and grandson of Hur, from the tribe of Judah, 3 and I have filled him with my power.* I have given him understanding, skill, and ability for every kind of artistic work — 4 for planning skilful designs and working them in gold, silver, and bronze; 5 for cutting jewels to be set; for carving wood; and for every other kind of artistic work. 6 I have also selected Oholiab son of Ahisamach, from the tribe of Dan, to work with him. I have also given great ability to all the other skilled workers, so that they can make everything I have commanded to be made: 7 the Tent of my presence, the Covenant Box and its lid, all the furnishings of the Tent, 8 the table and its equipment, the lampstand of pure gold and all its equipment, the altar for burning incense, 9 the altar for burnt offerings and all its equipment, the washbasin and its base, 10 the magnificent priestly garments for Aaron and his sons to use when they serve as priests, 11 the anointing oil, and the sweet-smelling incense for the Holy Place. In making all these things, they are to do exactly as I have commanded you."

30.29 HARMED BY THE POWER OF ITS HOLINESS: See 29.37.

See also: 30.18: Ex 38.8   **30.22–38:** Ex 37.29

31.3 power; or spirit.

Sabbath, the Day of Rest

12 The LORD commanded Moses 13 to say to the people of Israel, "Keep the Sabbath, my day of rest, because it is a sign between you and me for all time to come, to show that I, the LORD, have made you my own people. 14 You must keep the day of rest, because it is sacred. Whoever does not keep it, but works on that day, is to be put to death. 15 You have six days in which to do your work, but the seventh day is a solemn day of rest dedicated to me. Whoever does any work on that day is to be put to death. 16 The people of Israel are to keep this day as a sign of the covenant. 17 It is a permanent sign between the people of Israel and me, because I, the LORD, made heaven and earth in six days, and on the seventh day I stopped working and rested."

18 When God had finished speaking to Moses on Mount Sinai, he gave him the two stone tablets on which God himself had written the commandments.

The Gold Bull Calf

(Deut 9.6–29)

32 When the people saw that Moses had not come down from the mountain but was staying there a long time, they gathered round Aaron and said to him, "We do not know what has happened to this man Moses, who led us out of Egypt; so make us a god* to lead us."

2 Aaron said to them, "Take off the gold earrings which your wives, your sons, and your daughters are wearing, and bring them to me." 3 So all the people took off their gold earrings and brought them to Aaron. 4 He took the earrings, melted them, poured the gold into a mould, and made a gold bull calf.

The people said, "Israel, this is our god, who led us out of Egypt!"

5 Then Aaron built an altar in front of the gold bull calf and announced, "Tomorrow there will be a festival to honour the LORD." 6 Early the next morning they brought some animals to burn as sacrifices and others to eat as fellowship offerings. The people sat

down to a feast, which turned into an orgy of drinking and sex.

7 The LORD said to Moses, "Go back down at once, because your people, whom you led out of Egypt, have sinned and rejected me. 8 They have already left the way that I commanded them to follow; they have made a bull calf out of melted gold and have worshipped it and offered sacrifices to it. They are saying that this is their god, who led them out of Egypt. 9 I know how stubborn these people are. 10 Now, don't try to stop me. I am angry with them, and I am going to destroy them. Then I will make you and your descendants into a great nation."

11 But Moses pleaded with the LORD his God and said, "LORD, why should you be so angry with your people, whom you rescued from Egypt with great might and power? 12 Why should the Egyptians be able to say that you led your people out of Egypt, planning to kill them in the mountains and destroy them completely? Stop being angry; change your mind and do not bring this disaster on your people. 13 Remember your servants Abraham, Isaac, and Jacob. Remember the solemn promise you made to them to give them as many descendants as there are stars in the sky and to give their descendants all that land you promised would be their possession for ever." 14 So the LORD changed his mind and did not bring on his people the disaster he had threatened.

15 Moses went back down the mountain, carrying the two stone tablets with the commandments written on both sides. 16 God himself had made the tablets and had engraved the commandments on them.

17 Joshua heard the people shouting and said to Moses, "I hear the sound of battle in the camp."

18 Moses said, "That doesn't sound like a shout of victory or a cry of defeat; it's the sound of singing."

19 When Moses came close enough to the camp to see the bull calf and to see the people dancing, he was furious. There at the foot of the mountain, he threw down the tablets he was carrying and broke them. 20 He took the bull calf which they had made, melted it, ground it into fine

---

32.1 *a god; or* some gods.

See also: **31.15:** Ex 20.8–11, 23.12, 34.21, 35.2; Lev 23.3; Deut 5.12–14　**31.17:** Ex 20.11
32.1: Acts 7.40　**32.4:** 1 Kgs 12.28; Acts 7.41
32.6: 1 Cor 10.7

See also: **32.11–14:** Num 14.13–19
32.13: Gen 22.16–17, 17.8

powder, and mixed it with water. Then he made the people of Israel drink it. 21 He said to Aaron, "What did these people do to you, that you have made them commit such a terrible sin?"

22 Aaron answered, "Don't be angry with me; you know how determined these people are to do evil. 23 They said to me, 'We don't know what has happened to this man Moses, who brought us out of Egypt; so make us a god to lead us.' 24 I asked them to bring me their gold ornaments, and those who had any took them off and gave them to me. I threw the ornaments into the fire and out came this bull calf!"

25 Moses saw that Aaron had let the people get out of control and make fools of themselves in front of their enemies. 26 So he stood at the gate of the camp and shouted, "Everyone who is on the LORD's side come over here!" So all the Levites gathered round him, 27 and he said to them, "The LORD God of Israel commands every one of you to put on his sword and go through the camp from this gate to the other and kill his brothers, his friends, and his neighbours." 28 The Levites obeyed, and killed about three thousand men that day. 29 Moses said to the Levites, "Today you have consecrated yourselves* as priests in the service of the LORD by killing your sons and brothers, so the LORD has given you his blessing."

30 The next day Moses said to the people, "You have committed a terrible sin. But now I will again go up the mountain to the LORD; perhaps I can obtain forgiveness for your sin." 31 Moses then returned to the LORD and said, "These people have committed a terrible sin. They have made a god out of gold and worshipped it. 32 Please forgive their sin; but if you won't, then remove my name from the book in which you have written the names of your people."

33 The LORD answered, "It is those who have sinned against me whose names I will remove from my book. 34 Now go, lead the people to the place I told you about. Remember that my angel will guide you, but the time is coming when I will punish these people for their sin."

35 So the LORD sent a disease on the people, because they had caused Aaron to make the gold bull calf.

The LORD Orders Israel to Leave Mount Sinai

33 The LORD said to Moses, "Leave this place, you and the people you brought out of Egypt, and go to the land that I promised to give to Abraham, Isaac, and Jacob and to their descendants. 2 I will send an angel to guide you, and I will drive out the Canaanites, the Amorites, the Hittites, the Perizzites, the Hivites, and the Jebusites. 3 You are going to a rich and fertile land. But I will not go with you myself, because you are a stubborn people, and I might destroy you on the way."

4 When the people heard this, they began to mourn and did not wear jewellery any more. 5 For the LORD had commanded Moses to say to them, "You are a stubborn people. If I were to go with you even for a moment, I would completely destroy you. Now take off your jewellery, and I will decide what to do with you." 6 So after they left Mount Sinai, the people of Israel no longer wore jewellery.

The Tent of the LORD's Presence

7 Whenever the people of Israel set up camp, Moses would take the sacred Tent and put it up some distance away from the camp. It was called the Tent of the LORD's presence, and anyone who wanted to consult the LORD would go out to it. 8 Whenever Moses went out there, the people would stand at the door of their tents and watch Moses until he entered it. 9 After Moses had gone in, the pillar of cloud would come down and stay at the door of the Tent, and the LORD would speak to Moses from the cloud. 10 As soon as the people saw the pillar of cloud at the door of the Tent, they would bow down.

They would bow down (33.10)

32.29 *Some ancient translations* Today you have consecrated yourselves; *Hebrew* Consecrate yourselves today; *or* You have been consecrated today.

See also: 32.32: Ps 69.28; Rev 3.5

See also: 33.1: Gen 12.7, 26.3, 28.13

11 The LORD would speak with Moses face to face, just as someone speaks with a friend. Then Moses would return to the camp. But the young man who was his helper, Joshua son of Nun, stayed in the Tent.

The LORD Promises to be with his People

12 Moses said to the LORD, "It is true that you have told me to lead these people to that land, but you did not tell me whom you would send with me. You have said that you know me well and are pleased with me. 13 Now if you are, tell me your plans, so that I may serve you and continue to please you. Remember also that you have chosen this nation to be your own."

14 The LORD said, "I will go with you, and I will give you victory."

15 Moses replied, "If you do not go with us, don't make us leave this place. 16 How will anyone know that you are pleased with your people and with me if you do not go with us? Your presence with us will distinguish us from any other people on earth."

17 The LORD said to Moses, "I will do just as you have asked, because I know you very well and I am pleased with you."

18 Then Moses requested, "Please, let me see the dazzling light of your presence."

19 The LORD answered, "I will make all my splendour pass before you and in your presence I will pronounce my sacred name. I am the LORD, and I show compassion and pity on those I choose. 20 I will not let you see my face, because no one can see me and stay alive, 21 but here is a place beside me where you can stand on a rock. 22 When the dazzling light of my presence passes by, I will put you in an opening in the rock and cover you with my hand until I have passed by. 23 Then I will take my hand away, and you will see my back but not my face."

The Second Set of Stone Tablets
(Deut 10.1–5)

34 The LORD said to Moses, "Cut two stone tablets like the first ones, *and I will write on them the words* that were on the first tablets, which you broke. 2 Be ready tomorrow morning, and come up Mount Sinai to meet me there at the top. 3 No one is to come up with you; no one is

See also: **33.19:** Rom 9.15

to be seen on any part of the mountain; and no sheep or cattle are to graze at the foot of the mountain." 4 So Moses cut two more stone tablets, and early the next morning he carried them up Mount Sinai, just as the LORD had commanded.

5 The LORD came down in a cloud, stood with him there, and pronounced his holy name, the LORD.* 6 The LORD then passed in front of him and called out, "I, the LORD, am a God who is full of compassion and pity, who is not easily angered and who shows great love and faithfulness. 7 I keep my promise for thousands of generations* and forgive evil and sin; but I will not fail to punish children and grandchildren to the third and fourth generation for the sins of their parents."

8 Moses quickly bowed down to the ground and worshipped. 9 He said, "Lord, if you really are pleased with me, I ask you to go with us. These people are stubborn, but forgive our evil and our sin, and accept us as your own people."

The Covenant is Renewed
(Ex 23.14–19; Deut 7.1–5; 16.1–17)

10 The LORD said to Moses, "I now make a covenant with the people of Israel. In their presence I will do great things such as have never been done anywhere on earth among any of the nations. All the people will see what great things I, the LORD, can do, because I am going to do an awesome thing for you. 11 Obey the laws that I am giving you today. I will drive out the Amorites, the Canaanites, the Hittites, the Perizzites, the Hivites, and the Jebusites, as you advance. 12 Do not make any treaties with the people of the country into which you are going, because this could be a fatal trap for you. 13 Instead, tear down their altars, destroy their sacred pillars, and cut down the symbols of their goddess Asherah.

14 "Do not worship any other god, because I, the LORD, tolerate no rivals. 15 Do not make any treaties with the people of the country, because when they worship their pagan gods and sacrifice to them, they will invite you to join *them, and*

34.5 THE LORD: *See 3.14.*
34.7 thousands of generations; *or* thousands.
See also: **34.6–7:** Ex 20.5–6; Num 14.18; Deut 5.9–10, 7.9–10 **34.13:** Deut 16.21

you will be tempted to eat the food they offer to their gods. 16 Your sons might marry those foreign women, who would lead them to be unfaithful to me and to worship their pagan gods.

17 "Do not make and worship gods of metal.

18 "Keep the Festival of Unleavened Bread. As I have commanded you, eat unleavened bread for seven days in the month of Abib, because it was in that month that you left Egypt.

19 "Every firstborn son and firstborn male domestic animal belongs to me, 20 but you are to buy back every firstborn donkey by offering a lamb in its place. If you do not buy it back, break its neck. Buy back every firstborn son.

"No one is to appear before me without an offering.

21 "You have six days in which to do your work, but do not work on the seventh day, not even during ploughing time or harvest.

22 "Keep the Harvest Festival when you begin to harvest the first crop of your wheat, and keep the Festival of Shelters in the autumn when you gather your fruit.

23 "Three times a year all your men must come to worship me, the LORD, the God of Israel. 24 After I have driven out the nations before you and extended your territory, no one will try to conquer your country during the three festivals.

25 "Do not offer bread made with yeast when you sacrifice an animal to me. Do not keep until the following morning any part of the animal killed at the Passover Festival.

26 "Each year bring to the house of the LORD the first corn that you harvest.

"Do not cook a young sheep or goat in its mother's milk."

27 The LORD said to Moses, "Write these words down, because it is on the basis of these words that I am making a covenant with you and with Israel." 28 Moses stayed there with the LORD 40 days and nights,

eating and drinking nothing. He wrote on the tablets the words of the covenant — the Ten Commandments.

Moses Goes Down from Mount Sinai

29 When Moses went down from Mount Sinai carrying the Ten Commandments, his face was shining because he had been speaking with the LORD; but he did not know it. 30 Aaron and all the people looked at Moses and saw that his face was shining, and they were afraid to go near him. 31 But Moses called them, and Aaron and all the leaders of the community went to him, and Moses spoke to them. 32 After that, all the people of Israel gathered round him, and Moses gave them all the laws that the LORD had given him on Mount Sinai. 33 When Moses had finished speaking to them, he covered his face with a veil. 34 Whenever Moses went into the Tent of the LORD's presence to speak to the LORD, he took the veil off. When he came out, he would tell the people of Israel everything that he had been commanded to say, 35 and they would see that his face was shining. Then he would put the veil back on until the next time he went to speak to the LORD.

Regulations for the Sabbath

35 Moses called together the whole community of the people of Israel and said to them, "This is what the LORD has commanded you to do: 2 You have six days in which to do your work, but the seventh day is to be sacred, a solemn day of rest dedicated to me, the LORD. Anyone who does any work on that day is to be put to death. 3 Do not even light a fire in your homes on the Sabbath."

Offerings for the Sacred Tent
(Ex 25.1–9)

4 Moses said to all the people of Israel, "This is what the LORD has commanded: 5 Make an offering to the LORD. Everyone who wishes to do so is to bring an offering of gold, silver, or bronze; 6 fine linen; blue, purple, and red wool; cloth made of

See also: 34.17: Ex 20.4; Lev 19.4; Deut 5.8, 27.15
34.18: Ex 12.14–20; Lev 23.6–8; Num 28.16–25
34.19: Ex 13.2   34.20: Ex 13.13
34.21: Ex 20.9–10, 23.12, 31.15, 35.2; Lev 23.3;
Deut 5.13–14   34.22: Lev 23.15–21, 39.43;
Num 28.26–31   34.25: Ex 12.10
34.26: Deut 24.21, 26.2

See also: 34.29–35: 2 Cor 3.7–16
35.2: Ex 20.8–11, 23.12, 31.15, 34.21; Lev 23.3;
Deut 5.12–14

goats' hair; 7 rams' skin dyed red; fine leather; acacia wood; 8 oil for the lamps; spices for the anointing oil and for the sweet-smelling incense; 9 carnelians and other jewels to be set in the High Priest's ephod and in his breastpiece.

Articles for the Tent of the LORD's Presence
(Ex 39.32–43)

10 "All the skilled workers among you are to come and make everything that the LORD commanded: 11 the Tent, its covering and its outer covering, its hooks and its frames, its crossbars, its posts, and its bases; 12 the Covenant Box, its poles, its lid, and the curtain to screen it off; 13 the table, its poles, and all its equipment; the bread offered to God; 14 the lampstand for the light and its equipment; the lamps with their oil; 15 the altar for burning incense and its poles; the anointing oil; the sweet-smelling incense; the curtain for the entrance of the Tent; 16 the altar on which to burn offerings, with its bronze grating attached, its poles, and all its equipment; the washbasin and its base; 17 the curtains for the enclosure, its posts and bases; the curtain for the entrance of the enclosure; 18 the pegs and ropes for the Tent and the enclosure; 19 and the magnificent garments the priests are to wear when they serve in the Holy Place — the sacred clothes for Aaron the priest and for his sons."

The People Bring their Offerings

20 All the people of Israel left, 21 and everyone who wished to do so brought an offering to the LORD for making the Tent of the LORD's presence. They brought everything needed for use in worship and for making the priestly garments. 22 All who wanted to, both men and women, brought decorative pins, earrings, rings, necklaces, and all kinds of gold jewellery and dedicated them to the LORD. 23 Everyone who had fine linen; blue, purple, or red wool; cloth of goats' hair; rams' skin dyed red; or fine leather, brought it. 24 All who were able to contribute silver or bronze brought their offering for the LORD, and all who had acacia wood which could be used for any of the work brought it. 25 All the skilled women brought fine linen thread and thread of blue, purple,

and red wool, which they had made. 26 They also made thread of goats' hair. 27 The leaders brought carnelians and other jewels to be set in the ephod and the breastpiece 28 and spices and oil for the lamps, for the anointing oil, and for the sweet-smelling incense. 29 All the people of Israel who wanted to brought their offering to the LORD for the work which he had commanded Moses to do.

Workers to Make the Tent of the LORD's Presence
(Ex 31.1–11)

30 Moses said to the Israelites, "The LORD has chosen Bezalel, the son of Uri and grandson of Hur, from the tribe of Judah. 31 God has filled him with his power* and given him skill, ability, and understanding for every kind of artistic work, 32 for planning skilful designs and working them in gold, silver and bronze; 33 for cutting jewels to be set; for carving wood; and for every other kind of artistic work. 34 The LORD has given to him and to Oholiab son of Ahisamach, from the tribe of Dan, the ability to teach their crafts to others. 35 He has given them skill in all kinds of work done by engravers, designers, and weavers of fine linen; blue, purple, and red wool; and other cloth. They are able to do all kinds of work and are skilful designers.

36 "Bezalel, Oholiab, and all the other workers to whom the LORD has given skill and understanding, who know how to make everything needed to build the sacred Tent, are to make everything just as the LORD has commanded."

The People Bring Many Gifts

2 Moses called Bezalel, Oholiab, and all the other skilled men to whom the LORD had given ability and who were willing to help, and Moses told them to start working. 3 They received from him all the offerings which the Israelites had brought for constructing the sacred Tent. But the people of Israel continued to bring Moses their offerings every morning. 4 Then the skilled men who were doing the work went 5 and reported to Moses, "The people are bringing more than is needed for the work which the LORD commanded to be done."

35.31 power; or spirit.

6 So Moses sent a command throughout the camp that no one was to make any further contribution for the sacred Tent; so the people did not bring any more. 7 What had already been brought was more than enough to finish all the work.

Making the Tent of the LORD's Presence
(Ex 26.1–37)

8 The most skilled men among those doing the work made the Tent of the LORD's presence. They made it out of ten pieces of fine linen woven with blue, purple, and red wool and embroidered with figures of winged creatures. 9 Each piece was the same size, 12 metres long and 2 metres wide. 10 They sewed five of them together in one set and did the same with the other five. 11 They made loops of blue cloth on the edge of the outside piece in each set. 12 They put 50 loops on the first piece of the first set and 50 loops matching them on the last piece of the second set. 13 They made 50 gold hooks, with which to join the two sets into one piece.

14 Then they made a cover for the Tent out of eleven pieces of cloth made of goats' hair. 15 They made them all the same size, 13 metres long and 2 metres wide. 16 They sewed five of them together in one set and the other six in another set. 17 They put 50 loops on the edge of the last piece of one set and 50 loops on the edge of the other set. 18 They made 50 bronze hooks to join the two sets, so as to form one cover. 19 They made two more coverings, one of rams' skin dyed red and the other of fine leather, to serve as an outer cover.

20 They made upright frames of acacia wood for the Tent. 21 Each frame was 4 metres tall and 66 centimetres wide, 22 with two matching projections, so that the frames could be joined together. All the frames had these projections. 23 They made twenty frames for the south side 24 and 40 silver bases to go under them, two bases under each frame to hold its two projections. 25 They made twenty frames for the north side of the Tent 26 and 40 silver bases, two under each frame. 27 For the back of the Tent, on the west, they made six frames 28 and two frames for the corners. 29 These corner frames were joined at the bottom and connected all the way to the top. The two frames that formed the two corners were made in this way. 30 So there were eight frames and sixteen silver bases, two under each frame.

31 They made fifteen crossbars of acacia wood, five for the frames on one side of the Tent, 32 five for the frames on the other side, and five for the frames on the west end, at the back. 33 The middle crossbar, set halfway up the frames, extended from one end of the Tent to the other. 34 They covered the frames with gold and fitted them with gold rings to hold the crossbars, which were also covered with gold.

35 They made a curtain of fine linen, woven with blue, purple, and red wool and embroidered it with figures of winged creatures. 36 They made four posts of acacia wood to hold the curtain, covered them with gold, and fitted them with gold hooks. Then they made four silver bases to hold the posts. 37 For the entrance of the Tent they made a curtain of fine linen woven with blue, purple, and red wool and decorated with embroidery. 38 For this curtain they made five posts fitted with hooks, covered their tops and their rods with gold, and made five bronze bases for the posts.

Making the Covenant Box
(Ex 25.10–22)

37 Bezalel made the Covenant Box out of acacia wood, 110 centimetres long, 66 centimetres wide, and 66 centimetres high. 2 He covered it with pure gold inside and out and put a gold border all round it. 3 He made four carrying rings of gold for it and attached them to its four feet, with two rings on each side. 4 He made carrying poles of acacia wood, covered them with gold, 5 and put them through the rings on each side of the box. 6 He made a lid of pure gold, 110 centimetres long and 66 centimetres wide. 7 He made two winged creatures of hammered gold, 8 one for each end of the lid. He made them so that they formed one piece with the lid. 9 The winged creatures faced each other across the lid, and their outspread wings covered it.

Making the Table for the Bread Offered to God
(Ex 25.23–30)

10 He made the table out of acacia wood, 88 centimetres long, 44 centimetres wide, and 66 centimetres high. 11 He covered it with pure gold and put a gold border round it. 12 He made a rim 75 millimetres wide round it and put a gold border round the rim. 13 He made four carrying rings of gold for it and put them at the four corners, where the legs were. 14 The rings to hold the poles for carrying the table were placed near the rim. 15 He made the poles of acacia wood and covered them with gold. 16 He made the dishes of pure gold for the table: the plates, the cups, the jars, and the bowls to be used for the wine offering.

Making the Lampstand
(Ex 25.31–40)

17 He made the lampstand of pure gold. He made its base and its shaft of hammered gold; its decorative flowers, including buds and petals, formed one piece with it.

18 Six branches extended from its sides, three from each side. 19 Each of the six branches had three decorative flowers shaped like almond blossoms with buds and petals. 20 The shaft of the lampstand had four decorative flowers shaped like almond blossoms with buds and petals. 21 There was one bud below each of the three pairs of branches. 22 The buds, the branches, and the lampstand were a single piece of pure hammered gold. 23 He made seven lamps for the lampstand, and he made its tongs and trays of pure gold. 24 He used 35 kilogrammes of pure gold to make the lampstand and all its equipment.

Making the Altar for Burning Incense
(Ex 30.1–5)

25 He made an altar out of acacia wood, for burning incense. It was square, 45 centimetres long and 45 centimetres wide, and it was *90 centimetres high. Its projec*tions at the four corners formed one piece with it. 26 He covered its top, all four sides, and its projections with pure gold and put a gold border round it. 27 He made two gold carrying rings for it and attached them below the border on the two sides,

to hold the poles with which it was to be carried. 28 He made the poles of acacia wood and covered them with gold.

Making the Anointing Oil and the Incense
(Ex 30.22–38)

29 He also made the sacred anointing oil and the pure sweet-smelling incense, mixed like perfume.

Making the Altar for Burning Offerings
(Ex 27.1–8)

38 For burning offerings, he made an altar out of acacia wood. It was square, 2.2 metres long and 2.2 metres wide, and it was 1.3 metres high. 2 He made the projections at the top of the four corners, so that they formed one piece with the altar. He covered it all with bronze. 3 He also made all the equipment for the altar: the pans, the shovels, the bowls, the hooks, and the firepans. All this equipment was made of bronze. 4 He made a bronze grating and put it under the rim of the altar, so that it reached halfway up the altar. 5 He made four carrying rings and put them on the four corners. 6 He made carrying poles of acacia wood, covered them with bronze, 7 and put them in the rings on each side of the altar. The altar was made of boards and was hollow.

Making the Bronze Basin
(Ex 30.18)

8 He made the bronze basin and its bronze base out of the mirrors belonging to the women who served at the entrance of the Tent of the LORD's presence.

The Enclosure for the Tent of the LORD's Presence
(Ex 27.9–19)

9 For the Tent of the LORD's presence he made the enclosure out of fine linen curtains. On the south side the curtains were 44 metres long, 10 supported by twenty bronze posts in twenty bronze bases, with hooks and rods made of silver. 11 The enclosure was the same on the north side. 12 On the west side there were curtains 22 metres long, with ten posts and ten bases

See also: 37.29: Ex 30.22–38

and with hooks and rods made of silver.
13 On the east side, where the entrance
was, the enclosure was also 22 metres
wide. 14–15 On each side of the entrance
there were 6.6 metres of curtains, with
three posts and three bases. 16 All the curtains round the enclosure were made of
fine linen. 17 The bases for the posts were
made of bronze, and the hooks, the rods,
and the covering of the tops of the posts
were made of silver. All the posts round the
enclosure were connected with silver rods.
18 The curtain for the entrance of the
enclosure was made of fine linen woven
with blue, purple, and red wool and decorated with embroidery. It was 9 metres
long and 2 metres high, like the curtains of
the enclosure. 19 It was supported by four
posts in four bronze bases. Their hooks,
the covering of their tops, and their rods
were made of silver. 20 All the pegs for the
Tent and for the surrounding enclosure
were made of bronze.

Metals Used in the Tent of the Lord's Presence

21 Here is a list of the amounts of the
metals used in the Tent of the Lord's presence, where the two stone tablets were
kept on which the Ten Commandments
were written. The list was ordered by
Moses and made by the Levites who
worked under the direction of Ithamar son
of Aaron the priest.

22 Bezalel, the son of Uri and grandson of
Hur, from the tribe of Judah, made everything that the Lord had commanded.
23 His helper, Oholiab son of Ahisamach,
from the tribe of Dan, was an engraver,
a designer, and a weaver of fine linen and
of blue, purple, and red wool.

24 All the gold that had been dedicated
to the Lord for the sacred Tent weighed a
thousand kilogrammes, weighed according to the official standard. 25 The silver
from the census of the community
weighed 3,430 kilogrammes, weighed
according to the official standard. 26 This
amount equalled the total paid by all per-
sons enrolled in the census, each one paying the required amount, weighed
according to the official standard. There
were 603,550 men twenty years old or

older enrolled in the census. 27 Of the silver, 3,400 kilogrammes were used to
make the hundred bases for the sacred
Tent and for the curtain, 34 kilogrammes
for each base. 28 With the remaining 30
kilogrammes of silver Bezalel made the
rods, the hooks for the posts, and the covering for their tops. 29 The bronze which
was dedicated to the Lord amounted to
2,425 kilogrammes. 30 With it he made the
bases for the entrance of the Tent of the
Lord's presence, the bronze altar with its
bronze grating, all the equipment for the
altar, 31 the bases for the surrounding
enclosure and for the entrance of the
enclosure, and all the pegs for the Tent and
the surrounding enclosure.

Making the Garments for the Priests
(Ex 28.1–14)

39 With the blue, purple, and red
wool they made the magnificent
garments which the priests were to wear
when they served in the Holy Place. They
made the priestly garments for Aaron,
as the Lord had commanded Moses.

2 They made the ephod of fine linen;
blue, purple, and red wool; and gold
thread. 3 They hammered out sheets of
gold and cut them into thin strips to be
worked into the fine linen and into the
blue, purple, and red wool. 4 They made
two shoulder straps for the ephod and
attached them to its sides, so that it
could be fastened. 5 The finely woven
belt, made of the same materials, was
attached to the ephod so as to form one
piece with it, as the Lord had commanded Moses. 6 They prepared the carnelians and mounted them in gold
settings; they were skilfully engraved
with the names of the twelve sons of
Jacob. 7 They put them on the shoulder
straps of the ephod to represent the
twelve tribes of Israel, just as the Lord
had commanded Moses.

Making the Breastpiece
(Ex 28.15–30)

8 They made the breastpiece of the
same materials as the ephod and with
similar embroidery. 9 It was square and
folded double, 22 centimetres long and
22 centimetres wide. 10 They mounted

four rows of precious stones on it: in the first row they mounted a ruby, a topaz, and a garnet; 11 in the second row, an emerald, a sapphire, and a diamond; 12 in the third row, a turquoise, an agate, and an amethyst; 13 and in the fourth row, a beryl, a carnelian, and a jasper. These were mounted in gold settings. 14 Each of the twelve stones had engraved on it the name of one of the sons of Jacob, in order to represent the twelve tribes of Israel. 15 For the breastpiece they made chains of pure gold, twisted like cords. 16 They made two gold settings and two gold rings and attached the two rings to the upper corners of the breastpiece. 17 They fastened the two gold cords to the two rings 18 and fastened the other two ends of the cords to the two settings and in this way attached them in front to the shoulder straps of the ephod. 19 They made two rings of gold and attached them to the lower corners of the breastpiece, on the inside edge next to the ephod. 20 They made two more gold rings and attached them to the lower part of the front of the two shoulder straps of the ephod, near the seam and above the finely woven belt. 21 Just as the Lord had commanded Moses, they tied the rings of the breastpiece to the rings of the ephod with a blue cord, so that the breastpiece rested above the belt and did not come loose.

Making the Other Priestly Garments

(Ex 28.31–43)

22 The robe that goes under the ephod was made entirely of blue wool. 23 The hole for the head was reinforced with a woven binding to keep it from tearing. 24–26 All round its lower hem they put pomegranates of fine linen and of blue, purple, and red wool, alternating with bells of pure gold, just as the Lord had commanded Moses.

27 They made the shirts for Aaron and his sons, 28 and the turban, the caps, the linen shorts, 29 and the sash of fine linen and of blue, purple, and red wool, decorated with embroidery, as the Lord had commanded Moses. 30 They made the ornament, the sacred sign of dedication,

out of pure gold, and they engraved on it "Dedicated to the Lord". 31 They tied it to the front of the turban with a blue cord, just as the Lord had commanded Moses.

The Completion of the Work

(Ex 35.10–19)

32 All the work on the Tent of the Lord's presence was finally completed. The Israelites made everything just as the Lord had commanded Moses. 33 They brought to Moses the Tent and all its equipment, its hooks, its frames, its crossbars, its posts, and its bases; 34 the covering of rams' skin dyed red; the covering of fine leather; the curtain; 35 the Covenant Box containing the stone tablets, its poles, and its lid; 36 the table and all its equipment, and the bread offered to God; 37 the lampstand of pure gold, its lamps, all its equipment, and the oil for the lamps; 38 the gold altar; the anointing oil; the sweet-smelling incense; the curtain for the entrance of the Tent; 39 the bronze altar with its bronze grating, its poles, and all its equipment; the washbasin and its base; 40 the curtains for the enclosure and its posts and bases; the curtain for the entrance of the enclosure and its ropes; the pegs for the Tent; all the equipment to be used in the Tent; 41 and the magnificent garments the priests were to wear in the Holy Place — the sacred clothes for Aaron the priest and for his sons. 42 The Israelites had done all the work just as the Lord had commanded Moses. 43 Moses examined everything and saw that they had made it all just as the Lord had commanded. So Moses blessed them.

Setting Up and Dedicating the Tent of the Lord's Presence

40 The Lord said to Moses, 2 "On the first day of the first month set up the Tent of the Lord's presence. 3 Place in it the Covenant Box containing the Ten Commandments and put the curtain in front of it. 4 Bring in the table and place the equipment on it. Also bring in the lampstand and set up the lamps on it. 5 Put the gold altar for burning incense in front of the Covenant Box and hang the curtain at the entrance of the Tent. 6 Put in front of the Tent the altar for burning offerings. 7 Put the washbasin between the Tent and the altar and fill it with water. 8 Put up the surrounding enclosure and hang the curtain at its entrance.

9 "Then dedicate the Tent and all its equipment by anointing it with the sacred oil, and it will be holy. 10 Next, dedicate the altar and all its equipment by anointing it, and it will be completely holy. 11 Also dedicate the washbasin and its base in the same way.

12 "Bring Aaron and his sons to the entrance of the Tent, and tell them to take a ritual bath. 13 Dress Aaron in the priestly garments, anoint him, and in this way consecrate him, so that he can serve me as priest. 14 Bring his sons and put the shirts on them. 15 Then anoint them, just as you anointed their father, so that they can serve me as priests. This anointing will make them priests for all time to come."

16 Moses did everything just as the LORD had commanded. 17 So on the first day of the first month of the second year after they left Egypt, the Tent of the LORD's presence was set up. 18 Moses put down its bases, set up its frames, attached its crossbars, and put up its posts. 19 He spread out the covering over the Tent and put the outer covering over it, just as the LORD had commanded. 20 Then he took the two stone tablets and put them in the Covenant Box. He put the poles in the rings of the box and put the lid on it. 21 Then he put the box in the Tent and hung up the curtain. In this way he screened off the Covenant Box, just as the LORD had commanded.

22 He put the table in the Tent, on the north side outside the curtain, 23 and placed on it the bread offered to the LORD, just as the LORD had commanded. 24 He put the lampstand in the Tent, on the south side, opposite the table, 25 and there in the LORD's presence he lit the lamps, just as the LORD had commanded. 26 He put the gold altar in the Tent, in front of the curtain, 27 and burnt the sweet-smelling incense, just as the LORD had commanded. 28 He hung the curtain at the entrance of the Tent, 29 and there in front of the curtain he placed the altar for burning offerings. On it he sacrificed the burnt offering and the grain offering, just as the LORD had commanded. 30 He put the washbasin between the Tent and the altar and filled it with water. 31 Moses, Aaron, and his sons washed their hands and their feet there 32 whenever they went into the Tent or to the altar, just as the LORD had commanded. 33 Moses set up the enclosure round the Tent and the altar and hung the curtain at the entrance of the enclosure. So he finished all the work.

The Cloud over the Tent of the LORD's Presence
(Num 9.15–23)

34 Then the cloud covered the Tent and the dazzling light of the LORD's presence filled it. 35 Because of this, Moses could not go into the Tent. 36 The Israelites moved their camp to another place only when the cloud lifted from the Tent. 37 As long as the cloud stayed there, they did not move their camp. 38 During all their wanderings they could see the cloud of the LORD's presence over the Tent during the day and a fire burning above it during the night.

See also: **40.34:** 1 Kgs 8.10–11; Is 6.4; Ezek 43.4–5; Rev 15.8

LEVITICUS

INTRODUCTION

Leviticus contains regulations for worship and religious ceremonies in ancient Israel, and for the priests who were responsible for carrying out these instructions.

The main theme of the book is the holiness of God and the ways in which his people were to worship and live so as to maintain their relationship with him.

The best known words from the book are those which Jesus called the second great commandment: "Love your neighbour as you love yourself." (19.18)

Outline of Contents

Sacrifices Burnt Whole

1 The LORD called to Moses from the Tent of the LORD's presence and gave him the following rules ² for the Israelites to observe when they offer their sacrifices.

When anyone offers an animal sacrifice, it may be one of his cattle or one of his sheep or goats. ³ If he is offering one of his cattle as a burnt offering, he must bring a bull without any defects. He must present it at the entrance of the Tent of the LORD's presence so that the LORD will accept him. ⁴ The man shall put his hand on its head, and it will be accepted as a sacrifice to take away his sins. ⁵ He shall kill the bull there, and the Aaronite priests shall present the blood to the LORD and then throw it against all four sides of the altar which is at the entrance of the Tent. ⁶ Then he shall skin the animal and cut it up, ⁷ and the priests shall arrange firewood on the altar and light it. ⁸ They shall put on the fire the pieces of the animal, including the head and the fat. ⁹ The man must wash the internal organs and the hind legs, and the officiating priest will burn the whole sacrifice on the altar. The smell of this food offering is pleasing to the LORD.

¹⁰ If the man is offering one of his sheep or goats, it must be a male without any defects. ¹¹ He shall kill it on the north side of the altar, and the priests shall throw its blood on all four sides of the altar. ¹² After the man cuts it up, the officiating priest shall put on the fire all the parts, including the head and the fat. ¹³ The man must wash the internal organs and the hind legs, and the priest will present the sacrifice to the LORD and burn all of it on the altar. The smell of this food offering is pleasing to the LORD.

¹⁴ If the man is offering a bird as a burnt offering, it must be a dove or a pigeon. ¹⁵ The priest shall present it at the altar, wring its neck, and burn its head on the altar. Its blood shall be drained out against the side of the altar. ¹⁶ He shall remove the crop and its contents and throw them away on the east side of the altar where the ashes are put. ¹⁷ He shall take hold of its wings and tear its body open, without tearing the wings off, and then burn it whole on the altar. The smell of this food offering is pleasing to the LORD.

Grain Offerings

2 When anyone presents an offering of grain to the LORD, he must first grind it into flour. He must put olive oil and incense on it ² and bring it to the Aaronite priests. The officiating priest shall take a handful of the flour and oil and all of the incense and burn it on the altar as a token that it has all been offered to the LORD. The smell of this food offering is pleasing to the LORD. ³ The rest of the grain offering belongs to the priests; it is very holy, since it is taken from the food offered to the LORD.

4 If the offering is bread baked in an oven, it must be made without yeast. It may be thick loaves made of flour mixed with olive oil or biscuits brushed with olive oil.

5 If the offering is bread cooked on a griddle, it is to be made of flour mixed with olive oil but without yeast. 6 Crumble it up and pour the oil on it when you present it as an offering.

7 If the offering is bread cooked in a pan, it is to be made of flour and olive oil. 8 Bring it as an offering to the LORD and present it to the priest, who will take it to the altar. 9 The priest will take part of it as a token that it has all been offered to the LORD, and he will burn it on the altar. The smell of this food offering is pleasing to the LORD. 10 The rest of the offering belongs to the priests; it is very holy, since it is taken from the food offered to the LORD.

11 None of the grain offerings which you present to the LORD may be made with yeast; you must never use yeast or honey in food offered to the LORD. 12 An offering of the first corn that you harvest each year shall be brought to the LORD, but it is not to be burnt on the altar. 13 Put salt on every grain offering, because salt represents the covenant between you and God. (You must put salt on all your offerings.) 14 When you bring to the LORD an offering of the first corn harvested, offer roasted grain or ground meal. 15 Add olive oil and put incense on it. 16 The priest will burn that part of the meal and oil that is to serve as a token, and also all the incense, as a food offering to the LORD.

Fellowship Offerings

3 When anyone offers one of his cattle as a fellowship offering, it is to be a bull or a cow without any defects. 2 The man shall put his hand on the head of the animal and kill it at the entrance of the Tent of the LORD's presence. The Aaronite priests shall throw the blood against all four sides of the altar 3 and present the following parts of the animal as a food offering to the LORD: all the fat on the internal organs, 4 the kidneys and the fat on them, and the best part of the liver. 5 The priests shall burn all this on the altar along with the burnt offerings. The smell of this food offering is pleasing to the LORD.

6 If a sheep or goat is used as a fellowship offering, it may be male or female, but it must be without any defects. 7 If a man offers a sheep, 8 he shall put his hand on its head and kill it in front of the Tent. The priests shall throw its blood against all four sides of the altar 9 and present the following parts of the animal as a food offering to the LORD: the fat, the entire fat tail cut off near the backbone, all the fat covering the internal organs, 10 the kidneys and the fat on them, and the best part of the liver. 11 The officiating priest shall burn all this on the altar as a food offering to the LORD.

12 If a man offers a goat, 13 he shall put his hand on its head and kill it in front of the Tent. The priests shall throw its blood against all four sides of the altar 14 and present the following parts as a food offering to the LORD: all the fat on the internal organs, 15 the kidneys and the fat on them, and the best part of the liver. 16 The priest shall burn all this on the altar as a food offering pleasing to the LORD. All the fat belongs to the LORD. 17 No Israelite may eat any fat or any blood; this is a rule to be kept for ever by all Israelites wherever they live.

Offerings for Unintentional Sins

4 The LORD commanded Moses 2 to tell the people of Israel that anyone who sinned and broke any of the LORD's commands without intending to, would have to observe the following rules.

3 If it is the High Priest who sins and so brings guilt on the people, he shall present a young bull without any defects and sacrifice it to the LORD for his sin. 4 He shall bring the bull to the entrance of the Tent, put his hand on its head, and kill it there in the LORD's presence. 5 Then the High Priest shall take some of the bull's blood and carry it into the Tent. 6 He shall dip his finger in the blood and sprinkle it in front of the sacred curtain seven times. 7 Then he shall put some of the blood on the projections at the corners of the incense altar in the Tent. He shall pour out the rest of the blood at the base of the altar used for burning sacrifices, which is at the entrance of the Tent. 8 From this bull he shall take all the fat, the fat on the internal organs, 9 the kidneys and the fat on them, and the best part of the liver. 10 The priest shall take this

He shall bring the bull (4.4)

fat and burn it on the altar used for the burnt offerings, just as he does with the fat from the animal killed for the fellowship offering. 11 But he shall take its skin, all its flesh, its head, its legs, and its internal organs including the intestines, 12 carry it all outside the camp to the ritually clean place where the ashes are poured out, and there he shall burn it on a wood fire.

13 If it is the whole community of Israel that sins and becomes guilty of breaking one of the LORD's commands without intending to, 14 then as soon as the sin becomes known, the community shall bring a young bull as a sin offering. They shall bring it to the Tent of the LORD's presence; 15 the leaders of the community shall put their hands on its head, and it shall be killed there. 16 The High Priest shall take some of the bull's blood into the Tent, 17 dip his finger in it, and sprinkle it in front of the curtain seven times. 18 He shall put some of the blood on the projections at the corners of the incense altar inside the Tent *and pour out the rest of it* at the base of the altar used for burning sacrifices, which is at the entrance of the Tent. 19 Then he shall take all its fat and burn it on the altar. 20 He shall do the same thing with this bull as he does with the bull for the sin offering, and in this way he shall

make the sacrifice for the people's sin, and they will be forgiven. 21 Then he shall take the bull outside the camp and burn it, just as he burns the bull offered for his own sin. This is an offering to take away the sin of the community.

22 If it is a ruler who sins and becomes guilty of breaking one of the LORD's commands without intending to, 23 then as soon as his attention is called to the sin, he shall bring as his offering a male goat without any defects. 24 He shall put his hand on its head and kill it on the north side of the altar, where the animals for the burnt offerings are killed. This is an offering to take away sin. 25 The priest shall dip his finger in the blood of the animal, put it on the projections at the corners of the altar, and pour out the rest of it at the base of the altar. 26 Then he shall burn all its fat on the altar, just as he burns the fat of the animals killed for the fellowship offerings. In this way the priest shall offer the sacrifice for the sin of the ruler, and he will be forgiven.

27 If it is one of the common people who sins and becomes guilty of breaking one of the LORD's commands without intending to, 28 then as soon as his attention is called to the sin, he shall bring as his offering a female goat without any defects. 29 He shall put his hand on its head and kill it on the north side of the altar, where the animals for the burnt offerings are killed. 30 The priest shall dip his finger in the blood of the animal, put it on the projections at the corners of the altar, and pour out the rest of it at the base of the altar. 31 Then he shall remove all its fat, just as the fat is removed from the animals killed for the fellowship offerings, and he shall burn it on the altar so that the smell pleases the LORD. In this way the priest shall offer the sacrifice for the man's sin, and he will be forgiven.

32 If a man brings a sheep as a sin offering, it must be a female without any defects. 33 He shall put his hand on its head and kill it on the north side of the altar, where the animals for the burnt offerings are killed. 34 *The priest shall dip his finger in* the blood of the animal, put it on the projections at the corners of the altar, and pour out the rest of it at the base of the altar.

See also: 4.27–31: Num 15.27–28

35 Then he shall remove all its fat, just as the fat is removed from the sheep killed for the fellowship offerings, and he shall burn it on the altar along with the food offerings given to the Lord. In this way the priest shall offer the sacrifice for the man's sin, and he will be forgiven.

Cases Requiring Sin Offerings

5 Sin offerings are required in the following cases.

If someone is officially summoned to give evidence in court and does not give information about something he has seen or heard, he must suffer the consequences.

2 If someone unintentionally touches anything ritually unclean, such as a dead animal, he is unclean and guilty as soon as he realizes what he has done.

3 If someone unintentionally touches anything of human origin that is unclean, whatever it may be, he is guilty as soon as he realizes what he has done.

4 If someone makes a careless vow, no matter what it is about, he is guilty as soon as he realizes what he has done.

5 When a person is guilty, he must confess the sin, 6 and as the penalty for his sin he must bring to the Lord a female sheep or goat as an offering. The priest shall offer the sacrifice for the man's sin.

7 If a man cannot afford a sheep or a goat, he shall bring to the Lord as the payment for his sin two doves or two pigeons, one for a sin offering and the other for a burnt offering. 8 He shall bring them to the priest, who will first offer the bird for the sin offering. He will break its neck without pulling off its head 9 and sprinkle some of its blood against the side of the altar. The rest of the blood will be drained out at the base of the altar. This is an offering to take away sin. 10 Then he shall offer the second bird as a burnt offering, according to the regulations. In this way the priest shall offer the sacrifice for the man's sin, and he will be forgiven.

11 If a man cannot afford two doves or two pigeons, he shall bring one kilogramme of flour as a sin offering. He shall not put any olive oil or any incense on it, because it is a sin offering, not a grain offering. 12 He shall bring it to the priest, who will take a handful of it as a token that it has all been offered to the Lord, and he will burn it on the altar as a food offering. It is an offering to take away sin. 13 In this way the priest shall offer the sacrifice for the man's sin, and he will be forgiven. The rest of the flour belongs to the priest, just as in the case of a grain offering.

Repayment Offerings

14 The Lord gave the following regulations to Moses. 15 If anyone sins unintentionally by failing to hand over the payments that are sacred to the Lord, he shall bring as his repayment offering to the Lord a male sheep or goat without any defects. Its value is to be determined according to the official standard. 16 He must make the payments he has failed to hand over and must pay an additional twenty per cent. He shall give it to the priest, and the priest shall offer the animal as a sacrifice for the man's sin, and he will be forgiven.

17 If anyone sins unintentionally by breaking any of the Lord's commands, he is guilty and must pay the penalty. 18 He must bring to the priest as a repayment offering a male sheep or goat without any defects. Its value is to be determined according to the official standard. The priest shall offer the sacrifice for the sin which the man committed unintentionally, and he will be forgiven. 19 It is a repayment offering for the sin he committed against the Lord.

6 The Lord gave the following regulations to Moses. 2 An offering is to be made if anyone sins against the Lord by refusing to return what a fellow-Israelite has left as a deposit or by stealing something from him or by cheating him 3 or by lying about something that has been lost and swearing that he did not find it. 4–5 When a man sins in any of these ways, he must repay whatever he got by dishonest means. On the day he is found guilty, he must repay the owner in full, plus an additional twenty per cent. 6 He shall bring to the priest as his repayment offering to the Lord a male sheep or goat without any defects. Its value is to be determined according to the official standard. 7 The priest shall offer the sacrifice for the man's sin, and he will be forgiven.

See also: 6.1–7: Num 5.5–8

Sacrifices Burnt Whole

8 The LORD commanded Moses 9 to give Aaron and his sons the following regulations for burnt offerings. A burnt offering is to be left on the altar all night long, and the fire is to be kept burning. 10 Then the priest, wearing his linen robe and linen shorts, shall remove the greasy ashes left on the altar and put them at the side of the altar. 11 Then he shall change his clothes and take the ashes outside the camp to a ritually clean place. 12 The fire on the altar must be kept burning and never allowed to go out. Every morning the priest shall put firewood on it, arrange the burnt offering on it, and burn the fat of the fellowship offering. 13 The fire must always be kept burning on the altar and never allowed to go out.

Grain Offerings

14 The following are the regulations for grain offerings. An Aaronite priest shall present the grain offering to the LORD in front of the altar. 15 Then he shall take a handful of the flour and oil, and the incense on it, and burn it on the altar as a token that all of it has been offered to the LORD. The smell of this offering is pleasing to the LORD. 16–17 The priests shall eat the rest of it. It shall be made into bread baked without yeast and eaten in a holy place, the courtyard of the Tent of the LORD's presence. The LORD has given it to the priests as their part of the food offerings. It is very holy, like the sin offerings and the repayment offerings. 18 For all time to come any of the male descendants of Aaron may eat it as their continuing share of the food offered to the LORD. Anyone else who touches a food offering will be harmed by the power of its holiness.

19 The LORD gave Moses the following regulations 20 for the ordination of an Aaronite priest. On the day he is ordained, he shall present as an offering to the LORD one kilogramme of flour (the same amount as the daily grain offering), half in the morning and half in the evening. 21 It is to be mixed with oil and cooked on a griddle and then crumbled and presented as a grain offering, a smell pleasing to the LORD. 22 For all time to come this offering is to be made by every descendant of Aaron who is serving as High Priest. It shall be completely burnt as a sacrifice to the LORD. 23 No part of a grain offering that a priest makes may be eaten; all of it must be burnt.

Sin Offerings

24 The LORD commanded Moses 25 to give Aaron and his sons the following regulations for sin offerings. The animal for a sin offering shall be killed on the north side of the altar, where the animals for the burnt offerings are killed. This is a very holy offering. 26 The priest who sacrifices the animal shall eat it in a holy place, the courtyard of the Tent of the LORD's presence. 27 Anyone or anything that touches the flesh of the animal will be harmed by the power of its holiness. If any article of clothing is spattered with the animal's blood, it must be washed in a holy place. 28 Any clay pot in which the meat is boiled must be broken, and if a metal pot is used, it must be scrubbed and rinsed with water. 29 Any male of the priestly families may eat this offering; it is very holy. 30 But if any of the blood is brought into the Tent and used in the ritual to take away sin, the animal must not be eaten; it must be burnt.

Repayment Offerings

7 The following are the regulations for repayment offerings, which are very holy. 2 The animal for this offering is to be killed on the north side of the altar, where the animals for the burnt offerings are killed, and its blood is to be thrown against all four sides of the altar. 3 All its fat shall be removed and offered on the altar: the fat tail, the fat covering the internal organs, 4 the kidneys and the fat on them, and the best part of the liver. 5 The priest shall burn all the fat on the altar as a food offering to the LORD. It is a repayment offering. 6 Any male of the priestly families may eat it, but it must be eaten in a holy place, because it is very holy.

7 There is one regulation that applies to both the sin offering and the repayment offering: the meat belongs to the priest who offers the sacrifice. 8 The skin of an animal offered as a burnt offering belongs to the priest who offers the sacrifice. 9 Every grain offering that has been baked in an oven or prepared in a pan or on a griddle belongs to the priest who has offered it to God. 10 But all uncooked grain

offerings, whether mixed with oil or dry, belong to all the Aaronite priests and must be shared equally among them.

Fellowship Offerings

11 The following are the regulations for the fellowship offerings presented to the LORD. 12 If a man makes this offering as a thankoffering to God, he shall present, together with the animal to be sacrificed, an offering of bread made without yeast: either thick loaves made of flour mixed with olive oil or biscuits brushed with olive oil or cakes made of flour mixed with olive oil. 13 In addition, he shall offer loaves of bread baked with yeast. 14 He shall present one part of each kind of bread as a special contribution to the LORD; it belongs to the priest who takes the blood of the animal and throws it against the altar. 15 The flesh of the animal must be eaten on the day it is sacrificed; none of it may be left until the next morning.

16 If a man brings a fellowship offering in fulfilment of a vow or as his own free-will offering, not all of it has to be eaten on the day it is offered, but any that is left over may be eaten on the following day. 17 Any meat that still remains on the third day must be burnt. 18 If any of it is eaten on the third day, God will not accept the man's offering. The offering will not be counted to his credit but will be considered unclean, and whoever eats it will suffer the consequences. 19 If the meat comes into contact with anything ritually unclean, it must not be eaten, but must be burned.

Anyone who is ritually clean may eat the meat, 20 but if anyone who is not clean eats it, he shall no longer be considered one of God's people. 21 Also, if anyone eats the meat of this offering after he has touched anything ritually unclean, whether from a man or an animal, he shall no longer be considered one of God's people.

22 The LORD gave Moses the following regulations 23 for the people of Israel. No fat of cattle, sheep, or goats shall be eaten. 24 The fat of an animal that has died a natural death or has been killed by a wild animal must not be eaten, but it may be used for any other purpose. 25 Anyone who eats the fat of an animal that may be offered as a food offering to the LORD will no longer be considered one of God's people. 26 No matter where the Israelites live, they must never use the blood of birds or animals for food. 27 Anyone who breaks this law will no longer be considered one of God's people.

28 The LORD gave Moses the following regulations 29 for the people of Israel. Whoever offers a fellowship offering must bring part of it as a special gift to the LORD, 30 bringing it with his own hands as a food offering. He shall bring the fat of the animal with its breast and present it as a special gift to the LORD. 31 The priest shall burn the fat on the altar, but the breast shall belong to the priests. 32 The right hind leg of the animal shall be given as a special contribution 33 to the priest who offers the blood and the fat of the fellowship offering. 34 The breast of the animal is a special gift, and the right hind leg is a special contribution that the LORD has taken from the people of Israel and given to the priests. This is what the people of Israel must give to the priests for all time to come. 35 This is the part of the food offered to the LORD that was given to Aaron and his sons on the day they were ordained as priests. 36 On that day the LORD commanded the people of Israel to give them this part of the offering. It is a regulation that the people of Israel must obey for all time to come.

37 These, then, are the regulations for the burnt offerings, the grain offerings, the sin offerings, the repayment offerings, the ordination offerings, and the fellowship offerings. 38 There on Mount Sinai in the desert, the LORD gave these commands to Moses on the day he told the people of Israel to make their offerings.

The Ordination of Aaron and his Sons
(Ex 29.1–37)

8 The LORD said to Moses, 2 "Take Aaron and his sons to the entrance of the Tent of my presence and bring the priestly garments, the anointing oil, the young bull for the sin offering, the two rams, and the basket of unleavened bread. 3 Then call the whole community together there."

See also: 7.26–27: Gen 9.4; Lev 17.10–14, 19.26; Deut 12.16, 23, 15.23

4 Moses did as the LORD had commanded, and when the community had assembled, 5 he said to them, "What I am now about to do is what the LORD has commanded."

6 Moses brought Aaron and his sons forward and told them to take a ritual bath. 7 He put the shirt and the robe on Aaron and the sash round his waist. He put the ephod* on him and fastened it by putting its finely woven belt round his waist. 8 He put the breastpiece on him and put the Urim and Thummim* in it. 9 He placed the turban on his head, and on the front of it he put the gold ornament, the sacred sign of dedication, just as the LORD had commanded him.

10 Then Moses took the anointing oil and put it on the Tent of the LORD's presence and everything that was in it, and in this way he dedicated it all to the LORD. 11 He took some of the oil and sprinkled it seven times on the altar and its equipment and on the basin and its base, in order to dedicate them to the LORD. 12 He ordained Aaron by pouring some of the anointing oil on his head. 13 Next, Moses brought the sons of Aaron forward and put shirts on them, put sashes round their waists, and tied caps on their heads, just as the LORD had commanded.

14 Then Moses brought the young bull for the sin offering, and Aaron and his sons put their hands on its head. 15 Moses killed it and took some of the blood, and with his finger put it on the projections at the corners of the altar, in order to dedicate it. He then poured out the rest of the blood at the base of the altar. In this way he dedicated it and purified it. 16 Moses took all the fat on the internal organs, the best part of the liver, and the kidneys with the fat on them, and burnt it all on the altar. 17 He took the rest of the bull, including its skin, flesh, and intestines, and burnt it outside the camp, just as the LORD had commanded.

18 Next, Moses brought the ram for the burnt offering, and Aaron and his sons put their hands on its head. 19 Moses killed it *and threw the blood on all four sides* of the altar. 20–21 He cut the ram in pieces, washed the internal organs and the hind legs with water, and burnt the head, the fat, and all the rest of the ram on the altar, just as the LORD had commanded. This burnt offering was a food offering, and the smell was pleasing to the LORD.

22 Then Moses brought the second ram, which was for the ordination of priests, and Aaron and his sons put their hands on its head. 23 Moses killed it and took some of the blood and put it on the lobe of Aaron's right ear, on the thumb of his right hand, and on the big toe of his right foot. 24 Then he brought Aaron's sons forward and put some of the blood on the lobes of their right ears, on the thumbs of their right hands, and on the big toes of their right feet. Moses then threw the rest of the blood on all four sides of the altar. 25 He took the fat, the fat tail, all the fat covering the internal organs, the best part of the liver, the kidneys with the fat on them, and the right hind leg. 26 Then he took one loaf of bread from the basket of unleavened bread dedicated to the LORD, one loaf made with oil, and one biscuit, and he put them on top of the fat and the right hind leg. 27 He put all this food in the hands of Aaron and his sons, and they presented it as a special gift to the LORD. 28 Then Moses took the food from them and burnt it on the altar, on top of the burnt offering, as an ordination offering. This was a food offering, and the smell was pleasing to the LORD. 29 Then Moses took the breast and presented it as a special gift to the LORD. It was Moses' part of the ordination ram. Moses did everything just as the LORD had commanded.

30 Moses took some of the anointing oil and some of the blood that was on

In this way he consecrated them (8.30)

8.7 EPHOD: See Word List.
8.8 URIM AND THUMMIM: *Two objects used by the priest to determine God's will; it is not known precisely how they were used.*

the altar and sprinkled them on Aaron and his sons and on their clothes. In this way he consecrated them and their clothes to the LORD.

31 Moses said to Aaron and his sons, "Take the meat to the entrance of the Tent of the LORD's presence, boil it, and eat it there with the bread that is in the basket of ordination offerings, just as the LORD commanded. 32 Burn up any meat or bread that is left over. 33 You shall not leave the entrance of the Tent for seven days, until your ordination rites are completed. 34 The LORD commanded us to do what we have done today, in order to take away your sin. 35 You must stay at the entrance of the Tent day and night for seven days, doing what the LORD has commanded. If you don't, you will die. This is what the LORD has commanded me." 36 So Aaron and his sons did everything that the LORD had commanded through Moses.

Aaron Offers Sacrifices

9 The day after the ordination rites were completed, Moses called Aaron and his sons and the leaders of Israel. 2 He said to Aaron, "Take a young bull and a ram without any defects and offer them to the LORD, the bull for a sin offering and the ram for a burnt offering. 3 Then tell the people of Israel to take a male goat for a sin offering, a one-year-old calf, and a one-year-old lamb without any defects for a burnt offering, 4 and a bull and a ram for a fellowship offering. They are to sacrifice them to the LORD with the grain offering mixed with oil. They must do this because the LORD will appear to them today."

5 They brought to the front of the Tent everything that Moses had commanded, and the whole community assembled there to worship the LORD. 6 Moses said, "The LORD has commanded you to do all this, so that the dazzling light of his presence can appear to you." 7 Then he said to Aaron, "Go to the altar and offer the sin offering and the burnt offering to take away your sins and the sins of the people. Present this offering to take away the sins of the people, just as the LORD commanded."

8 Aaron went to the altar and killed the young bull which was for his own sin offering. 9 His sons brought him the blood, and he dipped his finger in it, put some of it on the projections at the corners of the altar, and poured out the rest of it at the base of the altar. 10 Then he burnt on the altar the fat, the kidneys, and the best part of the liver, just as the LORD had commanded Moses. 11 But he burnt the meat and the skin outside the camp.

12 He killed the animal which was for his own burnt offering. His sons brought him the blood, and he threw it on all four sides of the altar. 13 They handed him the head and the other pieces of the animal, and he burnt them on the altar. 14 Then he washed the internal organs and the hind legs and burnt them on the altar on top of the rest of the burnt offering.

15 After that, he presented the people's offerings. He took the goat that was to be offered for the people's sins, killed it, and offered it, as he had done with his own sin offering. 16 He also brought the animal for the burnt offering and offered it according to the regulations. 17 He presented the grain offering and took a handful of flour and burnt it on the altar. (This was in addition to the daily burnt offering.) 18 He killed the bull and the ram as a fellowship offering for the people. His sons brought him the blood, and he threw it on all four sides of the altar. 19 Aaron put the fat parts of the bull and the ram 20 on top of the breasts of the animals and carried it all to the altar. He burnt the fat on the altar 21 and presented the breasts and the right hind legs as the special gift to the LORD for the priests, as Moses had commanded.

22 When Aaron had finished all the sacrifices, he raised his hands over the people and blessed them, and then stepped down. 23 Moses and Aaron went into the Tent of the LORD's presence, and when they came out, they blessed the people, and the dazzling light of the LORD's presence appeared to all the people. 24 Suddenly the LORD sent a fire, and it consumed the burnt offering and the fat parts on the altar. When the people saw it, they all shouted and bowed down with their faces to the ground.

See also: 9.7: Heb 7.27   **See also: 9.18:** Lev 3.1–11   **9.22:** Num 6.22–26

The Sin of Nadab and Abihu

10 Aaron's sons Nadab and Abihu, each took his fire pan, put live coals in it, added incense, and presented it to the LORD. But this fire was not holy, because the LORD had not commanded them to present it. 2 Suddenly the LORD sent fire, and it burnt them to death there in the presence of the LORD. 3 Then Moses said to Aaron, "This is what the LORD was speaking about when he said, 'All who serve me must respect my holiness; I will reveal my glory to my people.' "* But Aaron remained silent.

4 Moses called Mishael and Elzaphan, the sons of Uzziel, Aaron's uncle, and said to them, "Come here and carry your cousins' bodies away from the sacred Tent and put them outside the camp." 5 So they came and took hold of the clothing on the corpses and carried them outside the camp, just as Moses had commanded.

6 Then Moses said to Aaron and to his sons Eleazar and Ithamar, "Do not leave your hair uncombed or tear your clothes to show that you are in mourning. If you do, you will die, and the LORD will be angry with the whole community. But all your fellow-Israelites are allowed to mourn this death caused by the fire which the LORD sent. 7 Do not leave the entrance of the Tent or you will die, because you have been consecrated by the anointing oil of the LORD." So they did as Moses said.

Rules for Priests

8 The LORD said to Aaron, 9 "You and your sons are not to enter the Tent of my presence after drinking wine or beer; if you do, you will die. This is a law to be kept by all your descendants. 10 You must distinguish between what belongs to God and what is for general use, between what is ritually clean and what is unclean. 11 You must teach the people of Israel all the laws which I have given to you through Moses."

12 Moses said to Aaron and his two remaining sons, Eleazar and Ithamar, "Take the grain offering that is left over *from the food offered to the LORD, make* unleavened bread with it and eat it beside the altar, because this offering is very holy.

13 Eat it in a holy place; it is the part that belongs to you and your sons from the food offered to the LORD. That is what the LORD commanded me. 14 But you and your families may eat the breast and the hind leg that are presented as the special gift and the special contribution to the LORD for the priests. You may eat them in any ritually clean place. These offerings have been given to you and your children as the part that belongs to you from the fellowship offerings of the people of Israel. 15 They shall bring the hind leg and the breast at the time the fat is presented as a food offering to the LORD. These parts belong to you and your children for ever, just as the LORD commanded."

16 Moses asked about the goat for the sin offering and learnt that it had already been burnt. This made him angry with Eleazar and Ithamar, and he demanded, 17 "Why didn't you eat the sin offering in a sacred place? It is very holy, and the LORD has given it to you in order to take away the sin of the community. 18 Since its blood was not brought into the sacred tent, you should have eaten the sacrifice there, as I commanded."

19 Aaron answered, "If I had eaten the sin offering today, would the LORD have approved? The people presented their sin offering to the LORD today, and they brought their burnt offering, but still these terrible things have happened to me." 20 When Moses heard this, he was satisfied.

Animals that may be Eaten
(Deut 14.3–21)

11 The Lord gave Moses and Aaron the following regulations 2 for the people of Israel. You may eat any land animal 3 that has divided hoofs and that also chews the cud, 4–6 but you must not eat camels, rock-badgers, or rabbits. They must be considered unclean; they chew the cud, but do not have divided hoofs. 7 Do not eat pigs. They must be considered unclean; they *have divided hoofs, but do* not chew the cud. 8 Do not eat these animals or even touch their dead bodies; they are unclean.

9 You may eat any kind of fish that has fins and scales, 10 but anything living in

---

10.3 I will reveal my glory to my people; *or* my people must honour me.

See also: **10.12–13:** Lev 6.14–18

See also: **10.14–15:** Lev 7.30–34   **10.17:** Lev 6.24–26

Unclean animals   (chapter 11)

the water that does not have fins and scales must not be eaten. 11 Such creatures must be considered unclean. You must not eat them or even touch their dead bodies. 12 You must not eat anything that lives in the water and does not have fins and scales.

13–19 You must not eat any of the following birds: eagles, owls, hawks, falcons; buzzards, vultures, crows; ostriches; seagulls, storks, herons, pelicans, cormorants;* hoopoes; or bats.

20 All winged insects are unclean, 21 except those that hop. 22 You may eat locusts, crickets, or grasshoppers. 23 But all other small things that have wings and also crawl must be considered unclean.

24–28 Whoever touches the dead bodies of the following animals will be unclean until evening: all animals with hoofs, unless their hoofs are divided and they chew the cud, and all four-footed animals with paws. Whoever carries their dead bodies must wash his clothes, but he will still be unclean until evening.

29–30 Moles, rats, mice, and lizards must be considered unclean. 31 Whoever touches them or their dead bodies will be unclean until evening. 32 And if their dead bodies fall on anything, it will be unclean. This applies to any article of wood, cloth, leather, or sacking, no matter what it is used for. It shall be dipped in water, but it will remain unclean until evening. 33 And if their bodies fall into a clay pot, everything that is in it shall be unclean, and you must break the pot. 34 Any food which could normally be eaten, but on which water from such a pot has been poured, will be unclean, and anything drinkable in such a pot is unclean. 35 Anything on which the dead bodies fall is unclean; a clay stove or oven shall be broken, 36 but a spring or a cistern remains clean, although anything else that touches their dead bodies is unclean. 37 If one of them falls on seed that is going to be sown, the seed remains clean. 38 But if the seed is soaking in water and one of them falls on it, the seed is unclean.

39 If any animal that may be eaten dies, anyone who touches it will be unclean until evening. 40 And if anyone eats any part of the animal, he must wash his clothes, but he will still be unclean until evening; anyone who carries the dead body must wash his clothes, but he will still be unclean until evening.

41 You must not eat any of the small animals that move on the ground, 42 whether they crawl, or walk on four legs, or have many legs. 43 Do not make yourselves unclean by eating any of these. 44 I am the LORD your God, and you must keep yourselves holy, because I am holy. 45 I am the LORD who brought you out of Egypt so that I could be your God. You must be holy, because I am holy.

11.13–19 *The identification of some of the birds in verses 13–19 is uncertain.*

See also: **11.44:** Lev 19.2; 1 Pet 1.16

46 This, then, is the law about animals and birds, about everything that lives in the water, and everything that moves on the ground. 47 You must be careful to distinguish between what is ritually clean and unclean, between animals that may be eaten and those that may not.

The Purification of Women after Childbirth

12 The LORD gave Moses the following regulations 2 for the people of Israel. For seven days after a woman gives birth to a son, she is ritually unclean, as she is during her monthly period. 3 On the eighth day, the child shall be circumcised. 4 Then it will be 33 more days before she is ritually clean from her loss of blood; she must not touch anything that is holy or enter the sacred Tent until the time of her purification is completed.

5 For fourteen days after a woman gives birth to a daughter, she is ritually unclean, as she is during her monthly period. Then it will be 66 more days before she is ritually clean from her loss of blood.

6 When the time of her purification is completed, whether for a son or daughter, she shall bring to the priest at the entrance of the Tent of the LORD's presence a one-year-old lamb for a burnt offering and a pigeon or a dove for a sin offering. 7 The priest shall present her offering to the Lord and perform the ritual to take away her impurity, and she will be ritually clean. This, then, is what a woman must do after giving birth.

8 If the woman cannot afford a lamb, she shall bring two doves or two pigeons, one for a burnt offering and the other for a sin offering, and the priest shall perform the ritual to take away her impurity, and she will be ritually clean.

Laws concerning Skin Diseases

13 The LORD gave Moses and Aaron these regulations. 2 If anyone has a sore on his skin or a boil or an inflammation which could develop into a dreaded skin disease, he shall be brought to the Aaronite priest. 3 The priest shall examine the sore, and if the hairs in it have turned white and the sore appears to be deeper

than the surrounding skin, it is a dreaded skin disease, and the priest shall pronounce the person unclean. 4 But if the sore is white and does not appear to be deeper than the skin round it and the hairs have not turned white, the priest shall isolate the person for seven days. 5 The priest shall examine him again on the seventh day, and if in his opinion the sore looks the same and has not spread, he shall isolate him for another seven days. 6 The priest shall examine him again on the seventh day, and if the sore has faded and has not spread, he shall pronounce him ritually clean; it is only a sore. The person shall wash his clothes and be ritually clean. 7 But if the sore spreads after the priest has examined him and pronounced him clean, he must appear before the priest again. 8 The priest will examine him again, and if it has spread, he shall pronounce him unclean; it is a dreaded skin disease.

9 If anyone has a dreaded skin disease, he shall be brought to the priest, 10 who will examine him. If there is a white sore on his skin which turns the hairs white and is full of pus, 11 it is a chronic skin disease. The priest shall pronounce him unclean; there is no need to isolate him, because he is obviously unclean. 12 If the skin disease spreads and covers the person from head to foot, 13 the priest shall examine him again. If he finds that it actually has covered the whole body, he shall pronounce the person ritually clean. If his whole skin has turned white, he is ritually clean. 14 But from the moment an open sore appears, he is unclean. 15 The priest shall examine him again, and if he sees an open sore, he shall pronounce him unclean. An open sore means a dreaded skin disease, and the person is unclean. 16 But when the sore heals and becomes white again, the person shall go to the priest, 17 who will examine him again. If the sore has turned white, he is ritually clean, and the priest shall pronounce him clean.

18 If anyone has a boil that has healed 19 and if afterwards a white swelling or a reddish-white spot appears where the boil was, he shall go to the priest. 20 The priest shall examine him, and if the spot seems to be deeper than the surrounding skin and the hairs in it have turned white, he shall pronounce him unclean. It is a dreaded skin

The priest shall examine him (13.20)

disease that has started in the boil. 21 But if the priest examines it and finds that the hairs in it have not turned white and that it is not deeper than the surrounding skin, but is light in colour, the priest shall isolate him for seven days. 22 If the spot spreads, the priest shall pronounce him unclean; he is diseased. 23 But if it remains unchanged and does not spread, it is only the scar left from the boil, and the priest shall pronounce him ritually clean.

24 In the case of a person who has been burnt, if the raw flesh becomes white or reddish-white, 25 the priest shall examine him. If the hairs in the spot have turned white and it appears deeper than the surrounding skin, it is a dreaded skin disease that has started in the burn, and the priest shall pronounce him unclean. 26 But if the hairs in it have not turned white and it is not deeper than the surrounding skin, but is light in colour, the priest shall isolate him for seven days. 27 The priest shall examine him again on the seventh day, and if it is spreading, it is a dreaded skin disease, and the priest shall pronounce him unclean. 28 But if the spot remains unchanged and does

not spread and is light in colour, it is not a dreaded skin disease. The priest shall pronounce him ritually clean, because it is only a scar from the burn.

29 When a man or a woman has a sore on the head or the chin, 30 the priest shall examine it. If it seems to be deeper than the surrounding skin and the hairs in it are yellowish and thin, it is a dreaded skin disease, and he shall pronounce the person unclean. 31 If, when the priest examines him, the sore does not appear to be deeper than the surrounding skin, but there are still no healthy hairs in it, he shall isolate him for seven days. 32 The priest shall examine the sore again on the seventh day, and if it has not spread and there are no yellowish hairs in it and it does not seem to be deeper than the surrounding skin, 33 the person shall shave the head except the area round the sore. The priest shall then isolate him for another seven days. 34 On the seventh day the priest shall again examine the sore, and if it has not spread and does not seem to be deeper than the surrounding skin, he shall pronounce him ritually clean. The person shall wash his clothes, and he will be clean. 35 But if the sore spreads after he has been pronounced clean, 36 the priest shall examine him again. If the sore has spread, he need not look for yellowish hairs; the person is obviously unclean. 37 But if in the priest's opinion the sore has not spread and healthy hairs are growing in it, the sore has healed, and the priest shall pronounce him ritually clean.

38 When a man or a woman has white spots on the skin, 39 the priest shall examine that person. If the spots are dull white, it is only a blemish that has broken out on the skin; the person is ritually clean.

40-41 If a man loses his hair at the back or the front of his head, this does not make him unclean. 42 But if a reddish-white sore appears on the bald spot, it is a dreaded skin disease. 43 The priest shall examine him, and if there is a reddish-white sore, 44 the priest shall pronounce him unclean, because of the dreaded skin disease on his head.

45 A person who has a dreaded skin disease must wear torn clothes, leave his hair uncombed, cover the lower part of his face, and call out, "Unclean, unclean!" 46 He remains unclean as long as he has the disease, and he must live outside the camp, away from others.

Laws concerning Mildew

47 When there is mildew* on clothing, whether wool or linen, 48 or on any piece of linen or wool cloth or on leather or anything made of leather, 49 if it is greenish or reddish, it is a spreading mildew and must be shown to the priest. 50 The priest shall examine it and put the object away for seven days. 51 He shall examine it again on the seventh day, and if the mildew has spread, the object is unclean. 52 The priest shall burn it, because it is a spreading mildew which must be destroyed by fire.

53 But if, when he examines it, the priest finds that the mildew has not spread on the object, 54 he shall order it to be washed and put away for another seven days. 55 Then he shall examine it, and if the mildew has not changed colour, even though it has not spread, it is still unclean; you must burn the object, whether the rot is on the front or the back. 56 But if, when the priest examines it again, the mildew has faded, he shall tear it out of the clothing or leather. 57 Then, if the mildew reappears, it is spreading again, and the owner shall burn the object. 58 If he washes the object and the spot disappears, he shall wash it again, and it will be ritually clean.

59 This, then, is the law about mildew on clothing, whether it is wool or linen, or on linen or wool cloth or on anything made of leather; this is how the decision is made as to whether it is ritually clean or unclean.

Purification after Having Skin Diseases

14 The LORD gave Moses 2 the following regulations about the ritual purification of a person cured of a dreaded skin disease. On the day he is to be pronounced clean, he shall be brought to the priest, 3 and the priest shall take him outside the camp and examine him. If the disease is healed, 4 the priest shall order two ritually clean birds to be brought, together with a piece of cedar wood, a red cord, and a sprig of hyssop. 5 Then the priest shall order one of the birds to be killed over a clay bowl containing fresh spring water. 6 He shall take the other bird and dip it, together with

the cedar wood, the red cord, and the hyssop, in the blood of the bird that was killed. 7 He shall sprinkle the blood seven times on the person who is to be purified from his skin disease, and then he shall pronounce him clean. He shall let the live bird fly away over the open fields. 8 The person shall wash his clothes, shave off all his hair, and have a bath; he will then be ritually clean. He may enter the camp, but he must live outside his tent for seven days. 9 On the seventh day he shall again shave his head, his beard, his eyebrows, and all the rest of the hair on his body; he shall wash his clothes and have a bath, and then he will be ritually clean.

10 On the eighth day he shall bring two male lambs and one female lamb a year old that are without any defects, three kilogrammes of flour mixed with olive oil, and a third of a litre of olive oil. 11 The priest shall take the person and these offerings to the entrance of the Tent of the LORD's presence. 12 Then the priest shall take one of the male lambs and together with the one-third of a litre of oil he shall offer it as a repayment offering. He shall present them as a special gift to the LORD for the priest. 13 He shall kill the lamb in the place where the animals for the sin offerings and the burnt offerings are killed. He must do this because the repayment offering, like the sin offering, belongs to the priest and is very holy. 14 The priest shall take some of the blood of the lamb and put it on the lobe of the right ear, on the thumb of the right hand, and on the big toe of the right foot of the one who is to be declared ritually clean. 15 The priest shall take some of the olive oil and pour it in the palm of his own left hand, 16 dip a finger of his right hand in it, and sprinkle some of it seven times there in the LORD's presence. 17 He shall take some of the oil that is in the palm of his hand and some of the blood of the lamb and put them on the lobe of the right ear, on the thumb of the right hand, and on the big toe of the right foot of the one who is to be declared ritually clean. 18 He shall put the rest of the oil that is in the palm of his hand on the person's head. In this way he shall perform the ritual of purification.

19 Then the priest shall offer the sin offering and perform the ritual of purification. After that, he shall kill the animal

---

13.47 MILDEW: *The Hebrew word for "dreaded skin disease" and "mildew" is the same.*

See also: 14.2: Mt 8.4; Mk 1.44; Lk 5.14, 17.14

for the burnt offering 20 and offer it with the grain offering on the altar. In this way the priest shall perform the ritual of purification, and the person will be ritually clean.

21 If he is poor and cannot afford any more, he shall bring for his purification only one male lamb as his repayment offering, a special gift to the LORD for the priest. He shall bring only one kilogramme of flour mixed with olive oil for a grain offering and a third of a litre of olive oil. 22 He shall also bring two doves or two pigeons, one for the sin offering and one for the burnt offering. 23 On the eighth day of his purification he shall bring them to the priest at the entrance of the Tent. 24 The priest shall take the lamb and the olive oil and present them as a special gift to the LORD for the priest. 25 He shall kill the lamb and take some of the blood and put it on the lobe of the person's right ear, on the thumb of his right hand, and on the big toe of his right foot. 26 The priest shall pour some of the oil into the palm of his own left hand 27 and with a finger of his right hand sprinkle some of it seven times there in the LORD's presence. 28 He shall put some of the oil on the same places as he put the blood: on the lobe of the person's right ear, on the thumb of his right hand, and on the big toe of his right foot. 29 The rest of the oil that is in his palm he shall put on the person's head and in this way perform the ritual of purification. 30 Then he shall offer one of the doves or pigeons 31 as the sin offering and the other as the burnt offering with the grain offering. In this way the priest shall perform the ritual of purification. 32 This is the law for the one who has a dreaded skin disease but who cannot afford the normal offerings required for his purification.

Mildew in Houses

33 The LORD gave Moses and Aaron 34–35 the following regulations about houses affected by spreading mildew. (These were to apply after the people of Israel entered the land of Canaan, which the LORD was going to give them as their possession.) If someone finds that the LORD has sent mildew on his house, then he must go and tell the priest about it. 36 The priest shall order everything to be moved out of the house before he goes to examine the mildew; otherwise everything in the house will be declared unclean. Then he shall go to the house 37 and examine the mildew. If there are greenish or reddish spots that appear to be eating into the wall, 38 he shall leave the house and lock it up for seven days. 39 On the seventh day he shall return and examine it again. If the mildew has spread, 40 he shall order the stones on which the mildew is found to be removed and thrown into some unclean place outside the city. 41 After that he must have all the interior walls scraped and the plaster dumped in an unclean place outside the city. 42 Then other stones are to be used to replace the stones that were removed, and new plaster will be used to cover the walls.

The stones … shall be removed (14.40)

43 If the mildew breaks out again in the house after the stones have been removed and the house has been scraped and plastered, 44 the priest shall go and look. If it has spread, the house is unclean. 45 It must be torn down, and its stones, its wood, and all its plaster must be carried out of the city to an unclean place. 46 Anyone who enters the house while it is locked up will be unclean until evening. 47 Anyone who lies down or eats in the house must wash his clothes.

48 If, when the priest comes to look, the mildew has not reappeared after the house has been replastered, he shall pronounce the house ritually clean, because the mildew has been completely removed. 49 To purify the house, he shall take two birds, some cedar wood, a red cord, and a sprig of hyssop. 50 He shall kill one of the birds over a

clay bowl containing fresh spring water. 51 Then he shall take the cedar wood, the hyssop, the red cord, and the live bird and shall dip them in the blood of the bird that was killed and in the fresh water. And he shall sprinkle the house seven times. 52 In this way he shall purify the house with the bird's blood, the fresh water, the live bird, the cedar wood, the hyssop, and the red cord. 53 Then he shall let the live bird fly away outside the city over the open fields. In this way he shall perform the ritual of purification for the house, and it will be ritually clean.

54 These are the laws about dreaded skin diseases; 55–56 sores, boils, or inflammations; and about mildew in clothes or houses. 57 These laws determine when something is unclean and when it is clean.

Unclean Bodily Discharges

15 The LORD gave Moses and Aaron the following regulations 2 for the people of Israel. When any man has a discharge from his penis, the discharge is unclean, 3 whether the penis runs with it or is stopped up by it. 4 Any bed on which he sits or lies is unclean. 5 Anyone who touches his bed 6 or sits on anything the man has sat on must wash his clothes and have a bath, and he remains unclean until evening. 7 Anyone who touches the man with the discharge must wash his clothes and have a bath, and he remains unclean until evening. 8 If the man with the discharge spits on anyone who is ritually clean, that person must wash his clothes and have a bath, and he remains unclean until evening. 9 Any saddle or seat on which the man with the discharge sits is unclean. 10 Anyone who touches anything on which the man sat is unclean until evening. Anyone who carries anything on which the man sat must wash his clothes and have a bath, and he remains unclean until evening. 11 If a man who has a discharge touches someone without first having washed his hands, that person *must wash his clothes and have a bath,* and he remains unclean until evening. 12 Any clay pot that the man touches must be broken, and any wooden bowl that he touches must be washed.

13 After the man is cured of his discharge, he must wait seven days and then wash his clothes and bathe in fresh spring water, and he will be ritually clean. 14 On the eighth day he shall take two doves or two pigeons to the entrance of the Tent of the LORD's presence and give them to the priest. 15 The priest shall offer one of them as a sin offering and the other as a burnt offering. In this way he will perform the ritual of purification for the man.

16 When a man has an emission of semen, he must bathe his whole body, and he remains unclean until evening. 17 Anything made of cloth or leather on which the semen falls must be washed, and it remains unclean until evening. 18 After sexual intercourse both the man and the woman must have a bath, and they remain unclean until evening.

19 When a woman has her monthly period, she remains unclean for seven days. Anyone who touches her is unclean until evening. 20 Anything on which she sits or lies during her monthly period is unclean. 21–23 Anyone who touches her bed or anything on which she has sat must wash his clothes and have a bath, and he remains unclean until evening. 24 If a man has sexual intercourse with her during her period, he is contaminated by her impurity and remains unclean for seven days, and any bed on which he lies is unclean.

25 If a woman has a flow of blood for several days outside her monthly period or if her flow continues beyond her regular period, she remains unclean as long as the flow continues, just as she is during her monthly period. 26 Any bed on which she lies and anything on which she sits during this time is unclean. 27 Anyone who touches them is unclean and must wash his clothes and have a bath; he remains unclean until evening. 28 After her flow stops, she must wait seven days, and then she will be ritually clean. 29 On the eighth day she shall take two doves or two pigeons to the priest at the entrance of the Tent of the LORD's presence. 30 The priest shall offer one of them as a sin offering and the other as a burnt offering, and in this way he will perform the ritual of purification for her.

31 The LORD told Moses to warn the people of Israel about their uncleanness, so that they would not defile the Tent of his presence, which was in the middle of the camp. If they did, they would be killed.

32 These are the regulations about a man who has a discharge or an emission of semen, 33 a woman during her monthly period, or a man who has sexual intercourse with a woman who is ritually unclean.

The Day of Atonement

16 The LORD spoke to Moses after the death of the two sons of Aaron who were killed when they offered unholy fire to the LORD. 2 He said, "Tell your brother Aaron that only at the proper time is he to go behind the curtain into the Most Holy Place, because that is where I appear in a cloud above the lid on the Covenant Box. If he disobeys, he will be killed. 3 He may enter the Most Holy Place only after he has brought a young bull for a sin offering and a ram for a burnt offering."

4 Then the LORD gave the following instructions. Before Aaron goes into the Most Holy Place, he must have a bath and put on the priestly garments: the linen robe and shorts, the belt, and the turban.

5 The community of Israel shall give Aaron two male goats for a sin offering and a ram for a burnt offering. 6 He shall offer a bull as a sacrifice to take away his own sins and those of his family. 7 Then he shall take the two goats to the entrance of the Tent of the LORD's presence. 8 There he shall draw lots, using two stones, one marked "for the LORD" and the other "for Azazel".* 9 Aaron shall sacrifice the goat chosen by lot for the LORD and offer it as a sin offering. 10 The goat chosen for Azazel shall be presented alive to the LORD and sent off into the desert to Azazel, in order to take away the sins of the people.

11 When Aaron sacrifices the bull as the sin offering for himself and his family, 12 he shall take a fire pan full of burning coals from the altar and two handfuls of fine incense and bring them into the Most Holy Place. 13 There in the LORD's presence he shall put the incense on the fire, and the smoke of the incense will hide the lid of the Covenant Box so that he will not see it and die. 14 He shall take some of the bull's blood and with his finger sprinkle it on the front of the lid and then sprinkle some of it seven times in front of the Covenant Box.

15 After that, he shall kill the goat for the sin offering for the people, bring its blood into the Most Holy Place, and sprinkle it on the lid and then in front of the Covenant Box, as he did with the bull's blood. 16 In this way he will perform the ritual to purify the Most Holy Place from the uncleanness of the people of Israel and from all their sins. He must do this to the Tent, because it stands in the middle of the camp, which is ritually unclean. 17 From the time Aaron enters the Most Holy Place to perform the ritual of purification until he comes out, there must be no one in the Tent. When he has performed the ritual for himself, his family, and the whole community, 18 he must then go out to the altar for burnt offerings and purify it. He must take some of the bull's blood and some of the goat's blood and put it all over the projections at the corners of the altar. 19 With his finger he must sprinkle some of the blood on the altar seven times. In this way he is to purify it from the sins of the people of Israel and make it holy.

The Scapegoat

20 When Aaron has finished performing the ritual to purify the Most Holy Place, the rest of the Tent of the LORD's presence, and the altar, he shall present to the LORD the live goat chosen for Azazel.* 21 He shall put both his hands on the goat's head and confess over it all the evils, sins, and rebellions of the people of Israel, and so transfer them to the goat's head. Then the goat is to be

The goat will carry all their sins away   (16.22)

16.8, 16.20 AZAZEL: *The meaning of this Hebrew word is unknown; it may be the name of a desert demon.*
See also: 16.2: Heb 6.19   **16.3:** Heb 9.7

16.20, 16.8 AZAZEL: *The meaning of this Hebrew word is unknown; it may be the name of a desert demon.*
See also: 16.15: Heb 9.12

driven off into the desert by someone appointed to do it. 22 The goat will carry all their sins away with him into some uninhabited land.

23 Then Aaron shall go into the Tent, take off the priestly garments that he had put on before entering the Most Holy Place, and leave them there. 24 He must bathe in a holy place and put on his own clothes. After that, he shall go out and offer the burnt offering to remove his own sins and those of the people. 25 He shall burn on the altar the fat of the animal for the sin offering. 26 The man who drove the goat into the desert to Azazel must wash his clothes and have a bath before he comes back into camp. 27 The bull and the goat used for the sin offering, whose blood was brought into the Most Holy Place to take away sin, shall be carried outside the camp and burnt. Skin, meat, and intestines shall all be burnt. 28 The one who burns them must wash his clothes and have a bath before he returns to camp.

Observing the Day of Atonement

29 The following regulations are to be observed for all time to come. On the tenth day of the seventh month the Israelites and the foreigners living among them must fast and must not do any work. 30 On that day the ritual is to be performed to purify them from all their sins, so that they will be ritually clean. 31 That day is to be a very holy day, one on which they fast and do no work at all. These regulations are to be observed for all time to come. 32 The High Priest, properly ordained and consecrated to succeed his father, is to perform the ritual of purification. He shall put on the priestly garments 33 and perform the ritual to purify the Most Holy Place, the rest of the Tent of the Lord's presence, the altar, the priests, and all the people of the community. 34 These regulations are to be observed for all time to come. This ritual must be performed once a year to purify the people of Israel from all their sins.

So Moses* did as the Lord had commanded.

16.34 Moses; *or* Aaron.

See also: 16.23: Ezek 44.19　　**16.27:** Heb 13.11
16.29–34: Lev 23.26–32; Num 29.7–11

The Sacredness of Blood

17 The Lord commanded Moses 2 to give Aaron and his sons and all the people of Israel the following regulations. 3–4 An Israelite who kills a cow or a sheep or a goat as an offering to the Lord anywhere except at the entrance of the Tent of the Lord's presence has broken the Law. He has shed blood and shall no longer be considered one of God's people. 5 The meaning of this command is that the people of Israel shall now bring to the Lord the animals which they used to kill in the open country. They shall now bring them to the priest at the entrance of the Tent and kill them as fellowship offerings. 6 The priest shall throw the blood against the sides of the altar at the entrance of the Tent and burn the fat to produce a smell that is pleasing to the Lord. 7 The people of Israel must no longer be unfaithful to the Lord by killing their animals in the fields as sacrifices to the goat-demons. The people of Israel must keep this regulation for all time to come.

8 Any Israelite or any foreigner living in the community who offers a burnt offering or any other sacrifice 9 as an offering to the Lord anywhere except at the entrance of the Tent shall no longer be considered one of God's people.

10 If any Israelite or any foreigner living in the community eats meat with blood still in it, the Lord will turn against him and no longer consider him one of his people. 11 The life of every living thing is in the blood, and that is why the Lord has commanded that all blood be poured out on the altar to take away the people's sins. Blood, which is life, takes away sins. 12 That is why the Lord has told the people of Israel that neither they nor any foreigner living among them shall eat any meat with blood still in it.

13 If any Israelite or any foreigner living in the community hunts an animal or a bird which is ritually clean, he must pour out its blood on the ground and cover it with earth. 14 The life of every living thing is in the blood, and that is why the Lord has told the people of Israel that they shall not eat any meat with blood still in it and that anyone who does so will no longer be considered one of his people.

See also: 17.10: Gen 9.4; Lev 7.26–27, 19.26;
Deut 12.16, 23, 15.23　　**17.11:** Heb 9.22

15 Any person, Israelite or foreigner, who eats meat from an animal that has died a natural death or has been killed by wild animals must wash his clothes, have a bath, and wait until evening before he is ritually clean. 16 If he does not, he must suffer the consequences.

Forbidden Sexual Practices

18 The LORD told Moses 2 to say to the people of Israel, "I am the LORD your God. 3 Do not follow the practices of the people of Egypt, where you once lived, or of the people in the land of Canaan, where I am now taking you. 4 Obey my laws and do what I command. I am the LORD your God. 5 Follow the practices and the laws that I give you; you will save your life by doing so. I am the LORD."

6 The LORD gave the following regulations. Do not have sexual intercourse with any of your relatives. 7 Do not disgrace your father by having intercourse with your mother. You must not disgrace your own mother. 8 Do not disgrace your father by having intercourse with any of his other wives. 9 Do not have intercourse with your sister or your stepsister, whether or not she was brought up in the same house with you. 10 Do not have intercourse with your granddaughter; that would be a disgrace to you. 11 Do not have intercourse with a half-sister; she, too, is your sister. 12–13 Do not have intercourse with an aunt, whether she is your father's sister or your mother's sister. 14 Do not have intercourse with your uncle's wife; she, too, is your aunt. 15 Do not have intercourse with your daughter-in-law 16 or with your brother's wife. 17 Do not have intercourse with the daughter or granddaughter of a woman with whom you have had intercourse; they may be related to you, and that would be incest. 18 Do not take your wife's sister as one of your wives, as long as your wife is living.

19 Do not have intercourse with a woman during her monthly period, because she is ritually unclean. 20 Do not have intercourse with another man's wife; that would make

you ritually unclean. 21 Do not hand over any of your children to be used in the worship of the god Molech, because that would bring disgrace on the name of God, the LORD. 22 No man is to have sexual relations with another man; God hates that. 23 No man or woman is to have sexual relations with an animal; that perversion makes you ritually unclean.

24 Do not make yourselves unclean by any of these acts, for that is how the pagans made themselves unclean, those pagans who lived in the land before you and whom the LORD is driving out so that you can go in. 25 Their actions made the land unclean, and so the LORD is punishing the land and making it reject the people who lived there. 26–27 They did all these disgusting things and made the land unclean, but you must not do them. All of you, whether Israelites or foreigners living with you, must keep the LORD's laws and commands, 28 and then the land will not reject you, as it rejected the pagans who lived there before you. 29 You know that whoever does any of these disgusting things will no longer be considered one of God's people.

30 And the LORD said, "Obey the commands I give and do not follow the practices of the people who lived in the land before you, and do not make yourselves unclean by doing any of these things. I am the LORD your God."

Laws of Holiness and Justice

19 The LORD told Moses 2 to say to the community of Israel, "Be holy, because I, the LORD your God, am holy. 3 Each of you must respect his mother and his father, and must keep the Sabbath, as I have commanded. I am the LORD your God.

4 "Do not abandon me and worship idols; do not make gods of metal and worship them. I am the LORD your God.

5 "When you kill an animal for a fellowship offering, keep the regulations that I have given you, and I will accept the offering. 6 The meat must be eaten on the day the animal is killed or on the next day. Any

See also: **18.5**: Neh 9.29; Ezek 18.9, 20.11–13; Lk 10.28; Rom 10.5; Gal 3.12   **18.8**: Lev 20.11; Deut 22.30, 27.20   **18.9**: Lev 20.17; Deut 27.22   **18.12–14**: Lev 20.19–20   **18.15**: Lev 20.12   **18.16**: Lev 20.21   **18.17**: Lev 20.14; Deut 27.23   **18.19**: Lev 20.18   **18.20**: Lev 20.10

See also: **18.21**: Lev 20.1–5   **18.22**: Lev 20.13   **18.23**: Ex 22.19; Lev 20.15–16; Deut 27.21   **19.2**: Lev 11.44–45; 1 Pet 1.16   **19.3**: Ex 20.8, 12; Deut 5.12, 16   **19.4**: Lev 26.1; Ex 20.23, 34.17; Deut 27.15

meat left on the third day must be burnt, 7 because it is ritually unclean, and if anyone eats it, I will not accept the offering. 8 Anyone who eats it will be guilty of treating as ordinary what is dedicated to me, and he will no longer be considered one of my people.

9 "When you harvest your fields, do not cut the corn at the edges of the fields, and do not go back to cut the ears of corn that were left. 10 Do not go back through your vineyard to gather the grapes that were missed or to pick up the grapes that have fallen; leave them for poor people and foreigners. I am the LORD your God.

11 "Do not steal or cheat or lie. 12 Do not make a promise in my name if you do not intend to keep it; that brings disgrace on my name. I am the LORD your God.

13 "Do not take advantage of anyone or rob him. Do not hold back the wages of someone you have hired, not even for one night. 14 Do not curse a deaf man or put something in front of a blind man so as to make him stumble over it. Obey me; I am the LORD your God.

15 "Be honest and just when you make decisions in legal cases; do not show favouritism to the poor or fear the rich. 16 Do not spread lies about anyone, and when someone is on trial for his life, speak out if your testimony can help him. I am the LORD.

17 "Do not bear a grudge against anyone, but settle your differences with him, so that you will not commit a sin because of him.* 18 Do not take revenge on anyone or continue to hate him, but love your neighbour as you love yourself. I am the LORD.

19 "Obey my commands. Do not cross-breed domestic animals. Do not plant two kinds of seed in the same field. Do not wear clothes made of two kinds of material.

20 "If a slave woman is the recognized concubine of a man and she has not been paid and freed, then if another man has sexual relations with her, they will be

punished but not* put to death, since she is a slave. 21 The man shall bring a ram to the entrance of the Tent of my presence as his repayment offering, 22 and with it the priest shall perform the ritual of purification to remove the man's sin, and God will forgive him.

23 "When you come into the land of Canaan and plant any kind of fruit tree, consider the fruit ritually unclean for the first three years. During that time you must not eat it. 24 In the fourth year all the fruit shall be dedicated as an offering to show your gratitude to me,* the LORD. 25 But in the fifth year you may eat the fruit. If you do all this, your trees will bear more fruit. I am the LORD your God.

26 "Do not eat any meat with blood still in it. Do not practise any kind of magic. 27 Do not cut the hair on the sides of your head or trim your beard 28 or tattoo yourselves or cut gashes in your body to mourn for the dead. I am the LORD.

29 "Do not disgrace your daughters by making them temple prostitutes;* if you do, you will turn to other gods and the land will be full of immorality. 30 Keep the Sabbath, and honour the place where I am worshipped. I am the LORD.

31 "Do not go for advice to people who consult the spirits of the dead. If you do, you will be ritually unclean. I am the LORD your God.

32 "Show respect for old people and honour them. Reverently obey me; I am the LORD.

33 "Do not ill-treat foreigners who are living in your land. 34 Treat them as you would a fellow-Israelite, and love them as you love yourselves. Remember that you were once foreigners in the land of Egypt. I am the LORD your God.

35 "Do not cheat anyone by using false measures of length, weight, or quantity.

19.20 they... not; *or* an investigation will be made but they will not be.
19.24 to show your gratitude to me; *or* in praise of me.
19.29 TEMPLE PROSTITUTES: *These women were found in Canaanite temples, where fertility gods were worshipped. It was believed that intercourse with these prostitutes assured fertile fields and herds.*

See also: **19.26:** Gen 9.4; Lev 7.26–27, 17.10–14; Deut 12.16, 23, 15.23, 18.10 **19.27–28:** Lev 2.5; Deut 14.1 **19.29:** Deut 23.17 **19.30:** Lev 26.2 **19.31:** Deut 18.11; 1 Sam 28.3; 2 Kgs 23.4; Is 8.19 **19.33–34:** Ex 22.21; Deut 24.17–18, 27.19 **19.35–36:** Deut 25.13–16; Prov 20.10; Ezek 45.10

19.17 so... him; *or so that you do not commit this sin* against him.
See also: **19.9–10:** Lev 23.22; Deut 24.19–22 **19.11:** Ex 20.15, 16; Deut 5.19, 20 **19.12:** Ex 20.7; Deut 5.11; Mt 5.33 **19.13:** Deut 24.14–15 **19.14:** Deut 27.18 **19.15:** Ex 23.6–8; Deut 16.19 **19.17:** Mt 18.15 **19.18:** Mt 5.43, 19.19, 22.39; Mk 12.31; Lk 10.27; Rom 13.9; Gal 5.14; Jas 2.8 **19.19:** Deut 22.9–11

Show respect for old people (19.32)

36 Use honest scales, honest weights, and honest measures. I am the LORD your God, and I brought you out of Egypt. 37 Obey all my laws and commands. I am the LORD."

Penalties for Disobedience

20 The LORD told Moses 2 to say to the people of Israel, "Any of you or any foreigner living among you who gives any of his or her children to be used in the worship of the god Molech shall be stoned to death by the whole community. 3 If anyone gives one of his children to Molech and makes my sacred Tent unclean and disgraces my holy name, I will turn against him and will no longer consider him one of my people. 4 But if the community ignores what he has done and does not put him to death, 5 I myself will turn against the man and his whole family and against all who join him in being unfaithful to me and worshipping Molech. I will no longer consider them my people.

6 "If anyone goes for advice to people who consult the spirits of the dead, I will turn against him and will no longer consider him one of my people. 7 Keep yourselves holy, because I am the LORD your God. 8 Obey my laws, because I am the LORD and I make you holy."

9 The LORD gave the following regulations. Anyone who curses his father or his mother shall be put to death; he is responsible for his own death.

10 If a man commits adultery with the wife of a fellow-Israelite, both he and the woman shall be put to death. 11 A man who has intercourse with one of his father's wives disgraces his father, and both he and the woman shall be put to death. They are responsible for their own death. 12 If a man has intercourse with his daughter-in-law, they shall both be put to death. They have committed incest and are responsible for their own death. 13 If a man has sexual relations with another man, they have done a disgusting thing, and both shall be put to death. They are responsible for their own death. 14 If a man marries a woman and her mother, all three shall be burnt to death because of the disgraceful thing they have done; such a thing must not be permitted among you. 15 If a man has sexual relations with an animal, he and the animal shall be put to death. 16 If a woman tries to have sexual relations with an animal, she and the animal shall be put to death. They are responsible for their own death.

17 If a man marries his sister or half-sister, they shall be publicly disgraced and driven out of the community. He has had intercourse with his sister and must suffer the consequences. 18 If a man has intercourse with a woman during her monthly period, both of them are to be driven out of the community, because they have broken the regulations about ritual uncleanness.

19 If a man has intercourse with his aunt, both of them must suffer the consequences for incest. 20 If a man has intercourse with his uncle's wife, he disgraces his uncle, and he and the woman will pay the penalty; neither of them will have children. 21 If a man marries his brother's wife, they will die childless. He has done a ritually unclean thing and has disgraced his brother.

22 The LORD said, "Keep all my laws and commands, so that you will not be rejected by the land of Canaan, into which I am bringing you. 23 Do not adopt the customs of people who live there; I am driving out those pagans so that you can enter the land. They have disgusted me with all their

See also: 20.9: Ex 21.17; Mt 15.4; Mk 7.10

See also: 20.10: Ex 20.14; Lev 18.20; Deut 5.18
20.11: Lev 18.8; Deut 22.30, 27.20 **20.12:** Lev 18.15
20.13: Lev 18.22 **20.14:** Lev 18.17; Deut 27.23
20.15–16: Ex 22.19; Lev 18.23; Deut 27.21
20.17: Lev 18.9; Deut 22.22 **20.18:** Lev 18.19
20.19–20: Lev 18.12–14 **20.21:** Lev 13.16

evil practices. 24 But I have promised you this rich and fertile land as your possession, and I will give it to you. I am the LORD your God, and I have set you apart from the other nations. 25 So then, you must make a clear distinction between animals and birds that are ritually clean and those that are not. Do not eat unclean animals or birds. I have declared them unclean, and eating them would make you unclean. 26 You shall be holy and belong only to me, because I am the LORD and I am holy. I have set you apart from the other nations so that you would belong to me alone.

27 "Any man or woman who consults the spirits of the dead shall be stoned to death; any person who does this is responsible for his own death."

The Holiness of the Priests

21 The LORD commanded Moses to say to the Aaronite priests, "No priest is to make himself ritually unclean by taking part in the funeral ceremonies when a relative dies, 2 unless it is his mother, father, son, daughter, brother, 3 or unmarried sister living in his house. 4 He shall not make himself unclean at the death of those related to him by marriage.*

5 "No priest shall shave any part of his head or trim his beard or cut gashes on his body to show that he is in mourning. 6 He must be holy and must not disgrace my name. He offers food offerings to me, and he must be holy. 7 A priest shall not marry a woman who has been a prostitute or a woman who is not a virgin or who is divorced; he is holy. 8 The people must consider the priest holy, because he presents the food offerings to me. I am the LORD; I am holy and I make my people holy. 9 If a priest's daughter becomes a prostitute, she disgraces her father; she shall be burnt to death.

10 "The High Priest has had the anointing oil poured on his head and has been consecrated to wear the priestly garments, so he must not leave his hair uncombed or tear *his clothes to show that he is in mourning.* 11–12 He has been dedicated to me and is not to make himself ritually unclean nor is he to defile my sacred Tent by leaving it and

entering a house where there is a dead person, even if it is his own father or mother. 13 He shall marry a virgin, 14 not a widow or a divorced woman or a woman who has been a prostitute. He shall marry only a virgin from his own clan. 15 Otherwise, his children, who ought to be holy, will be ritually unclean. I am the LORD and I have set him apart as the High Priest."

16 The LORD commanded Moses 17 to say to Aaron, "None of your descendants who has any physical defect may present the food offering to me. This applies for all time to come. 18 No man with any physical defect may make the offering: no one who is blind, lame, disfigured, or deformed; 19 no one with a crippled hand or foot; 20 no one who is a hunchback or a dwarf; no one with any eye or skin disease; and no eunuch. 21 No descendant of Aaron the priest who has any physical defect may present the food offering to me. 22 Such a man may eat the food offered to me, both the holy food offering and the very holy food offering, 23 but because he has a physical defect, he shall not come near the sacred curtain or approach the altar. He must not profane these holy things, because I am the LORD and I make them holy."

24 This, then, is what Moses said to Aaron, the sons of Aaron, and to all the people of Israel.

The Holiness of the Offerings

22 The LORD commanded Moses 2 to say to Aaron and his sons, "You must not bring disgrace on my holy name, so treat with respect the sacred offerings that the people of Israel dedicate to me. I am the LORD. 3 If any of your descendants, while he is ritually unclean, comes near the sacred offerings which the people of Israel have dedicated to me, he can never again serve at the altar. This applies for all time to come. I am the LORD.

4 "None of the descendants of Aaron who has a dreaded skin disease or a discharge may eat any of the sacred offerings *until he is ritually clean. Any priest is unclean if he touches anything which is* unclean through contact with a corpse or if he has an emission of semen 5 or if he has touched an unclean animal or person. 6 Any priest who becomes unclean remains unclean until evening, and even then he

---

21.4 *Verse 4 in Hebrew is unclear.*
See also: 21.5: Lev 19.27–28; Deut 14.1

may not eat any of the sacred offerings until he has had a bath. 7 After the sun sets he is clean, and then he may eat the sacred offerings, which are his food. 8 He shall not eat the meat of any animal that has died a natural death or has been killed by wild animals; it will make him unclean. I am the LORD.

9 "All priests shall observe the regulations that I have given. Otherwise, they will be guilty and die, because they have disobeyed the sacred regulations. I am the LORD and I make them holy.

10 "Only a member of a priestly family may eat any of the sacred offerings; no one else may eat them — not even someone staying with a priest or hired by him. 11 But a priest's slaves, bought with his own money or born in his home, may eat the food the priest receives. 12 A priest's daughter who marries someone who is not a priest may not eat any of the sacred offerings. 13 But a widowed or divorced daughter who has no children and who has returned to live in her father's house as a dependant may eat the food her father receives as a priest. Only a member of a priestly family may eat any of it.

14 "If any person who is not a member of a priestly family eats any of the sacred offerings without intending to, he must repay the priest its full value plus an additional twenty per cent. 15 The priests shall not profane the sacred offerings 16 by letting any unauthorized person eat them; this would bring guilt and punishment on such a person. I am the LORD and I make the offerings holy.

17 The LORD commanded Moses 18 to give Aaron and his sons and all the people of Israel the following regulations. When any Israelite or any foreigner living in Israel presents a burnt offering, whether in fulfilment of a vow or as a freewill offering, the animal must not have any defects. 19 To be accepted, it must be a male without any defects. 20 If you offer any animal that has any defect, the LORD will not accept it. 21 When anyone presents a fellowship offering to the LORD, whether in fulfilment of a vow or as a freewill offering, the animal must be without any defect if it is to be accepted. 22 Do not offer to the LORD any animal that is blind or crippled or mutilated, or that has a running sore or a skin eruption or scabs. Do not offer any such animals on the altar as a food offering. 23 As a freewill offering you may offer an animal that is stunted or not perfectly formed, but it is not acceptable in fulfilment of a vow. 24 Do not offer to the LORD any animal whose testicles have been crushed, cut, bruised, or torn off. This is not permitted in your land.

25 Do not offer as a food offering any animal obtained from a foreigner. Such animals are considered defective and are not acceptable.

26–27 When a calf or a lamb or a kid is born, it must not be taken from its mother for seven days, but after that it is acceptable as a food offering. 28 Do not sacrifice a cow and its calf or a sheep and its lamb or a goat and its kid on the same day. 29 When you offer a sacrifice of thanksgiving to the LORD, follow the rules so that you will be accepted; 30 eat it the same day and leave none of it until the next morning.

31 The LORD said, "Obey my commands; I am the LORD. 32 Do not bring disgrace on my holy name; all the people of Israel must acknowledge me to be holy. I am the LORD and I make you holy; 33 and I brought you out of Egypt to become your God. I am the LORD."

The Religious Festivals

23 The LORD gave Moses 2 the following regulations for the religious festivals, when the people of Israel are to gather for worship. 3 You have six days in which to do your work, but remember that the seventh day, the Sabbath, is a day of rest. On that day do not work, but gather for worship. The Sabbath belongs to the LORD, no matter where you live. 4 Proclaim the following festivals at the appointed times.

Passover and Unleavened Bread
(Num 28.16–25)

5 The Passover, celebrated to honour the LORD, begins at sunset on the fourteenth day of the first month. 6 On the fifteenth day the Festival of Unleavened Bread begins, and for

---

See also: **22.20:** Deut 17.1

See also: **23.3:** Ex 20.8–10, 23.12, 31.15, 34.21, 35.2; Deut 5.12–14   **23.5:** Ex 12.1–13; Deut 16.1–2
23.6–8: Ex 12.14–20, 23.15, 34.18; Deut 16.3–8

seven days you must not eat any bread made with yeast. 7 On the first of these days you shall gather for worship and do none of your daily work. 8 Offer your food offerings to the LORD for seven days. On the seventh day you shall again gather for worship, but you shall do none of your daily work.

9–10 When you come into the land that the LORD is giving you and you harvest your corn, take the first sheaf to the priest. 11 He shall present it as a special offering to the LORD, so that you may be accepted. The priest shall present it the day after the Sabbath. 12 On the day you present the offering of corn, also sacrifice as a burnt offering a one-year-old male lamb that has no defects. 13 With it you shall present two kilogrammes of flour mixed with olive oil as a food offering. The smell of this offering is pleasing to the LORD. You shall also present with it an offering of one litre of wine. 14 Do not eat any of the new corn, whether raw, roasted, or baked into bread, until you have brought this offering to God. This regulation is to be observed by all your descendants for all time to come.

The Harvest Festival
(Num 28.26–31)

15 Count seven full weeks from the day after the Sabbath on which you bring your sheaf of corn to present to the LORD. 16 On the fiftieth day, the day after the seventh Sabbath, present to the LORD another new offering of corn. 17 Each family is to bring two loaves of bread and present them to the LORD as a special gift. Each loaf shall be made of two kilogrammes of flour baked with yeast and shall be presented to the Lord as an offering of the first corn to be harvested. 18 And with the bread the community is to present seven one-year-old lambs, one bull, and two rams, none of which may have any defects. They shall be offered as a burnt offering to the LORD, together with a grain offering and a wine offering. The smell of this offering is pleasing to the LORD. 19 Also offer one male goat as a sin offering and two one-year-old male lambs as a fellowship offering. 20 The priest shall present the bread with the two lambs as a special gift to the LORD for the priests. These offerings are holy. 21 On that day do

Leave them for poor people (23.22)

none of your daily work, but gather for worship. Your descendants are to observe this regulation for all time to come, no matter where they live.

22 When you harvest your fields, do not cut the corn at the edges of the fields, and do not go back to cut the ears of corn that were left; leave them for poor people and foreigners. The LORD is your God.

The New Year Festival
(Num 29.1–6)

23–24 On the first day of the seventh month observe a special day of rest, and come together for worship when the trumpets sound. 25 Present a food offering to the LORD and do none of your daily work.

The Day of Atonement
(Num 29.7–11)

26–27 The tenth day of the seventh month is the day when the annual ritual is to be performed to take away the sins of the people. On that day do not eat anything at all; come together for worship, and present a food offering to the Lord. 28 Do no work on that day, because it is the day for performing the ritual to take away sin. 29 Anyone who eats anything on that day will no longer be considered one of God's people. 30 And if anyone does any work on that day, the LORD himself will put him to death. 31 This regulation applies to all your descendants, no matter where they live. 32 From sunset on the ninth day of the month to sunset on the tenth observe this day as a special day of rest, during which nothing may be eaten.

See also: 23.15–21: Ex 23.16, 34.22; Deut 16.9–12

See also: 23.22: Lev 19.9–10; Deut 24.19–22
23.26–32: Lev 16.29–34

The Festival of Shelters
(Num 29.12–40)

33–34 The Festival of Shelters begins on the fifteenth day of the seventh month and continues for seven days. 35 On the first of these days come together for worship and do none of your daily work. 36 Each day for seven days you shall present a food offering. On the eighth day come together again for worship and present a food offering. It is a day for worship, and you shall do no work.

37 (These are the religious festivals on which you honour the LORD by gathering together for worship and presenting food offerings, burnt offerings, grain offerings, sacrifices, and wine offerings, as required day by day. 38 These festivals are in addition to the regular Sabbaths, and these offerings are in addition to your regular gifts, your offerings in fulfilment of vows, and your freewill offerings that you give to the LORD.)

39 When you have harvested your fields, celebrate this festival for seven days, beginning on the fifteenth day of the seventh month. The first day shall be a special day of rest. 40 On that day take some of the best fruit from your trees, take palm branches and the branches of leafy trees, and begin a religious festival to honour the LORD your God. 41 Celebrate it for seven days. This regulation is to be kept by your descendants for all time to come. 42 All the people of Israel shall live in shelters for seven days, 43 so that your descendants may know that the LORD made the people of Israel live in simple shelters when he led them out of Egypt. He is the LORD your God.

44 So in this way Moses gave the people of Israel the regulations for observing the religious festivals to honour the LORD.

Taking Care of the Lamps
(Ex 27.20–21)

24 The LORD told Moses 2 to give the following orders to the people of Israel: Bring some pure olive oil of the finest quality for the lamps in the Tent, so that a light may be kept burning regularly. 3 Each evening Aaron shall light them and keep them burning until morning, there in the LORD's presence outside the curtain in front of the Covenant Box, which is in the Most Holy Place. This regulation is to be observed for all time to come. 4 Aaron shall take care of the lamps on the lampstand of pure gold and must see that they burn regularly in the LORD's presence.

The Bread Offered to God
5 Take twelve kilogrammes of flour and bake twelve loaves of bread. 6 Put the loaves in two rows, six in each row, on the table covered with pure gold. which is in the LORD's presence. 7 Put some pure incense on each row, as a token food offering to the LORD to take the place of bread. 8 Every Sabbath, for all time to come, the bread must be placed in the presence of the LORD. This is Israel's duty for ever. 9 The bread belongs to Aaron and his descendants, and they shall eat it in a holy place, because this is a very holy part of the food offered to the LORD for the priests.

An Example of Just and Fair Punishment
10–11 There was a man whose father was an Egyptian and whose mother was an Israelite named Shelomith, the daughter of Dibri from the tribe of Dan. There in the camp this man quarrelled with an Israelite. During the quarrel he cursed God, so they took him to Moses, 12 put him under guard, and waited for the LORD to tell them what to do with him.

13 The LORD said to Moses, 14 "Take that man out of the camp. Everyone who heard him curse shall put his hands on the man's head to testify that he is guilty, and then the whole community shall stone him to death. 15 Then tell the people of Israel that anyone who curses God must suffer the consequences 16 and be put to death. Any Israelite or any foreigner living in Israel who curses the LORD shall be stoned to death by the whole community.

17 "Anyone who commits murder shall be put to death, 18 and anyone who kills an animal belonging to someone else must replace it. The principle is a life for a life.

19 "If anyone injures another person, whatever he has done shall be done to him. 20 If he breaks a bone, one of his bones shall

See also: 23.33–36: Deut 16.13–15

See also: 24.5–6: Ex 25.30 **24.9:** Mt 12.4; Mk 2.26; Lk 6.4 **24.17:** Ex 21.12
24.20: Ex 21.23–25; Deut 19.21; Mt 5.38

be broken; if he blinds him in one eye, one of his eyes shall be blinded; if he knocks out a tooth, one of his teeth shall be knocked out. Whatever injury he causes another person shall be done to him in return. 21 Whoever kills an animal shall replace it, but whoever kills a human being shall be put to death. 22 This law applies to all of you, to Israelites and to foreigners living among you, because I am the LORD your God."

23 When Moses had said this to the people of Israel, they took the man outside the camp and stoned him to death. In this way the people of Israel did what the LORD had commanded Moses.

The Seventh Year
(Deut 15.1–11)

25 The LORD spoke to Moses on Mount Sinai and commanded him 2 to give the following regulations to the people of Israel. When you enter the land that the LORD is giving you, you shall honour the LORD by not cultivating the land every seventh year. 3 You shall sow your fields, prune your vineyards, and gather your crops for six years. 4 But the seventh year is to be a year of complete rest for the land, a year dedicated to the LORD. Do not sow your fields or prune your vineyards. 5 Do not even harvest the corn that grows by itself without being sown, and do not gather the grapes from your unpruned vines; it is a year of complete rest for the land. 6 Although the land has not been cultivated during that year, it will provide food for you, your slaves, your hired men, the foreigners living with you, 7 your domestic animals, and the wild animals in your fields. Everything that it produces may be eaten.

The Year of Restoration

8 Count seven times seven years, a total of 49 years. 9 Then, on the tenth day of the seventh month, the Day of Atonement, send someone to blow a trumpet throughout the whole land. 10 In this way you shall set the fiftieth year apart and proclaim freedom to all the inhabitants of the land. During this year all property that has been sold shall be restored to the original owner or his descendants, and anyone who has been sold as a slave shall return to his family.

See also: **24.22:** Num 15.16 **25.1–7:** Ex 23.10–11

11 You shall not sow your fields or harvest the corn that grows by itself or gather the grapes in your unpruned vineyards. 12 The whole year shall be sacred for you; you shall eat only what the fields produce of themselves.

13 In this year all property that has been sold shall be restored to its original owner. 14 So when you sell land to your fellow-Israelite or buy land from him, do not deal unfairly. 15 The price is to be fixed according to the number of years the land can produce crops before the next Year of Restoration. 16 If there are many years, the price shall be higher, but if there are only a few years, the price shall be lower, because what is being sold is the number of crops the land can produce. 17 Do not cheat a fellow-Israelite, but obey the LORD your God.

The Problem of the Seventh Year

18 Obey all the LORD's laws and commands, so that you may live in safety in the land. 19 The land will produce its crops, and you will have all you want to eat and will live in safety.

20 But someone may ask what there will be to eat during the seventh year, when no fields are sown and no crops gathered. 21 The LORD will bless the land in the sixth year so that it will produce enough food for two years. 22 When you sow your fields in the eighth year, you will still be eating what you harvested during the sixth year, and you will have enough to eat until the crops you plant that year are harvested.

Restoration of Property

23 Your land must not be sold on a permanent basis, because you do not own it; it belongs to God, and you are like foreigners who are allowed to make use of it.

24 When land is sold, the right of the original owner to buy it back must be recognized. 25 If an Israelite becomes poor and is forced to sell his land, his closest relative is to buy it back. 26 Anyone who has no relative to buy it back may later become prosperous and have enough to buy it back. 27 In that case he must pay to the man who bought it a sum that will make up for the years remaining until the next Year of Restoration, when he would in any event recover his land. 28 But if he does not have enough money to buy the land back, it remains

under the control of the man who bought it until the next Year of Restoration. In that year it will be returned to its original owner.

29 If someone sells a house in a walled city, he has the right to buy it back during the first full year from the date of sale. 30 But if he does not buy it back within the year, he loses the right of repurchase, and the house becomes the permanent property of the purchaser and his descendants; it will not be returned in the Year of Restoration. 31 But houses in unwalled villages are to be treated like fields; the original owner has the right to buy them back, and they are to be returned in the Year of Restoration. 32 However, Levites have the right to buy back at any time their property in the cities assigned to them. 33 If a house in one of these cities is sold by a Levite and is not bought back, it must be returned in the Year of Restoration,* because the houses which the Levites own in their cities are their permanent property among the people of Israel. 34 But the pasture land round the Levite cities shall never be sold; it is their property for ever.

Loans to the Poor

35 If a fellow-Israelite living near you becomes poor and cannot support himself or herself, you must provide for them as you would for hired servants, so that they can continue to live near you. 36 Do not charge them any interest, but obey God and let your fellow-Israelites live near you. 37 Do not make them pay interest on the money you lend them, and do not make a profit on the food you sell them. 38 This is the command of the LORD your God, who brought you out of Egypt in order to give you the land of Canaan and to be your God.

Release of Slaves

39 If a fellow-Israelite living near you becomes so poor that he sells himself to you as a slave, you shall not make him do the work of a slave. 40 He shall stay with you as a hired servant and serve you until the next Year of Restoration. 41 At that time he and his children shall leave you and

You must provide for them   (25.35)

return to his family and to the property of his ancestors. 42 The people of Israel are the LORD's slaves, and he brought them out of Egypt; they must not be sold into slavery. 43 Do not treat them harshly, but obey your God. 44 If you need slaves, you may buy them from the nations round you. 45 You may also buy the children of the foreigners who are living among you. Such children born in your land may become your property, 46 and you may leave them as an inheritance to your sons, whom they must serve as long as they live. But you must not treat any of your fellow-Israelites harshly.

47 Suppose a foreigner living with you becomes rich, while a fellow-Israelite becomes poor and sells himself as a slave to that foreigner or to a member of his family. 48 After he is sold, he still has the right to be bought back. One of his brothers 49 or his uncle or his cousin or another of his close relatives may buy him back; or if he himself earns enough, he may buy his own freedom. 50 He must consult the one who bought him, and they must count the years from the time he sold himself until the next Year of Restoration and must set the price for his release on the basis of the wages paid to a hired servant. 51-52 He must refund a part of the purchase price according to the number

---

25.33 *Probable text* If a house… Restoration; *Hebrew unclear.*

See also: **25.35:** Deut 15.7–8   **25.37:** Ex 22.25; Deut 23.19–20   **25.39–46:** Ex 21.2–6; Deut 15.12–18 of years left, 53 as if he had been hired on an annual basis. His master must not treat him harshly. 54 If he is not set free in any of these ways, he and his children must be set free in the next Year of Restoration. 55 An Israelite cannot be a permanent slave, because the people of Israel are the LORD's slaves. He brought them out of Egypt; he is the LORD their God.

Blessings for Obedience
(Deut 7.12–24; 28.1–14)

26 The LORD said, "Do not make idols or set up statues, stone pillars, or carved stones to worship. I am the LORD your God. 2 Keep the religious festivals and honour the place where I am worshipped. I am the LORD.

3 "If you live according to my laws and obey my commands, 4 I will send you rain at the right time, so that the land will produce crops and the trees will bear fruit. 5 Your crops will be so plentiful that you will still be harvesting corn when it is time to pick grapes, and you will still be picking grapes when it is time to sow corn. You will have all that you want to eat, and you will live in safety in your land.

6 "I will give you peace in your land, and you will sleep without being afraid of anyone. I will get rid of the dangerous animals in the land, and there will be no more war there. 7 You will be victorious over your enemies; 8 five of you will be able to defeat a hundred, and a hundred will be able to defeat ten thousand. 9 I will bless you and give you many children; I will keep my part of the covenant that I made with you. 10 Your harvests will be so plentiful that they will last for a year, and even then you will have to throw away what is left of the old harvest to make room for the new. 11 I will live among you in my sacred tent, and I will never turn away from you. 12 I will be with you; I will be your God, and you will be my people. 13 I, the LORD your God, brought you out of Egypt so that you would no longer be slaves. I broke the power that held you down and I let you walk with your head held high."

See also: 26.1: Ex 20.4; Lev 19.4; Deut 5.8, 16.21–22, 27.1   26.3–5: Deut 11.13–15, 28.1–14   26.12: 2 Cor 6.16

Punishment for Disobedience
(Deut 28.15–68)

14 The LORD said, "If you will not obey my commands, you will be punished. 15 If you refuse to obey my laws and commands and break the covenant I have made with you, 16 I will punish you. I will bring disaster on you — incurable diseases and fevers that will make you blind and cause your life to waste away. You will sow your seed, but it will do you no good, because your enemies will conquer you and eat what you have grown. 17 I will turn against you, so that you will be defeated, and those who hate you will rule over you; you will be so terrified that you will run when no one is chasing you.

18 "If even after all this you still do not obey me, I will increase your punishment seven times. 19 I will break your stubborn pride; there will be no rain, and your land will be dry and as hard as iron. 20 All your hard work will do you no good, because your land will not produce crops and the trees will not bear fruit.

21 "If you still continue to resist me and refuse to obey me, I will again increase your punishment seven times. 22 I will send dangerous animals among you, and they will kill your children, destroy your livestock, and leave so few of you that your roads will be deserted.

23 "If after all this punishment you still do not listen to me, but continue to defy me, 24 then I will turn on you and punish you seven times harder than before. 25 I will bring war on you to punish you for breaking our covenant, and if you gather in your cities for safety, I will send incurable diseases among you, and you will be forced to surrender to your enemies. 26 I will cut off your food supply, so that ten women will need only one oven to bake all the bread they have. They will ration it out, and when you have eaten it all, you will still be hungry.

27 "If after all this you still continue to defy me and refuse to obey me, 28 then in my anger I will turn on you and again make your punishment seven times worse than before. 29 Your hunger will be so great that you will eat your own children. 30 I will destroy your places of worship on the hills, tear down your incense altars, and throw your dead

bodies on your fallen idols. In utter disgust 31 I will turn your cities into ruins, destroy your places of worship, and refuse to accept your sacrifices. 32 I will destroy your land so completely that the enemies who occupy it will be shocked at the destruction. 33 I will bring war on you and scatter you in foreign lands. Your land will be deserted, and your cities left in ruins. 34–35 Then the land will enjoy the years of complete rest that you would not give it; it will lie abandoned and get its rest while you are in exile in the land of your enemies.

36 "I will make those of you who are in exile so terrified that the sound of a leaf blowing in the wind will make you run. You will run as if you were being pursued in battle, and you will fall when there is no enemy near you. 37 You will stumble over one another when no one is chasing you, and you will be unable to fight against any enemy. 38 You will die in exile, swallowed up by the land of your enemies. 39 The few of you who survive in the land of your enemies will waste away because of your own sin and the sin of your ancestors.

40 "But your descendants will confess their sins and the sins of their ancestors, who resisted me and rebelled against me, 41 and made me turn against them and send them into exile in the land of their enemies. At last, when your descendants are humbled and they have paid the penalty for their sin and rebellion, 42 I will remember my covenant with Jacob and with Isaac and with Abraham, and I will renew my promise to give my people the land. 43 First, however, the land must be rid of its people, so that it can enjoy the complete rest, and they must pay the full penalty for having rejected my laws and my commands. 44 But even then, when they are still in the land of their enemies, I will not completely abandon or destroy them. That would put an end to my covenant with them, and I am the LORD their God. 45 I will renew the covenant that I made with their ancestors when I showed all the nations my power by bringing my people out of Egypt, in order that I, the LORD, might be their God."

46 All these are the laws and commands that the LORD gave to Moses on Mount Sinai for the people of Israel.

Laws concerning Gifts to the LORD

27 The LORD gave Moses 2 the following regulations for the people of Israel. When a person has been given to the LORD in fulfilment of a special vow, that person may be set free by the payment of the following sums of money, 3–7 according to the official standard:

— adult male, twenty to sixty years old: 50 pieces of silver
— adult female: 30 pieces of silver
— young male, five to twenty years old: 20 pieces of silver
— young female: 10 pieces of silver
— infant male under five: 5 pieces of silver
— infant female: 3 pieces of silver
— male above sixty years of age: 15 pieces of silver
— female above sixty: 10 pieces of silver

8 If anyone who made the vow is too poor to pay the standard price, he or she shall bring the person to the priest, and the priest will set a lower price, according to the ability of that person to pay.

9 If the vow concerns an animal that is acceptable as an offering to the LORD, then every gift made to the LORD is sacred, 10 and anyone who made the vow may not substitute another animal for it. If he does, both animals belong to the LORD. 11 But if the vow concerns a ritually unclean animal, which is not acceptable as an offering to the LORD, the man shall take the animal to the priest. 12 The priest shall fix a price for it, according to its good or bad qualities, and the price will be final. 13 If the person wishes to buy it back, he must pay the price plus an additional twenty per cent.

14 When someone dedicates his house to the LORD, the priest shall fix the price according to its good or bad points, and the price will be final. 15 If the one who dedicated the house wishes to buy it back, he must pay the price plus an additional twenty per cent.

16 If someone dedicates part of his land to the LORD, the price shall be fixed according to the amount of seed it takes to sow it, at the rate of ten pieces of silver for

See also: 26.42: Gen 17.7–8, 26.3–4, 28.13–14

every twenty kilogrammes of barley.
17 If he dedicates the land immediately
after a Year of Restoration, the full price
applies. 18 If he dedicates it later, the priest
shall estimate the cash value according to
the number of years left until the next Year
of Restoration, and fix a reduced price.
19 If the one who dedicated the field
wishes to buy it back, he or she must pay
the price plus an additional twenty per
cent. 20 If they sell the field to someone
else without first buying it back from the
LORD, they lose the right to buy it back.
21 At the next Year of Restoration the field
will become the LORD's permanent property; it shall belong to the priests.

22 If someone dedicates to the LORD a
field that he has bought, 23 the priest shall
estimate its value according to the number
of years until the next Year of Restoration,
and the person must pay the price that
very day; the money belongs to the LORD.
24 At the Year of Restoration the field shall
be returned to the original owner or to his
descendants.

25 All prices shall be fixed according to
the official standard.

26 The firstborn of an animal already
belongs to the LORD, so no one may dedicate it to him as a freewill offering. A calf,

a lamb, or a kid belongs to the LORD,
27 but the firstborn of an unclean animal
may be bought back at the standard price
plus an additional twenty per cent. If it is
not bought back, it may be sold to someone else at the standard price.

28 No one may sell or buy back what he
has unconditionally dedicated* to the LORD,
whether it is a human being, an animal, or
land. It belongs permanently to the LORD.
29 Not even a human being who has been
unconditionally dedicated may be bought
back; he must be put to death.

30 One-tenth of all the produce of the
land, whether grain or fruit, belongs to the
LORD. 31 If a man wishes to buy any of it
back, he must pay the standard price plus
an additional twenty per cent. 32 One out
of every ten domestic animals belongs to
the LORD. When the animals are counted,
every tenth one belongs to the LORD. 33 The
owner may not arrange the animals so that
the poor animals are chosen, and he may
not make any substitutions. If he does substitute one animal for another, then both
animals will belong to the LORD and may not
be bought back.

34 These are the commands that the LORD
gave Moses on Mount Sinai for the people
of Israel.

27.28 UNCONDITIONALLY DEDICATED: *Anything dedicated in this way belonged completely to the LORD and could not be used; it had to be destroyed.*

See also: 27.28: Num 18.14 **27.30–33:** Num 18.21; Deut 14.22–29

NUMBERS

INTRODUCTION

Numbers tells the story of the Israelites during the nearly forty years from the time they left Mount Sinai until they reached the eastern border of the land that God had promised to give them. The name of the book refers to a prominent feature of the story, that is, the census which Moses took of the Israelites at Mount Sinai before their departure, and again in Moab, east of the Jordan, about a generation later. In the period between the two censuses the Israelites went to Kadesh Barnea on the southern border of Canaan, but failed to enter the promised land from there. After spending many years in that area, they went to the region east of the River Jordan, where part of the people settled and where the rest prepared to cross the river into Canaan.

Numbers is an account of a people who were often discouraged and afraid in the face of hardship, and who rebelled against God and against Moses, the man God appointed to lead them. It is the story of God's faithful, persistent care for his people in spite of their weakness and disobedience, and of Moses' steadfast, if sometimes impatient, devotion both to God and to his people.

Outline of Contents

The Israelites prepare to leave Mount Sinai   1.1—9.23
  a. The first census   1.1—4.49
  b. Various laws and rules   5.1—8.26
  c. The second Passover   9.1—23
From Mount Sinai to Moab   10.1—21.35
Events in Moab   22.1—32.42
Summary of the journey from Egypt to Moab   33.1—49
Instructions before crossing the Jordan   33.50—36.13

The First Census of Israel

1 On the first day of the second month in the second year after the people of Israel left Egypt, the LORD spoke to Moses there in the Tent of his presence in the Sinai Desert. He said, 2 "You and Aaron are to take a census of the people of Israel by clans and families. List the names of all the men 3 twenty years old or older who are fit for military service. 4 Ask one clan chief from each tribe to help you." 5–16 These are the men, leaders within their tribes, who were chosen from the community for this work:

Tribe	Clan chief
Reuben	Elizur son of Shedeur
Simeon	Shelumiel son of Zurishaddai
Judah	Nahshon son of Amminadab
Issachar	Nethanel son of Zuar
Zebulun	Eliab son of Helon
Ephraim	Elishama son of Ammihud
Manasseh	Gamaliel son of Pedahzur
Benjamin	Abidan son of Gideoni
Dan	Ahiezer son of Ammishaddai
Asher	Pagiel son of Ochran
Gad	Eliasaph son of Deuel
Naphtali	Ahira son of Enan

17 With the help of these twelve men Moses and Aaron 18 called together the whole community on the first day of the second month and registered all the people by clans and families. The names of all the men twenty years old or older were recorded and counted, 19 as the LORD had commanded. In the Sinai Desert, Moses registered the people. 20–46 The men

See also: 1.1–46: Num 26.1–51

twenty years old or older who were fit for military service were registered by name according to clan and family, beginning with the tribe of Reuben, Jacob's eldest son. The totals were as follows:

Tribe	Number
Reuben	46,500
Simeon	59,300
Gad	45,650
Judah	74,600
Issachar	54,400
Zebulun	57,400
Ephraim	40,500
Manasseh	32,200
Benjamin	35,400
Dan	62,700
Asher	41,500
Naphtali	53,400
Total:	603,550

47 The Levites were not registered with the other tribes, 48 because the LORD had said to Moses, 49 "When you take a census of the men fit for military service, do not include the tribe of Levi. 50 Instead, put the Levites in charge of the Tent of my presence and all its equipment. They shall carry it and its equipment, serve in it, and set up their camp round it. 51 Whenever you move your camp, the Levites shall take the Tent down and set it up again at each new camping place. Anyone else who comes near the Tent shall be put to death. 52 The rest of the Israelites shall set up camp, company by company, each man with his own group and under his own banner. 53 But the Levites shall camp round the Tent to guard it, so that no one may come near and cause my anger to strike the community of Israel." 54 So the people of Israel did everything that the LORD had commanded Moses.

The Arrangement of the Tribes in Camp

2 The LORD gave Moses and Aaron following instructions. 2 When the Israelites set up camp, each man will camp under the banner of his division and the flag of his own clan. The camp is to be set up all round the Tent.

3-9 On the east side, those under the banner of the division of Judah shall camp in their groups, under their leaders, as follows:

Tribe	Leader	Number
Judah	Nahshon son of Amminadab	74,600
Issachar	Nethanel son of Zuar	54,400
Zebulun	Eliab son of Helon	57,400
	Total:	186,400

The division of Judah shall march first.

10-16 On the south, those under the banner of the division of Reuben shall camp in their groups, under their leaders, as follows:

Tribe	Leader	Number
Reuben	Elizur son of Shedeur	46,500
Simeon	Shelumiel son of Zurishaddai	59,300
Gad	Eliasaph son of Deuel	45,650
	Total:	151,450

The division of Reuben shall march second.

17 Then, between the first two divisions and the last two the Levites are to march carrying the Tent. Each division shall march in the same order as they camp, each in position under its banner.

18-24 On the west, those under the banner of the division of Ephraim shall camp in their groups, under their leaders, as follows:

Tribe	Leader	Number
Ephraim	Elishama son of Ammihud	40,500
Manasseh	Gamaliel son of Pedahzur	32,200
Benjamin	Abidan son of Gideoni	35,400
	Total:	108,100

The division of Ephraim shall march third.

25-31 On the north, those under the banner of the division of Dan shall camp in their groups, under their leaders, as follows:

Tribe	Leader	Number
Dan	Ahiezer son of Ammishaddai	62,700
Asher	Pagiel son of Ochran	41,500
Naphtali	Ahira son of Enan	53,400
	Total:	157,600

The division of Dan shall march last.